W9-BKW-204

3 1170 00105 9058

DATE DUE

SEP 1 2 1994			
OCT 1 2 1994			
MAY - 8 1995			
APR 1 8 1996			
JAN 2 1 1997			
APR 4 1998			
DEC 3 1998			
MAR 9 2000			
FEB 2 3 2002			
OCT 2 6 2003			
GAYLORD			PRINTED IN U.S.A.

Building
Model Ships From
Scratch

No. 907
$12.95

Building
Model Ships From
By Kent Porter   Scratch

6 23 82
PoR

Glenview Public Library
1930 Glenview Road
Glenview Illinois

TAB BOOKS
Blue Ridge Summit, Pa. 17214

FIRST EDITION

FIRST PRINTING—JANUARY 1977

Copyright © 1977 by TAB BOOKS

Printed in the United States
of America

Reproduction or publication of the content in any manner, without express permission of the publisher, is prohibited. No liability is assumed with respect to the use of the information herein.

Library of Congress Cataloging in Publication Data

Porter, Kent.
   Building model ships from scratch.

   Includes index.
   1.   Ship models.   I.   Title.
VM298.P63   623.82'01   76-45071
ISBN 0-8306-7907-3
ISBN 0-8306-6907-8 pbk.

C. A. P.

NOV 0 9 1977

Contents

Introduction

At one time or another you may have looked at an elaborately detailed model of a sailing ship, built from scratch, and thought, "Wow! Wish I could do that. But I know it's too hard."

It's a lot easier than you think—and that is the point of this book. Building from scratch is not as easy as building a ship model from a plastic kit, of course, but the rewards are proportional to the efforts you put into it.

Viewed as a finished work, a ship model appears astonishingly complex, but the construction itself is done one easy step at a time. The model is actually an accumulation of tiny details executed with loving care. It does not require tremendous skill to build a ship from scratch, nor even inordinate manual dexterity. Anyone with a reasonable amount of patience and average ability with the hands can turn out a magnificent piece of artwork.

There are two secrets to building from scratch: *method* and *time*.

Building sailing ship models from scratch is an ideal hobby. It takes very little space, a few inexpensive tools, and surprisingly little money. For an impressive 36-inch clipper model, the material investment will fall in the range of $50 to $75, which can be spread out quite thinly over the period of construction time. The only other thing you need, in generous quantities, is time. The crux of the activity lies in the method, which I have tried to lay out as clearly as possible in this book.

8

Models are crafted slowly and painstakingly, through trial and error, by hands no different than yours. This does not mean the model was built in exhausting, consecutive hours during which the craftsman was hunched in tedious labor. It means only that a long time elapsed from start to finish. My experience indicates that a couple of hours a night, broken in two by a short break, will yield steady, visible progress. At this rate, it takes about a year to build a three-masted square rigger.

Your own work habits will have a great influence over the lapse of time from the first stick to the last knot, as will the size and complexity of the ship itself. I once built a schooner in three weeks, but then built a six-foot barkentine model over a period of 17 months, at the expense of well over 600 hours of work. These are extremes, of course.

Building a ship model from scratch has traditionally been regarded as a man's hobby, yet there are a number of models that have been built by women. As a matter of fact, if fancy needlework and the experience of factory assembly lines are any indication, women are probably better at fine detail work than are men.

Certainly there is no reason why women should not build ship models. Children, however, are another story. Preadolescents are physically capable of building a model, though the low level of eye-hand coordination typical in preteens may place a really fine job out of reach. The problem is more one of attention. Few young children are capable of sustaining an interest in a long-term project such as a ship model. If a child wants to build a model ship, I suggest he or she stick with plastic kits at least until age 14. The reward in building from kits appears much sooner and it's good training for the real thing later on.

The stores are filled with kits for everything imaginable, including ship models. So why build from scratch at all? All the reasons for building from scratch reduce to the common denominator of satisfaction.

You can buy a plastic kit from the great variety available and turn out a very nice model in a fraction of the time needed for an equivalent ship built from scratch. Having done so, you can take pride in the result, and others will be impressed. But you will have created nothing new. A plastic kit is merely assembled from parts mass-produced by someone else, and engineered for ease of assembly.

You can also buy a wooden kit from one of the makers of high-quality kits, and the construction would in many ways be the same as that of building from scratch. Your product will be marvelous and will be indistinguishable from a ship built from scratch. It will also be virtually indistinguishable from hundreds or thousands of others built from the same kit.

The craftsman who builds from scratch is a total creator. He or she does not leave the selection of ships to others, nor the construction methods, nor the materials. Those who build from scratch start with nothing, except perhaps a set of plans. They finish with a unique creation. The satisfaction of this creation—of being able to say "I *made* that!"—is something rare and rewarding. The goal of this book is to have you share in that satisfaction.

I started building from scratch in my early teens and have since turned out enough ship models to have lost count at age 20. I have attempted to set forth what I have learned so that it can be followed like a set of instructions that will take you through the logical progression from selecting a model to putting it on display. But I've provided several alternative methods for hull construction, as well as options at various points elsewhere, so that you can make the ultimate choices yourself. Also included are chapters on maritime history and ship modeling in general, instructions for every aspect of building from scratch, and drawings to illustrate all the steps.

Each chapter is devoted to a major stage in construction and subdivided into activities within that stage. I suggest you read the book from cover to cover before beginning construction. I also suggest that you skim each chapter again as you enter each stage so that you will know where you are headed.

Don't let the occasional complexity of written instructions frighten you—bear in mind, that it is often easier to do something than to tell others how to do it. A quick and easy operation, such as the tying of a knot, can take a whole paragraph to explain, but five seconds to execute.

I hope that by the time you complete your first ship, you will have learned that the process is easier than it looks. I also hope that you will have experienced the unparalleled satisfaction of creating a magnificent ship model from scratch.

Kent Porter

Chapter 1

About Sailing Ships

Whenever the subject of ships comes up, one almost invariably hears the term "the sailing ship era," as though that were some period in history whose beginning and end were defined by the punctuation marks of events. "The sailing ship era," in fact, almost exactly corresponds to the era of recorded civilization.

A BRIEF HISTORY

No one knows when or where a man first noticed that paddle boats were prone to blow with the wind—or when he decided to take advantage of it. We do know that vases unearthed from Egyptian tombs of 8000 years ago show paintings of boats under sail. Because the Egyptians, commendably concerned with posterity, tended to record the commonplaces of their world, we can assume that the harnessing of the wind was already fairly widespread in the earliest days of civilization.

The evolution of the sailing ship follows the evolution of society. It was a slow process of growth, characterized by long periods of relative stability and complacency, and sudden jerks of innovation.

The Prototype

For at least 4400 years, the Egyptians spread sails on their little reed boats. Then, about 1600 B.C., they built wooden ships nearly a hundred feet long propelled by a great square sail that could be raised and lowered.

Others copied these ships. The Phoenicians, whose only significant innovation to the ship was the keel, spread their civilization throughout the known world by seafaring in vessels copied from the Egyptians' wooden marvel. The Greeks and Romans, beneficiaries of the Phoenecian trade in goods and ideas, copied the Phoenician ships and established navies for commerce and warfare.

Nothing further happened to naval architecture for a very long time. In the first millenium A.D., the Vikings, either on their own or by some unrecorded contact with Mediterranean seafarers, developed a type of vessel very like those of the south. The Norsemen did make one improvement; their ships were *clinker-built*. This means the edges of the hull strakes (See Glossary for any unfamiliar terms) overlapped much like clapboard siding. This innovation made for a very strong, light, seaworthy vessel, which enabled the Vikings to make their epic voyages.

Other improvements appeared from time to time. Around 1200 A.D., the Mediterranean people produced a two-masted vessel carrying lateen sails. Half a century later King Henry III of England made warships by mounting temporary castles with crenelated battlements on the ends of barge-like merchantmen. Essentially, however, all ships built for 3000 years after the Egyptians launched the first wooden vessel were primarily galleys, dependent upon long oars for propulsion. The single mast with its single square sail was an incidental means of propulsion that relieved the oarsman when the wind happened to be over the stern.

The Revolution

Then, a century-long revolution in naval architecture began. In 1356, the French first mounted cannon on ships. At the same time, they increased the number of masts from one to three. These immensely superior vessels startled France's enemies into imitation and innovation.

Around 1380, the *carrack* appeared. It was a totally new type of ship carrying three masts, with a long projecting platform over the bow and a large overhanginging castle aft. The carrack had three deck levels, with a high poop deck astern and a sunken main deck amidships. She carried two sails on the mainmast, and a lateen sail on the mizzen mast. Her hull was the first to have the characteristic of tumblehome, a narrowing above the waterline. This narrowing was intended to inhibit boarders in combat, but it has the more practical influence of stabilizing the vessel.

Carracks became a standard of ship design for the next three centuries. Tubby and slow, they were nonetheless tremendously seaworthy vessels. The carrack *Santa Maria* brought Columbus to the New World in 1492, and the Pilgrims came to Plymouth 128 years later on the carrack *Mayflower*.

IMPROVEMENTS

Improvements in armament and ship design soon forced improvements elsewhere. In the period 1400—1500, rigging became so standardized and perfected that it had changed very little by the time the clippers started beating around the Horn four centuries later. With increasing ship size, the demand for taller and taller masts soon outgrew the supply of suitable trees and the shipwrights began lashing extensions to the tops of the masts.

The Spanish Armada brought us the galleon in the 1580s. This ship was primarily a refinement of the carrack. In fact, the two were nearly indistinguishable above the waterline. But underwater there was a significant difference. Gone was the tubbiness and dragging square stern of the carrack. It was replaced by a sleek fish-like form that made the galleon astonishingly fast for its time.

At about the same time, the European powers began a 17th Century arms race that resulted in a steady increase in the size of ships and the development of a ship specialized for warfare. A few true warships had been built in the past, such as the *Great Harry* of 1515, but these were exceptions. All ships carried guns for protection from pirates and enemies of the flag, and even as late as 1800, merchantmen and warships were fairly interchangeable.

Among large vessels, the warship type began developing with the launch of the *Sovereign of the Seas* in 1637. She was among the first of the ships of the line, a vessel with several gun decks, intended to intimidate as much by her lavish display of gilded wealth, as by her bristling fire power. By 1670, the heavy warships had so proliferated, that the British began classifying them according to their *rate*, or number of gun decks.

A century later, all sailing warships were still rated on the basis of a number of guns. The *U.S. Constellation*, for example, was rated a 36-gun frigate. Without exception, however, naval vessels were overarmed, so that the *Constellation*, though rated a 36, actually carried 49 at one point in her career. The *Constitution*, rated a 44, mounted 52 guns.

With the advent of the carronade, a short-range but powerful gun, it became commom practice not to count them as guns, and usually to carry as many long guns as the rate indicated. Thus the *Constellation* carried 36 truck guns and 12 carronades. The extra gun which made her armament 49 was a long 24-pounder lashed on the forecastle and occasionally rolled to the railing for use as a chase gun.

The vast floating arsenals afloat in 1670, however, were clumsy, topheavy vessels whose lineage is directly traceable to the galleon. The high poop stayed high, but the ship grew larger and larger in relation to it, until the poop became the quarterdeck. The *Victory*, a 1767 "liner" still in existence in Portsmouth, England, exhibits the galleon influence in her lines.

Until quite recently, ship building was more an art than a science. The shipwrights worked from experience and a general agreement of dimensions rather than from drawings, as they do today. It's not surprising that the ships of the line were cranky, unstable vessels. Their sides rose as much as thirty feet off the water, carrying a hundred or so guns, each weighing a ton apiece. The ships also carried rigging, provisions, personnel, and ammunition. Every time a new ship was launched, everyone watched to see if she would capsize, and no vessel was regarded as truly seaworthy until she'd had a couple of years to prove herself.

The loss of the *Vasa*, which capsized and sank in Stockholm harbor the first time she was under sail in 1628, was not at all unusual for the time. It only comes to modern attention because she has been raised and put on display. The annals of maritime history are filled with ships that went missing in deep water under perfectly normal conditions. Many of them were later reputed to be cranky and were supposedly victims of an unscientific technology.

Yankee Ingenuity

It was the Americans who first began to bring some elements of science to naval architecture. Almost from the first colonization, the Americans had been producing vessels for domestic use and for the British market. The first steps Americans took in systematizing ship building came in the direction of specialization. Fishing boats had long existed in Europe and elsewhere, but the Americans perceived a need for special vessel types; the deep, capacious, stable type for Grand Banks fishing; the flat-bottom bugeye skipjack that still plies Chesapeake Bay, last of the working sailing vessels, and others. Light coastal traders working the tortuous, shoal-studded harbors of New England demanded a rig more suited to adverse breezes than the square-sailed vessel could offer, and so the schooner was developed.

In time, many other specialized vessels came from America, designed for the peculiar requirements of certain trade routes and cargos. Much was borrowed from England, a great deal more than she took.

The American revolution forced a new type of shipbuilding problem on the rebellious colonists. England, wary of giving away her secrets, had never permitted the construction of a warship in these or any other colonies. As the rattling of sabres grew steadily louder in 1775, the colonies undertook the construction of a fleet of frigates.

Very experienced in the merchant line, but utterly inexperienced when it came to warships, the American yards produced a rather pitiful collection of vessels, which in turn produced a most uninspiring string of defeats, and disasters. In April, 1776, for example, the entire Continental Navy was bested by one small British frigate off Block Island.

The only really fine Continental frigate was the *Hancock*, which was captured by the British after only a few months of service. And she turned out to be of such poor materials that she rapidly rotted to a hulk. Luckily for us, the Revolution did not depend on naval prowess.

In the 1970s when the need for an American navy again arose, the country resolved to make a better showing. The government hired as its chief designer, Philadelphia Quaker Joshua Humphreys, a self-declared master shipwright who had never been to sea but who knew ships like few others. The government retained Josiah Fox as his assistant. He was a young British immigrant who had taken his apprenticeship as a naval architect in the Royal Dockyards at Portsmouth. These two men transformed the art of ship design into a science. Of the first three ships they produced, two are still afloat, and based at the cities of their construction: the *Constitution* at Boston and the *Constellation* at Baltimore. The other, the *United States*, was scuttled during the Civil War, seven decades after her launch. It was later raised for a few more years of service.

These American frigates were systematically designed as fighting machines. They were fast, maneuverable, and capable of engaging much larger vessels. The British didn't like them. In fact, the British claimed the ships were "unfair" because they were ships of the line disguised as frigates. The British copied them all the same. So did the French, Spanish, Portuguese, Scandinavians, Ottomans, and anyone else who had a taste for sea power.

Humphreys and Fox and their disciple William Doughty became world-renowned authorities on naval architecture, a fame that grew to legendary proportions as their ships compiled an impressive series of victories over superior vessels. Humphreys and Fox passed to their associates the principles they had developed.

In the brief decade and a half between the end of the Revolution and the end of the 18th Century, America had become the foremost trading nation of the world, and now she was becoming a naval power as well. By 1805, in our first foreign war, the American frigates defeated the Barbary pirates. This was something the Europeans had been unable to do since Roman times. In the War of 1812, the same Humphreys/Fox frigates defeated the mighty British Navy.

By that time, the science of naval architecture had created a worldwide demand for superior American ships, which were faster, and carried more cargo more safely, than any vessels on earth. With all this interest in maritime matters, new research went forward.

Thomas Truxtun, first captain of the *Constellation*, published works on the masting and sparring of vessels. James Barron, another naval captain, patented a means of ventilating ships. In Baltimore, a significant and extremely fast new vessel type called the Baltimore clipper started tumbling from the ways.

America, until the advent of the frigates, had always been a producer of small merchant craft. Now she started turning out large commercial vessels to sell overseas, and to operate under the American flag.

In the 1830s a large, fast vessel called the *packet ship* appeared. A packet is defined as any vessel that operates according to a schedule. But these packets were also unique in that they had a sharp bow, commodious holds, and extensive passenger accommodations.

In 1836, Maryland merchant Isaac McKim expanded the Baltimore clipper from a two-masted *schooner* into a three-masted *square rigger*. He called the vessel *Ann McKim* after his wife. It was a beautiful vessel and extraordinarily fast, but because of her narrow hull she could carry so little cargo that she was a commercial failure.

Others, however, saw promise in her. By the late 1840s men like William Webb were carrying the best of the packets and the features of the *Ann McKim* in a showy vessel they called the *clipper ship*. The result was the legendary decade of the clipper.

The Clippers

Clippers were a fad. They were lovely, graceful racehorses which, like most thoroughbreds, had serious flaws of character. Fast as they were, they didn't carry nearly as much cargo as slower ships of equivalent size. They ran wet, rolling and pitching and taking on water to the incessant misery of passengers and crew. Their vast acreage of canvas required huges crews—50 and more men—and the lightweight construction needed frequent overhaul, all of which ran operating expenses very high.

Those most enamoured of clippers were the landsmen who delighted in their comings and goings, and the wealthy investors who wagered large sums on their performance. Neither of these groups had to sail on them.

The clipper ship era began in earnest with the California gold rush. No land route yet bridged the continent, so prospectors and shippers were willing to pay high rates to make the three-and-a-half month run around Cape Horn. In the beginning, clippers made immense profits for their owners. An average clipper costs about $50,000 and could reasonably be expected to turn a $100,000 profit on her first voyage.

Profits like that attracted investors. In 1850, 24 clippers were launched; by 1853, the peak year, the number of launchings had risen to 120. Clipper-watching became a national mania on the scale of today's pro football following, with stars and superstars among the captains and builders, and running times between various points published daily in papers.

Passengers in 1854 reported that it was possible to sail from New York to San Francisco without ever losing sight of at least one other clipper on the horizon. Impelled by the prospects of glamour and fat bonuses, captains drove their ships unmercifully to beat the records.

By 1856 it was all over. Thirty-eight clippers came off the ways that year; half that many would be launched over the next three years combined. In all, 443 clippers were built in this country during the nine-year craze that fizzled out completely in 1859.

Many things conspired to kill the clipper: a general economic depression, the railroad, the drying-up of the gold rush, apprehensions over the growing prospects of civil war. One of the most significant factors was the clipper itself. So many entered the California trade that competition drove freight and passenger rates down below the break-even point. The ships themselves required large dollops of operating capital to pay the oversized crews and repair the damage caused by captains who had forgotten how to take in sail. As maintenance expenses grew with the age of the ship, and as revenues simultaneously fell, clippers became a source of poverty rather than wealth.

Many clippers were sold to disreputable houses that cut back the excessive sparring, engaged a small ragtag crew, and used them as guano boats and as ferries for chinese laborers destined for slavery on distant islands. A few were sold to the British, whose clipper era came later than ours. But American clippers proved unsatisfactory for the British routes. By the turn of the century a handful still worked in the coastal trade.

A search in the 1930s turned up a number of hulls bearing fanciful clipper names like *Flying Mist, Queen of the Seas,* and *Wings of the Wind.* They were serving as garbage scows. Today, of all those hundreds of high-spirited, ill-tempered, but beautiful vessels, only one survives. It is the China tea clipper *Cutty Sark* based in England.

It is not true that the age of sail came to a close with the death of the clipper. Certainly steam had by then begun to cut deeply into the shipping market. But steam had already made inroads before the clipper appeared, and it would be many years before it finally displaced sail altogether. Steam had the decided advantage of independence from the wind, but this advantage was far outweighed by the disadvantages of small cargo capacity, filth, fire hazards, and great expense. All of these factors aroused stubborn resistance among shippers and potential passengers.

Almost unnoticed in the shadows beyond the glare of clipper publicity, other sailing vessels were coming into their own. The whaler, for example, a stubby, blocky vessel capable of making voyages several years long with only a handful of seamen, matured into a distinctive and ideal type during this period. The coastal trading schooner came into full flower as a highly maneuverable shoaldraft vessel that carried great amounts of cargo on deck and below. These ships operated until well into the 20th Century.

Though the clipper died, she left an ancestor, the Downeaster freighting ship. Downeasters were large square-rigged vessels with fuller hulls and fewer sails than clippers, but with nearly as much speed. They required smaller crews and less maintenance, being more stoutly built. A number were built in the last decades of the 19th Century, but because of competition with schooners and steam they never became a great commercial success. In terms of square-rigger development, however, they represent the peak.

By the year 1890, steam had become an accepted fact of maritime life, but there were still numerous hold-outs. Among shippers and seamen, one was either a steam man or a sail man, and passions flared over the issue. Steamships had gotten very large by then, introducing economies of scale hard to match in sailing vessels. In response, the sail men focused their attention on the schooner.

The Schooners

Schooners were handy sailers. The nature of the rig enabled them to work well even to windward. Using power winches, one or two men could handle the immense sail on each mast. Schooners quickly grew to sizes comparable with steamers. Five and six masts were common, tended by astonishingly small crews. The *Thomas W. Lawson*, launched in 1901, was the largest sailing ship ever built in this country. She had seven masts, carried 11,000 tons of cargo, and needed a crew of only 17.

Schooners had a place on the seas for many years. They were used heavily in the lumbering trade of the Pacific

Northwest, as coasters and island traders, and to a lesser extent for transoceanic traffic. They transported men and equipment during World War I. The Navy still used at least one schooneer, the *Lanikai*, in World War II. Up until 1941 schooners were a fairly common sight in American coastal waters. But then, fear of U-boat attacks beached many of these ships. A small number remained in service until the 1950s.

You can still find a few schooners, rotting and forgotten by all but vandals, in quiet corners of some seaports. Their gaunt remains contrast with the great cranes and the massive vessels that threaten to gobble up our irreplaceable fossil fuel. The schooner skeletons serve as a reminder that the age of sail is over.

VESSEL TYPES

For the model ship builder, American vessels of the 19th Century offer the richest standards. The sailing ship reached its pinnacle at this time and many original plans still survive. Copies of these plans are readily obtainable.

Hobby companies, museums, nautical societies, and even the federal government have researched and adapted some of these plans for modelers' use. Contemporary newspapers, books, magazines, registry certificates, and other documents still exist to provide the modeler with information about a particular vessel's appearance, characteristics, movements, and exploits.

American waters witnessed a startling variety of hulls and rigs in the last century. As a rule, ships were referred to by their rig unless they had a peculiar hull that differentiated them from other vessels of similar rig. The Baltimore clipper, for example, carried schooner rig but was seldom called a schooner.

The following pages will describe by sketch and text the most common vessel types of the 19th Century.

The Brig

The *brig* is a common two-masted vessel. Brigs were handy utility vessels, suited to almost any role from coastal knockabouts to transoceanic commerce. Their respectable speed, adequate cargo capacity, and low crew and maintenance expense made brigs extremely popular with merchants. As warships, they boasted excellent maneuverability and carried arms well. Brigs were always small vessels, seldom exceeding 100 feet in length. Even so, they were the workhorses of the seafaring trades.

A brig always carries tow masts, fore and main, with square sails on both, and a large gaff-rigged spanker on the main.

Early in the century, a distinction was made between a brig and a *snow*. On a brig, the spanker attached directly to the lower mainmast. The snow had a secondary mast from deck to doubling, to carry the spanker. With time, this esoteric distinction disappeared, and all two-masted square-riggers came to be called brigs.

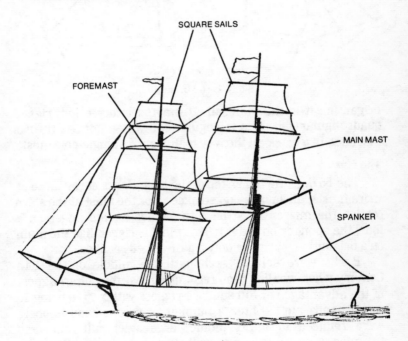

Fig. 1-1. The brig.

The Brigantine

Brigantines are first cousins to the brigs. A brigantine is also called a hermaphrodite brig because it is a cross between a brig and a schooner.

On a brigantine, the foremast carries square sails just like a brig, but the main carries only a large fore-and-aft rigged sail. On a brig, this sail is called the spanker, but on a

Fig. 1-2. The brigantine.

brigantine it is the mainsail. It may be either a gaff-rigged quadrangular sail, or a triangular sail whose luff has fittings that slide in a track all the way to the top of a single-pole mast.

The Bark

The *bark* is the big sister of the brig. Barks carry three or more masts, all square-rigged except for the mast at the stern (called the mizzen mast on a three-master, the jigger on a four, the spanker on a five). This mast is rigged like the main on a brigantine, carrying only a gaff-rigged spanker.

Barks were seldom seen until the middle of the 19th Century when whaling men recognized that they offered most of the advantages of full squuare-riggers without requiring so many hands aloft. Later a number of second-hand clippers were reduced to barks. Some large steel hull four- and five-masters were built, primarily by the British and Germans late in the century. In this country the bark never achieved much popularity except among whalers. The Coast Guard's famed training ship *Eagle* is a bark.

The Barkentine

Barkentines very closely resemble multi-masted schooners, the difference being that a barkentine carries square sails on the foremast. Barkentines have from three to six masts. The foremast is generally shorter than the others, which are of uniform height. The order of masts is fore, main, mizzen, jigger, spanker, driver, and pusher.

The barkentine achieved popularity late in the 1800's, when crew expenses became an important competitive factor. Barkentines had a slight edge over schooners in being able to spread more canvas to a trailing wind, but the more elaborate foremast rig entailed greater expense to the owner.

Barkentines were among the last of the big sailing ships. Many operated into the 1920s and 1930s. The famed Coast Guard cutter *Bear*, whose nine decades of service ended with her sinking in 1963, was a barkentine. The Spanish still operate a barkentine as a training vessel.

The Schooner

Schooner is a catch-all name to describe a great variety of fore-and-aft rigged vessels ranging from fishing boats to mammoth bulk carriers. A schooner must have at least two masts. Some have had as many as seven.

In two-masters, the foremast is shorter than the main, but on ships of three or more masts, each is usually the same height. The sails are generally gaff-rigged.

Some of the small schooners carried one or two square sails on the foremast, and a few had them on the main as well. These were called topsail schooners. Occasionally a two-mast

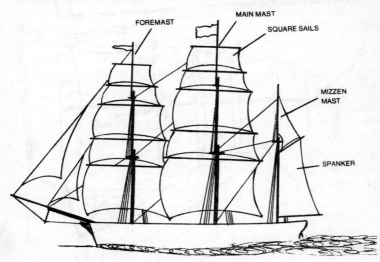

Fig. 1-3. The bark.

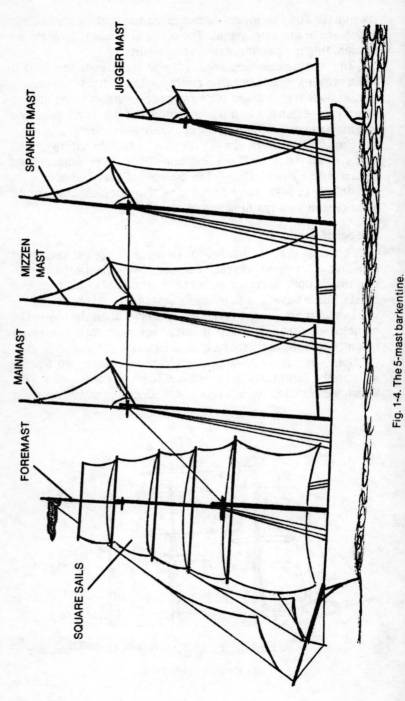

Fig. 1-4. The 5-mast barkentine.

JIGGER MAST

SPANKER MAST

MIZZEN MAST

MAINMAST

FOREMAST

SQUARE SAILS

schooner with a complete set of square sails turns up. It's very easy to confuse this rig with a brig. The only difference between the two is that the schooner carries a large fore-and-aft sail on both masts and the brig carries one only on the main.

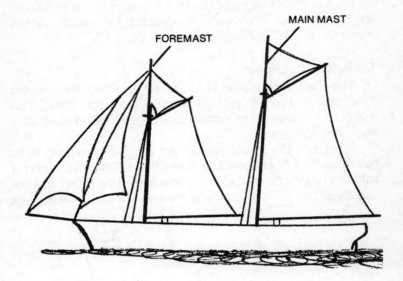

2-MASTER

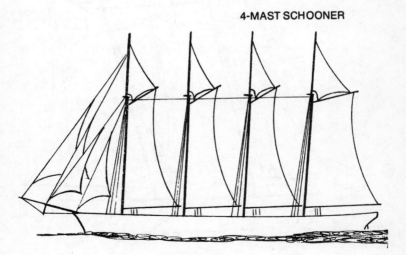

Fig. 1-5. Schooners.

The schooner rig was an American development that answered the need for handiness in the frivolous winds of the New England coastline. It proved to be suitable for sailing anywhere, and spread throughout the world. The rig was the most successful ever devised, for it outlived every other rig in the crucial test of day-to-day use. Even today, new schooners are in operation and being constructed for use as yachts, research vessels, and fishing ships.

The Baltimore Clipper

The *Baltimore clipper* is a special type of topsail schooner developed in the Chesapeake Bay in the early 1800s. This schooner's masts were extremely tall and raked back at a startling, jaunty angle.

What sets the Baltimore clipper off most, however, is its hull form. The sharp bow has distinctive hollows that contrast with the roundness of the traditional apple bow found on most vessels of the period. Long and narrow, the hull sweeps back

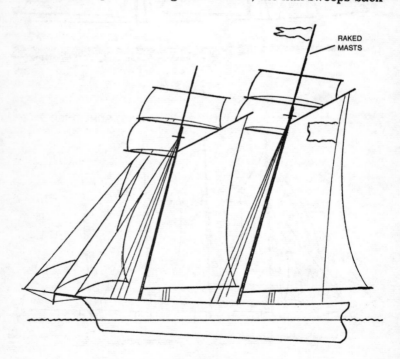

RAKED MASTS

Fig. 1-6. The Baltimore clipper.

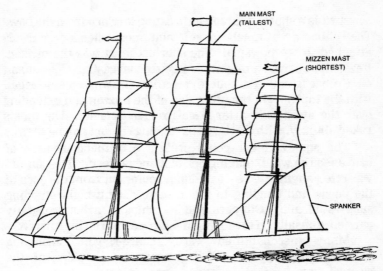

MAIN MAST
(TALLEST)

MIZZEN MAST
(SHORTEST)

SPANKER

Fig. 1-7. The 3-masted square rigger.

into a deep run that draws several feet more water than the bow. The sleek hull form and extensive sparring of the Baltimore clipper made her one of the swiftest of all sailing vessels.

Because of her swiftness, the Baltimore clipper became a favorite of the Revenue Service. Her great speed was a decided asset in the control of smuggling and piracy along American shores. For the same reason, this type of ship was also the favorite of those smugglers and pirates, and also of slave transporters. Her narrow hull prevented her from gaining much importance in the cargo trade, but the Baltimore clipper was around for a long time in other capacites.

The Square-Rigger

Square-rigger, in its broadest sense, applies to all vessels carrying square sails. In conventional usage the term denotes a fully rigged three-master. This rig was the standard of the heavy ocean-going vessels from the day of the carrack until the decline of the Downeaster.

On square-riggers of the 18th and 19th Centuries, the tallest mast was the main, which stood a little abaft the midpoint of the hull. Next in height was the foremast which, in addition to square sails, supported a group of long triangular sails running forward to the bowsprit and jibboom. The

27

bowsprit is a short, stout mast thrusting forward from the bow. The jibboom, a much longer and more slender spar, is attached to the bowsprit. The shortest mast was the mizzen. Few ships carried a mizzen course (the largest and lowest sail on a mast is called a course). Rather, the mizzen sail began with the topsail. On the after side of the mizzen and extending over the stern was a large gaff-rigged spanker. The masts raked slightly, with a cobweb of running rigging among them.

The square-rigger could present a tremendous area of canvas to the wind, making her fast and powerful. This spread was often augmented by extending booms out from the ends of the yards and bending to them narrow lightweight studding sails (stunsails). Clippers and warships in a hurry usually carried stunsails on the fore and main, seldom on the mizzen.

Many merchantmen were square-riggers, including virtually all clippers and Downeasters. Warships of the sloop-of-war, frigate, and liner classes were also square-riggers.

Chapter 2
About Building From Scratch

Building ships from scratch is probably one of the least expensive hobbies, and produces some of the most spectacular results. There are no kits to buy, no costly tools, no fees to pay to others, no exotic materials to purchase. Also, no special facilities have to be set up for the model shipyard.

Because the construction of a model ship takes time, the cost of materials can be spread out to the point where it costs almost nothing to create a magnificent vessel that will be a source of pride for the rest of your life and perhaps for generations to come.

There are, of course, some start-up expenses. To do a good job, you need good tools and good materials. Since the costs of engaging in the hobby are so low and the results so long-lasting, you can easily justify buying good tools and materials. With reasonable care, decent tools should last for years. Those tools you need to construct your first ship will probably be all the tools you'll ever need. Scraps and remnants, too, can be carried over from one ship to another.

Years ago, for instance, I bought a couple of yards of fine white cotton for sails. The cotton has provided suits of sails for six ships now, including a big six-foot barkentine, and there is still enough for at least as many more. I also have a desk drawer full of odds and ends of wood strips, paints, rigging threads, and other modeler's necessaries, some probably dating from a dozen ships ago. Scraps are an invaluable resource, and they keep the cost of future vessels low.

TOOLS

To start building from scratch, there are a few basic tools you must have. If you have built ships from kits, you probably already have some of the tools. The basic instrument set consists of:

> X-acto or equivalent knife with no. 11 blades
> X-acto or equivalent knife with No. 24 blades
> several packets of No. 11 and 24 blades
> pin vise (small drill) and several #70 bits
> ruler, preferably with inch and metric scales
> set of dividers
> protractor
> fingernail file
> good pair of manicure or surgical scissors
> several needle threaders
> set of French curves (described in chapter 4)
> two dental forceps, 6″ long, with hooked tips

Most of these tools can be purchased in any hobby shop. I don't specifically recommend X-acto products, but they are easily obtained. Needle threaders are available in sewing shops. The best kind usually come three to a package and look like the one shown in Fig. 2-1. Bend the two ends downward

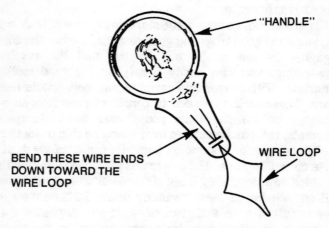

"HANDLE"

BEND THESE WIRE ENDS
DOWN TOWARD THE
WIRE LOOP

WIRE LOOP

Fig. 2-1. Needle threader.

where the wire passes through the holder, and the threader will last a long time.

The hooked-tip dental forceps are essential. No other kind of tweezers or forceps works as well. I bought mine through a dentist. Three of them cost me $5. You can also buy them from surgical suppliers.

A word on knife blades: A dull blade does not cut. It tears. And the result is never as neat and satisfying as it ought to be. Don't be economy-minded when it comes to blades. If you work every night on your ship, change blades every other night even if the blade still seems to be sharp.

Some other tools you might find helpful are:

> spring-type clothespins
> wood carving set
> needlenose pliers
> small wire cutters
> small vise that clamps on a table edge

A jigsaw is also very useful. A few years ago I purchased an inexpensive jigsaw, the kind with a tiltable table for the work to lie on, and it has been a great aid in cutting parts. The beginner can do without it quite nicely (as can the more experienced shipwright), but it saves a lot of time and trouble when making frame members and other curvy parts.

MATERIALS

Balsa is generally not a very good material for models, contrary to popular opinion and the practice of some kit makers. Balsa is soft and grainy, which makes it weak, hard to finish, and unsuitable for small parts. Balsa does, however, have some uses.

A model of the *Flying Fish* that I made has some frame members and other structural parts made of balsa, and balsa was also used for some of the railings and moldings. Since it is so soft, it curves easily without breaking, as long as you treat it gently. But place no great reliance on balsa.

Wood

The best material for those who build model ships from scratch is strip basswood. You can buy it in strips ranging from 1/32" × 1/32" up to about 1/4" × 3" in most hobby shops, usually in the model train area. It's strong, cheap, easily worked, and produces a good realistic appearance. Sometimes basswood is referred to as strip pine or modelers' hardwood. It can be used for almost everything on a ship model—hull planking, decks, rails, channels, gunwales, etc.,—and you can even round it for use as spars.

Once in a great while, you will need to carve some exotic or unusual fitting. Or, if you're a purist, you'll need to make all the parts of the ship. In those cases, buy a piece of boxwood. It costs about twice as much as basswood, but for intricate carved work it can't be beaten. The grain is extremely fine, which makes it ideal for working in all sorts of detail without fear of breaking the work.

Some modelers like mahogany as a basic material. This is a matter of taste. Personally, I find it entirely too grainy, almost like a hard balsa, and it's about one and a half times the cost of basswood. If you want the mahogany color, I suggest you use basswood and stain it.

Glue

The selection of glues is important. After all, the glue holds the model together, and if you choose a poor or cheap cement, you may eventually have a pile of sticks to show for your efforts. For sheer holding power that will last a long time, use a liquid contact cement formulated for wood and porous surfaces, such as Weldwood. It's best to buy a pint can and apply the cement with a paint brush. If it gets thick and dark, thin it with a lacquer thinner containing toluene.

Contact cement, as the name implies, bonds on contact. You apply it to the two surfaces to be joined, let it dry five minutes or so, until tacky to the touch, and then join the pieces. Ordinarily, you don't have to clamp it unless it's a joint that involves unavoidable strain (sharply curved hull planking, for example). Care must be taken in bringing the surfaces together in proper alignment, since they bond immediately and won't slide around. If you do make a mistake, you can usually get the pieces apart without damage, but then you have to start all over with a new coat of cement.

Contact cement is ideal for bonding flat surfaces, but it's not satisfactory on small jobs, or for joining metal and wood. Such jobs include fastening down deck fittings and gluing small parts together. In those cases, use a good-quality hobby glue like Ambroid or Duco. Always use this type of cement sparingly. Extra cement bulging around a joint is sloppy, and such a job will look sloppy no matter what you do to remedy it.

On the other hand, don't use too little glue, because the joint won't hold. How much to use is a matter of experience, but in general a small drop per penny-sized area will do nicely. Use only enough so that when the parts are pressed together the glue will spread out and almost completely cover the joined surfaces without oozing out.

I also suggest the use of casein glue in specific types of joints. Casein is a very good glue that produces an almost unbreakable bond. The main reason I do not recommend it for general use is the difficulty of working with it. Casein ordinarily comes in a powder form that has to be mixed with water. It is slow-drying and the joint has to be clamped, which makes casein very cumbersome.

Paint

Paints are also important. Probably the best for most modeling purposes are railroad paints. They form a good, smooth, dull surface. Avoid plastic dopes and other glossy paints which would create shiny surfaces and make a model look chintzy. If you can only get the color you want in gloss paint, give the surface a second coat of clear flat dope, but be sure to try this treatment on a piece of scrap first, because some dopes curdle under clear flat. For all painted surfaces apply a base primer coat of Gesso. This is a flat white acrylic paint used by artists for preparing canvas. Since it never yellows, it also makes a great white finish.

Some surfaces, such as decks, should not be painted. If you want a natural surface, apply a coat of shellac to seal the wood against humidity. For stained surfaces, you should use modelers' stain (Flo-stain, for example, which is sold with railroad paints). Don't use furniture wiping stain, which simply doesn't work on small parts. Modelers' stain is like paint. You just apply it. It comes in all the common wood tones, and one small bottle will last a long time. After the stain is dry, shellac the surface. Use a thin shellac, not one that leaves a hard shiny finish. If you can't find shellac, you can substitute an ordinary satin-sheen varnish.

Sandpaper

Sanding is required only on occasion, or when shaping parts on the hull. Sailing ships were usually pretty crudely painted and a bit of roughness about the finish on a model enhances its realism. On the other hand, a hull usually needs a good sanding to smooth out the planking. It also needs a couple of coats of paint to make the color uniform. For the preliminary sanding, use a medium-grade sandpaper, followed by a very fine grade like 00 or 000. To sand the first coat of paint, use the fine grade again, or if it's a solid hull and not planked, use fine steel wool.

Plastic

Although purists may shudder, plastic makes a very fine material for some jobs. You can buy miniature steel beams in I-beam and angle iron shapes, which are useful on later-vintage models. You can also get plastic sheet in various thicknesses and widths, from which to cut strips. Plastic can't be beaten as a material for decorative moldings and other parts that have to adhere to sharply curved surfaces.

Household Items

For some of your materials, you won't have to leave the house. Round toothpicks, for example, make excellent posts, upper yards, and stanchions. The lowly 3" × 5" card is very useful for making smooth white cabin sides, part templates, and a multitude of other parts. Cellophane wrappers from cigarette packages and boxed food items make good windows. Sewing thread is perfectly suitable for some rigging needs. Use paper clips for ladder rails and staples for window bars. Cigar smokers should look to their cigar bands for elaborate curly-cued goldwork nicely tailored to trailboard and stern decorations.

I once modified the propellor from my son's rubber-band-powered toy airplane for the screw on a big steam auxiliary. Be on the lookout. With enough ingenuity, you could probably find everything you need for a ship model in your own home.

As an illustration of what ingenuity can produce (not a suggestion that you try to imitate it, though!) there stands a collection of ship models in the Naval Academy Museum in Annapolis, Maryland. These are collectively referred to as prisoner-of-war models because most were made by French and British seamen captured in the series of wars around 1800. The models are made entirely of bones left over from the prisoners' rations, carefully carved and shaved down to form planks, spars, guns, and all the other parts of warships. Some were, or still are, rigged with the hair of the prisoners plaited, and wound to form miniature ropes. The men who made them had no tools save their seamen's dirks. This is not mentioned, of course, to suggest you try making a copy of one of these astonishing models, but rather to give you some idea of the possibilities for model use in even the most unlikely substances.

Still, you will buy most of your materials. When you do buy, spend a little extra for good materials, so that the model you are creating will last long enough to become an heirloom.

PURCHASED PARTS

If you've been worried about making all those thousands of tiny parts that constitute the detail on a sailing ship model, worry no more. You can buy most or all of them already made.

If you want to be a purist, carve your own belaying pins (about 150 for the average three-master), shape your own stanchions (about 30 per ship), bend your own eyebolts, and turn and drill your own deadeyes. Meanwhile, the rest of us will build a half-dozen ships. There is no more shame in using some purchased parts than there is in buying do-it-yourself items from the hardware store. In fact, using these parts is only common sense.

Most model ship fittings are made of "white metal," which is cast solder, or of brass, either turned or stamped. The white metal parts usually have casting flash on them and will need to be trimmed and filed. Because the white metal is soft, it works easily with a hobby knife. Metals do not take a finish well unless primed. Use a flat gray metal primer, which is sold with model railroad paints.

Many hobby shops carry prepackaged parts. The bigger shops stock thousands of parts on a piece-by-piece basis, which is much better and generally more economical; if you only need one, why buy a dozen? The biggest shops carry more than one brand on a piece-part basis, so you can usually get anything you need.

Not everyone, though, is lucky enough to live within reach of a hobby supermarket. And even if you do, they won't always have exactly what you need. This makes it occasionally necessary to order your parts by mail from the manufacturers and mail-order distributors.

I use three different brands of parts, and I've ordered, with good any speedy results, from all three makers. They are: Model Shipways,Inc., 39 West Fort Lee Road, Bogota, New Jersey 07603; Marine Model Company, Inc., Halesite, Long Island, New York 11743; and A. J. Fisher, Inc., 1002 Etowah Avenue, Royal Oak, Michigan 48067.

There are other brands as well, but I'm not familiar with them. Ship parts are also marketed through some nautical curio firms. Such companies regularly advertise in hobby magazines and regional publications, such as *Yankee Magazine*.

These firms all produce catalogs containing illustrations of parts, available dimensions, and prices. The catalogs also contain a lot of miscellaneous items like parts boxes, tapered spars, decals, case kits, and the like. Most of the catalogs will cost about a dollar, but I think they are worth it as a reference. It's a good idea to have several catalogs on hand, in fact, because no one maker carries everything you'll need for most ships. And even if you buy from a hobby shop, you can shop in advance through the catalog, know what you'll have to pay, and simplify the purchase by having the maker and part number when you walk into the store.

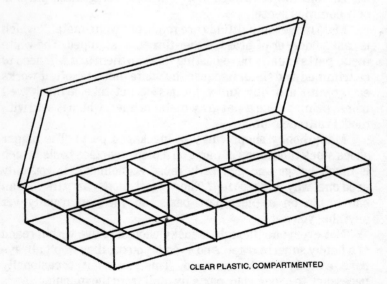

CLEAR PLASTIC, COMPARTMENTED

Fig. 2-2. Parts box.

You should also buy a clear plastic box with lots of small compartments for your parts, as shown in Fig. 2-2. These can usually be obtained from craft shops, sewing stores, and some jewelers. Use the compartments to keep your parts separated by size and type. If you have more kinds of parts than compartments, mix dissimilar parts in the same compartment. In no circumstance should you combine different sizes of the same part.

One of the most useful parts you'll need is lill pins. These are small pins about half the size of ordinary sewing pins. They are supposedly sold in sewing shops, but I've never found them there. Manufacturers make all the parts and most hobby shops carry them. Buy several dozen.

THE MODEL SHIPYARD

Another of the nice things about building ships from scratch is that you don't need any special place in which to do it. It's great if you do have a workshop, of course, but all you really need is a drawer for your tools and materials, and a board to work on.

The board is an essential. It provides a flat surface, and you can cut, paint, make scrap piles, and generally mess it up without fear of marring a table top. It's a good idea to set aside an out-of-sight, level place, such as a closet shelf, for storing the board. This enables you to leave some of the tools and materials currently in use on the board, without having to put them all away at the end of each construction session.

Use a drawer to store things not needed at the particular stage in the ship's construction. It will probably soon turn into a rat's nest, since the oddments and paraphernalia of ship building don't lend themselves to neatness and order. But placed in a drawer, the items will at least be out of harm's way and that of your spouse's wrath.

Wood storage can be a problem, since most strip materials come in lengths between 18″ and 3′, but there is an easy solution. Usually hobby shops wrap strip purchases in paper, and tape the wrapping into a tube form. When you get it home, cut only the last inch or so off the tube, and it becomes a perfect wood holder. Try to keep different sizes in different tubes, so things don't get mixed up. This way you can mark the top of each tube to show the size of the strips it contains. Find an unseen but accessible place for the tubes: a corner in a closet, under the sofa, behind a chair.

It's a good idea to pick the place where your ship will be displayed before you begin to build it. This is discussed in greater detail in Chapter 3 and again in Chapter 13. As an interesting conversation piece, the unfinished vessel can be stored there between work sessions. It's fascinating to watch it take shape and to imagine how it will look when completed, and the incompleteness of it will keep you working toward that end.

I often work on a TV tray. Once I built a six-foot model mostly on two TV trays set end to end, but after a certain point the arrangement made me nervous and I switched to a card table. Either one is perfectly suitable, so long as it is stable. By setting up in front of the television set in the evening, you can watch a lot of TV in a productive manner. Just make certain you have plenty of light.

PLANS

It's impossible to build a scale model ship without a set of plans. You cannot build an accurate replica from a photo or painting no matter how hard you try. But where do you get the plans for a ship?

The easiest sources to find are the same companies that make parts. All of them are primarily in the kit business, but they sell plans separately, and these plans are ideal in being scaled and noted specifically for modelers. They are also quite economical, ranging from a dollar or so for small vessels up to five or six dollars for a big clipper. Many are also suitable for framing after you're completed the building.

The disadvantage of using kit plans, though, is that you produce a model just like hundreds of others made from that kit. One of the great things about building from scratch is the lack of limitations on what you can build. For non-kit plans, you have to look around a little, but the result is bound to be something out of the ordinary and perhaps one of its kind.

One excellent source for such drawings is the maritime museums that abound along the eastern seaboard. The gift shop at the Whaling Museum in New Bedford, Massachusetts, for example, carries modelers' plans for at least a dozen vessels, some of them sold in different scales. The same is true of Mystic Seaport, Connecticut; the Mariners' Museum at Norfolk, Virginia; and any number of others.

If you'd like to get truly authentic, you can check with the state archives of any coastal state. Nearly all have fallen heir, at one time or another, to builders' drafts passed on by dying shipyards. If they haven't, the archivists can tell you who has collections in their states. You can also check listings of maritime museums and libraries. Model Shipways sells the *Nautical Museum Directory* for $1.85, and some of the nautical histories have appendixes listing these museums. *America's Maritime Heritage*, by Eloise Engle and Arnold S. Lott, for example, has an appendix that includes nautical museums.

Some states have public or private societies dedicated to the preservation of their seafaring traditions, such as the Peabody Museum in Salem, Massacusetts. These organizations usually publish a list of drafts in their possession, and they will sell photocopies of the plans at some fee per square foot. This is also the case with the National Archives in Washington, D.C., which has extensive holdings of warship plans going all the way back to the 1790's.

Another excellent source is the Smithsonian Institute in Washington, D.C., and you can "shop" for their plans without going farther than the public library.

One of the nation's finest naval historians is Howard I. Chappelle, author of numerous books on American naval architecture. Chappelle retired a few years ago from the Smithsonian, leaving a great legacy of ship plans, many of which appear in his books. Any draft you find in *The History of American Sailing Ships, The History of the American Sailing Navy*, and other Chappelle books, can be ordered at a per-square-foot charge from the Smithsonian Institute, Division of Naval History, Washington, D.C. The institute has other drawings such as an extraordinary 1/4″ scale rendering of the famed revenue cutter *Bear*. If you write, or better yet call, you will find the people there most considerate and helpful. Also, their model-makers cheerfully give advice to hobbyists who call.

In browsing through ship books, you may fall in love with a vessel whose plans appear with the source unnamed: if the plans shown in the book are clear enough, and large enough to get an accurate measure, you can use them to build a model using the scale-conversion techniques discussed in Chapter 4. The job, though somewhat tedious, is not especially difficult and if carefully done it will yield a satisfactory model.

If you are interested in warships, a good source for plans is the Historian of the British Navy at Portsmouth, England. The

British Navy made, for posterity, admiralty drafts of every captured vessel ever brought into His Majesty's Royal Dockyards. This listing includes many American naval and privateering vessels. The British have been more scrupulous about preserving their drafts than we have, with the result that their files on certain significant American vessels (e.g. *Hancock, President,* and *Chesapeake*) are better than ours. If the ship you want to build was taken by the British, write the Historian and ask if the drafts are available. Ask, also, for a price guide. You will have to pay with a money order in pounds sterling, but this can be easily arranged with your bank.

The age of sail produced thousands of vessels. The plans for a great many of these vessels still exist. To locate them, exercise a bit of investigative imagination. The process can be almost as much fun and as absorbing as the selection and building of your ship.

Chapter 3

Selecting Your Model

When you select a ship model kit, you are picking one of the ships someone else thinks you ought to build. The modeler who builds from scratch is freed from the judgment of others; his choice of a ship is subject only to the availability of plans, and to practical considerations.

A PLACE TO DISPLAY IT

As soon as you have decided to build a ship model, ask yourself where it will ultimately stand. On the mantle? In a bookcase? Atop the piano? This must be your first decision, because the amount of space available will determine the size and scale of the model.

Environmental requirements have much to do with selecting the place to display your model. Avoid places in the direct flow of air from registers. Extremes in temperature cause the wood to warp and will eventually break the cement bonds. Sunlight will do the same thing and will also bleach paints. Choose a place where humidity is fairly low and constant, to prevent the wood from swelling and shrinking. Stay away from dusty places.

One of the favorite spots to display a ship is on the mantle. There is nothing wrong with the mantle, so long as the fireplace draws properly. Check it. Tape a sheet of paper so it hangs down from the mantle's edge, then light a fire in the fireplace. If the paper moves from heat currents, the mantle is a poor choice—unless you seldom use your fireplace. It's also a poor choice if the width is inadequate to hold the model without ramming a yardarm into the wall.

The spot you choose should be away from traffic that might bump, snag, or jar the ship. On the other hand, don't hide the model either. It should stand where it can be seen and admired. Almost everyone has some out-of-the-mainstream corner that would be perfect for displaying a proud vessel.

There should be adequate light, so that your craftsmanship can be clearly seen. The viewer should be able to see the ship from one side and both ends.

THE MATTER OF SCALE

The matter of scale is extremely important, and should be carefully considered. It affects not only the dimensions of your model, but the availability of parts as well.

You would be wise to stay with one of three standard scales, which are 1/8″, 3/16″, and 1/4″. These notations mean that 1/8″ = 1′, 3/16″ = 1′, and 1/4″ = 1′. Some kit plans come in other scales, such as 3/32″, 1/12″, etc. It's extremely difficult to find parts for such odd-size scales. You can also find plans in 1/16″ scale, but such a small scale is hard to work with and usually produces a toy-like result.

As a matter of practice, most historical and builders' plans for ships are drawn in 1/4″ scale. This has led to the convention of construction museum models in the same scale. That's fine for museums, which have the room for large models. Most homes, however, are better suited to 1/8″ scale, which will yield a clipper model of around 36″. The same model in 3/16″ scale will be 54″, and in 1/4″ scale it will be 72″ long.

Parts in 1/8″ scale are the most plentiful, but you can usually find most things in 3/16″ and 1/4″ also, at a slightly higher price. Fortunately, as you will see in Chapter 4, scale conversion is not difficult, so don't let differences between plan and model scales deter you.

If you are planning to build from a kit plan, the maker's catalog will tell you the overall dimensions of the model. You may find that this ship is either too large or too small for your needs. In that case, apply the scale conversion factors in chapter 4 to the dimensions of the model to find its size in other scales.

Let's say, for example, that you have a space 24″ long, and you are considering building a model 30″ long in 3/16″ scale. To make the model smaller, you must select the next smaller standard scale, which is 1/8″. Looking in the table on page in Chapter 4, you find a 3/16″ to 1/8″ conversion factor of .67. To change scales, you multiply the "from-scale" dimension by the conversion factor, so:

$$\begin{array}{r} 30″ \text{ length of model in 3/16″ scale} \\ \underline{\times .67} \quad \text{conversion factor 3/16″ to 1/8″} \\ 20″ \text{ length of model in 1/8″ scale.} \end{array}$$

The model, with scale conversions, will fit your space nicely.

In shopping for a ship from actual vessel plans, the process of establishing model size is a little more involved. In Anglo-American naval architecture, the length given for a ship is somewhat arbitrary and never truly expresses the vessel's real size. Ship plans usually give a length expressed as LOA (length overall), LWL (load waterline), LBP (length between perpendiculars), or length on the range of the gun deck. For the purposes of estimating model size, any of these figures is suitable as a starting point.

Suppose your eye is caught by the *Hancock*, a frigate appearing in Chappelle's *History of American Sailing Ships*, and you want to estimate its size as a model. On the draft you find the length on the range of the lower deck given at 136′ 7″, which rounds to 137′. To convert feet to actual inches at different scales, use the following factors:

1/8″ scale	Feet divided by 8
3/16″ scale	Feet divided by 5.33
1/4″ scale	Feet divided by 4

To find the principal dimensions (length, height, and width) of a *Hancock* model in ⅛″ scale, then:

1. Find scaled length by dividing 137 by 8 = 17.125″. Estimate model's actual length by adding 50% = 25.69″, or about 26″.
2. Height of model = length less 10% = 23.5″
3. Width of model (square-rigged only) = length divided by 4 = 6.5″.

These are, of course, only approximations to help you match the ship to the available space. Ships vary widely in dimensions, with a corresponding variation in model size. The 50% added to length, for instance, is to accommodate the bowsprit and stern overhang. If your vessel has no bowsprit, add only 25%. If it is fore-and-aft rigged only, divide the model length by 6 to find its approximate width. If the estimated dimensions are not satisfactory, you can find the effect of changing scales by applying the scale conversion factors in Chapter 4.

THINGS TO LOOK (OUT) FOR

Building ships from scratch is easier than it looks, but that does not mean you ought to start off with a big three-masted square-rigger. Choose something fairly simple for a first ship, to familiarize yourself with the techniques and the materials.

Building bows and sterns can often be a problem. Ships built before 1820 had apple bows, which were essentially round in shape. Planking such bows can be frustrating for the veteran model builder, and terribly discouraging for a novice. It's best to select a sharp-prowed vessel, since clipper-type bows are clean and easy. Round sterns are all curves and they require some intricate carpentry. Pick a ship with a square stern first.

Avoid elaborate decorations. Sailing warships in general, and also some big pre-1800 merchant vessels were festooned with fancy carvings. They make beautiful models, but you could spend longer decorating a fancy stern than building all the rest of the ship.

Most ship plans include a drawing of the stern elevation. Study it closely, and check your catalogs to see if they carry any decorations resembling those in the drawing. If not, and if you don't think you can fashion the decorations yourself, file that ship away for a future project.

The rig is another consideration. It's advisable not to try a three-master for your first effort in building from scatch, unless it's a simple schooner rig or unless you've built a wooden kit ship before, because skill in rigging can only be acquired through experience. The experience is best attained on a fairly simple rig.

These constraints limit your choice for a first ship somewhat, but the limitations are by no means narrow. There are a vast number of plans available for sharp-prowed, square-sterned brigs, brigantines, barkentines, Baltimore clippers, and schooners, all of which make handsome models. Once you have completed your first ship, then you can forget about these considerations and build whatever you please, because you'll have the necessary skills and experience.

RESEARCHING YOUR SHIP

Any ship becomes more intriguing if you know her history: what she did, where she went, who built her for whom, how her career ended. Knowledge of the ship's architecture and of her history will make the model come alive for you and through you, it will come alive for others.

This sort of knowledge is gained through research, which is a lot more fun than it probably sounds. There are authoritative works on maritime history in nearly every public library of any size, and they make fascinating reading. Every one is a compilation of the lore of the sea: mutinies, exotic ports, shipwrecks, storms, heroism, unexplained mysteries. Most also describe the evolution of naval architecture to fit specific needs.

For general reading on the subject, some of the best sources are *The History of American Sailing Ships* by Chappelle, and *American Heritage History of Seafaring America*. If your interest lies in American warships, check Chappelle's *History of the American Sailing Navy*. A brief resume of every U.S. naval vessel can be obtained from the Navy Department's *Dictionary of American Naval Fighting Ships*, which is arranged by ship name in alphabetical order.

The great social movements that culminated in the clipper ship and all the voyages of these romantic vessels are laid out in highly entertaining format in Carl C. Cutler's classic *Greyhounds of the Sea*. There are many other sources, both general and specific, which can be found in your public library.

Naturally, not every ship that ever sailed will be found in the maritime histories. Unless you are building a famed clipper or warship, chances are good that the details of your ship's career have not been recorded in modern works. Don't let this discourage your research, though. Armed with only sketchy knowledge of your vessel—her type, home port, year of launch, builder, owner, all of which are ordinarily included on the drafts—you can learn a great deal about her without ever seeing her name in print.

Let's say, for example, that you are building a small sharp-prowed brig of 1847, launched and registered in a New England port. A bit of browsing in the maritime histories will soon lead to the certainty that she was engaged in the cut-throat Triangle Trade, which demanded cheap, fast vessels capable of carrying large cargos.

Further study of the Triangle will reveal your ship's ports of call, her approximate running times port-to-port, her likely scrapes with pirates, the navigation hazards she faced, her occasional illicit cargo of slaves, and her probable "retirement" after ten years or so to work the South America—New England trade routes.

This may not be the detailed, specific knowledge you could get if you built, for example, the *Constitution*, but it will make your model much more enjoyable. That's what modeling is all about.

Chapter 4

All About Plans

To convert lines on a flat piece of paper into a lovely three-dimensional vessel, you need first to know how to read a ship plan, and then you'll have to decide which hull-building technique to use so that if necessary you can draw working plans.

HOW TO READ A SHIP PLAN

Until the 1700s, ships were mostly built by skilled artisans who created the hull form as they worked. Their plans came from experience and existed only in their minds. The growth of British sea power in the 1700s brought about a corresponding increase in the interest in naval architecture. One result was the development of a uniform technique for accurately recording what a vessel looked like and how her hull was contoured. This record was soon extended into a tool for ship design.

The Americans quickly adopted the British system, since the Colonies were major producers of ships for His Majesty's Empire. We made some minor changes in the system, but for the most part the British and American methods are the same. Today, they are used as standards throughout the world.

A hull is all curves in three dimensions, and is represented on plans through the presentation of three views: side, top, and end. The curves are represented by imaginary lines showing

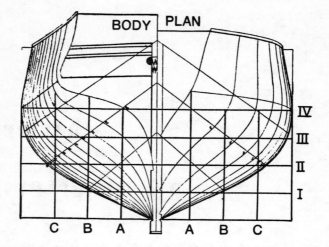

Fig. 4-1. Example of a draft.

what would result if a huge saw cut through the vessel in a horizontal or vertical position. The continuity of the curves is achieved by making these imaginary cuts at fairly regular intervals (see Fig. 4-1).

If a saw were to cut the hull from end to end vertically, it would slice off very long pieces. Viewing the hull from the end or the top, the cuts would appear as parallel lines. The shapes of these slices could be observed by viewing them from the side. The shapes are represented by the curves drawn on the side elevation of the hull plan. They are called the *buttock lines*. For modelling purposes, the actual buttock lines are not important, but their locations as seen from the top (parallel lines from bow to stern) and the end (parallel vertical lines) are important references.

If the hull were to be cut from end to end, horizontally by a saw, it would be sliced into layers appearing parallel from the sides and ends. But each layer would have a distinctive curving shape when viewed from above. These curves, called the *lifts*, appear on the top view of the hull. The position of each lift is shown by the parallel lines on the end and side views. If you choose to construct your model using a laminated method (detailed later), the lifts will serve as patterns.

If the hull were to be cut from side to side at regular vertical intervals by a saw at right angles to the keel, it will be sliced into slabs, much like a loaf of bread. The shape of these slabs, or *sections* as they are properly called, can be seen in the end view of the hull. The position of each section can be seen in the top and side views. For the plank-on-frame method of construction, (detailed later), the section lines serve as patterns for frame members, and in any model built from scratch they are the most important reference points on the ship.

The end view of the hull is called the body plan. (See Fig. 4-2). It is actually a composite view of the hull's port half. Because a ship is symmetrical, it is only necessary to show one side to illustrate the section shapes. Since a ship tapers fore and aft from a point of maximum breadth, a view from both ends must be shown. Thus the right half of the body plan shows a front view of the hull's port side from the prow to the widest point on the ship; the left half of the body plan shows a stern view of the hull's port side to the widest point. In this way, the shape of one half of every section of the hull is shown, and the form of the hull at its widest point can be seen.

One of the main differences between the British and American systems of naval draftsmanship is the location of hull lines. In the British system, the cuts of the imaginary saw occur on the outside of the hull planking, where the saw enters the wood. In the American system, the hull lines are shown from the inside of the planking, as the cuts would be seen from the interior of the vessel. Thus the British show the size of the entire hull, while the Americans' plans are for the frame without planking.

Each of the lines—lifts, buttocks, and sections—is designated with a letter, symbol, or Roman numeral. Usually the lines are referred to by dissimilar designations to differentiate among them. For example, sections may be numbered, lifts lettered, and buttocks given Roman numerals. Almost always, the section at the point of maximum breadth is designated by the symbol c.

The lines represent the curvatures and overall form of the hull, and are used to build the hull of the model. Once the hull is built, we turn to other drawings on the plans for details.

Often builders' drafts include a drawing called "inboard works." This drawing shows the ship from one side or the other, with the hull planking and frames cut away to reveal the arrangement of decks, cabins, bulkheads, windlasses, and other fixtures below deck. Unless you plan to leave your

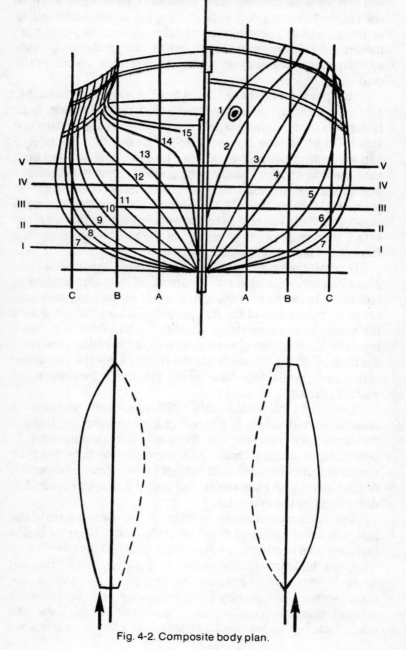

Fig. 4-2. Composite body plan.

model's hatches open for a glimpse "down below," most of the inboard works plan is of little value. The only useful part shows a side view of the deck furniture (cabins, hatches, railings, etc.) on the exterior decks. On modelers' plans, the inboard works plan is usually replaced by a side view of the deck with the railing removed, which is really only an inboard works plan with the unnecessary parts eliminated. (See Fig. 4-3).

The purpose of this side view is to show you how high things stand and what they look like so that you can reproduce them in miniature. Their position on the deck and their length and breadth are obtained from the deck layout, a view of the deck from above. These two views are almost always presented side by side with their section lines and thus all features lined up, the one directly above the other. This arrangement enables you, with a vertical flick of the eye, to see the same object in two different perspectives.

OTHER PLANS

The unused area on modelers' plans, and sometimes even an extra sheet, is often devoted to the small details and drawings and notes that describe the peculiarities of the ship.

Naval architects, however, are not usually as concerned with the efficient use of paper, and such things as fife rails, anchors, and launches appear on separate drawings. These details are important, but you should only buy builders' detail drawings for the things you can't get from other more necessary drawings, such as decks and inboard works. If you don't exercise a bit of judgment in the puchase of detail drawings, you can easily go to expensive extremes, acquiring irrelevant drafts you'll never use. As an example, in the listing of reconstruction drafts for the frigate *Constellation* (which is well suited to modeling) are included sets of drawings of the head rails for $2.50, of the fife rails for $2.50, and of several guns for $5.50. Modelers can learn enough from other drawings to make the various railings. The guns are purely standard for the period and are sold in a variety of scales by the partsmakers.

Other drawings you will need are rigging and belaying plans. The main rigging plan is usually a side view of the vessel with the yards turned to run fore-and-aft, so that you can determine the dimensions of all spars. Also shown on this plan are the standing (supportive) rigging and some of the

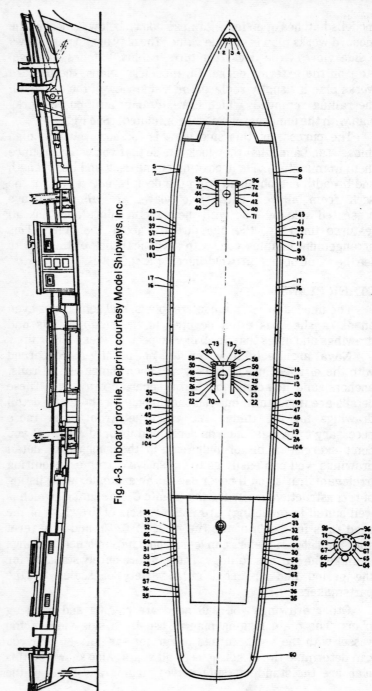

Fig. 4-3. Inboard profile. Reprint courtesy Model Shipways, Inc.

Fig. 4-4. Belaying plan. Reprint courtesy Model Shipways, Inc.

running (movable) rigging. Another set of plans shows each mast from the aft side with sail-handling rigging in place, plus certain details such as crosstrees, caps, platforms, and special rigging notes.

The belaying plan illustrated in Fig. 4-4 shows where each running line is tied off. The plan is useful during construction of hull details because it shows the location of the pin rails and the number of mounted belaying pins. All of these rigging drawings will be discussed in greater detail in a later chapter.

METHODS OF HULL CONSTRUCTION

The hull is the most important part of any model because it is the largest part of the ship and the foundation for all other ports. There are three basic ways of constructing a ship's hull: solid, laminated, and plank-on-frame. Each has certain unique characteristics that will be discussed in more detail in Chapters 5 and 6, but the selection of one particular method is one of the first major decisions you must make.

Solid Hull

Making a *solid hull* is, in my opinion, unsuitable for any ship larger than a lifeboat. Using this method, you start out with a block of wood and whittle it to a rough shape, then sand it down until its contours match the drafts. The method is unsuitable for several reasons. First, it's easy to cut off too much wood, possible ruining the work and making it necessary to start again. Second, there can be no points of reference within a block of wood, so it's difficult to measure where you are versus where you ought to be. Third, it is almost impossible to get the curves the same on both sides, since you are working without points of reference. And fourth, solid wooden blocks are prone to swell and crack, an event likely to create utter frustration after all the agonies of carving. See Fig. 4-5.

I have carved a solid hull. It took an entire weekend and a week of evenings to do it, yet it was a job that could have been accomplished in a few hours using other techniques. A friend spent months carving hulls for a five-foot schooner; "hulls" is plural, because he carved three before one finally came out right. Neither he nor I will be carving any more large solid hulls.

Most of the wooden ship kits such as those sold by Marine Models and Model Shipways have rough-shaped solid hulls.

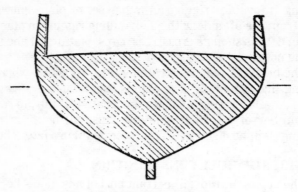

Fig. 4-5. Solid hull cross section.

These kit makers shape the hulls with a special machine that works with a jig to direct the cutting heads. Those building from scratch don't have the benefit of such devices, and should probably avoid solid hulls altogether.

Laminated Hull

Laminated techniques produce a solid or semi-solid hull, but without the agonies of carving from a block. The method is described in detail in Chapter 5, but in general, you transfer the lift lines from the hull plan to sheets of wood of the proper thickness (usually 2′ reduced to scale), cut the pieces, and then cement them together to form a stack in the rough shape of a hull (see Fig. 4-6).

The horizontal curves are created by the shapes of the layers. The vertical curves are made in stair-steps. You carve down the steps to approximate roundness, then sand until the

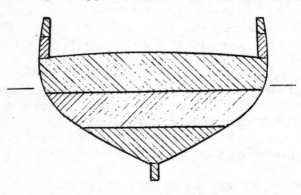

Fig. 4-6. Laminated hull cross section.

lift lines disappear. Ordinarily you laminate as high as the lift lines go on the plan, or to the height of the lowest visible deck, and build up the sides from there.

Built-Up Hull

A variation on this technique is the *built-up* method, also called bread-and-butter. (See Fig. 4-7.) In this method, which is detailed in Chapter 5 you also cut pieces to the shapes of lift-lines, but then you cut a parallel curve 1/2″ to 1″ inside the lift line (depending on how much overlap is needed).

When assembled in laminated fashion, the result is a hull that appears solid, but is actually hollow. This permits you to install inboard works, such as a cargo hold visible down a hatch. Care must be taken with this technique, though, to establish points of reference inside the hull to insure the curved planks are placed properly.

Laminating is certainly the fastest way to construct a hull. For anything from small launches up to hulls of around 18″, it is probably the best construction technique.

If you plan to plank the hull (you should—real ships were planked, not solid), balsa is suitable as a laminating material. It keeps the hull lightweight. Be sure to seal it inside and out before planking and building up the sides.

In general, laminated hulls are not especially susceptible to cracking like solid hulls, but balsa is so porous it can act like a sponge. Laminating uses a lot of wood, and for larger hulls it can be quite expensive. For any hull over 15″ and for all over 18″, you should consider the plank-on-frame method.

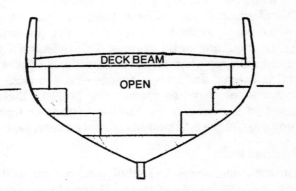

Fig. 4-7. Built-up hull section.

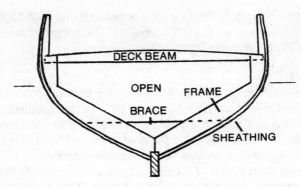

Fig. 4-8. Plank-on-frame section.

Plank-On-Frame

Plank-on-frame is considered by many to be terribly difficult. I have found it to be quite simple, very economical, and amazingly strong. It has the added appeal of duplicating the construction techniques used in actual shipbuilding. (See Fig. 4-8.)

Plank-on-frame has several steps, which are detailed in Chapter 6. In general, using the body plan of the ship, you make frame patterns for each section and cut pieces to the patterns. Next the frames are cemented and braced in place along a keel. The framework is then sheathed in 1/32″-thick balsa, and the planking is applied with contact cement. The result is a lightweight, tremendously strong hull with deck beams in place and plenty of room for inboard works. The process takes very little longer than other techniques, and for models with a hull length over 18″ it's almost necessary.

The plank-on-frame method, however, has one problem that must be addressed; it's easy to twist the framework during the mounting of the frames. This twist usually eludes the casual admirer when the model is done, but *you* will know the hull is twisted and so will anyone else who looks closely. There are some ways to correct this problem that will be discussed in the chapter on building a plank-on-frame hull. One, however, is the combination technique described next.

Combination Hulls

The combination method of hull construction, as the name implies, involves the use of more than one basic technique of hull building. I developed the method myself, and it is presented in detail in Chapter 6. I have found that the most useful combination is that of laminated and plank-on-frame. (See Fig. 4-9.) Combining the two solves the twist problem of plank-on-frame hulls and builds up difficult structures such as round bows and sterns.

I used the combination method in building the *Hancock*. The hull is quite small, only about 16″ long, but I wanted to run a gun deck the entire length of the ship, even under the large quarterdeck, with a finished captain's cabin visible through the windows across the stern.

Because of the small size of the ship and because I wanted to avoid the twist problem, I laminated balsa sheets 3/16″ thick up to the last lift below the gun deck, and built up the topsides using plank-on-frame.

The ship's bow is round and gets rounder with height, a fact which would have made planking a chore. Even thin basswood strips don't like sharp curves, and 1/32″ balsa sheet will break when bent sharply.

On a larger model, the roundness would not have been such a problem, but on this small vessel the planking had to be fastened securely to something solid. So I built up the round bow by continuing the lamination upwards to the level of the foredeck. To avoid having a wall visible through the large deck opening amidships, I put the lamination forward of the mainmast and glued onto the backside of it a piece of black construction paper cut to size. This keeps the lamination invisible even through open gunports. See Fig. 4-10.

It's quite easy to combine laminated and plank-on-frame, and the technique is explained in Chapter 6. If you choose to

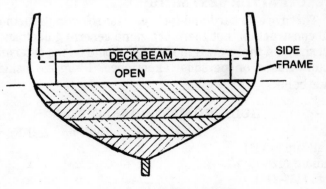

Fig. 4-9. Combination hull section.

Fig. 4-10. Laminated hull of Hancock model with built-up bow. Note black paper on after side of raised bow. This will be a combination hull.

laminate the bottom, pick one of the lifts as the demarcation. Use the lamination technique to build up to that point, and make frames only for the portion of the ship above the lift. Before you cement on the frames, the laminated part will look something like an aircraft carrier, and will provide a nice level surface to keep the hull from developing a twist. Make certain that the demarcation lift you select is wide enough in the bow and stern to mount the frames securely.

SELECTING THE BEST METHOD

There are no hard-and-fast rules for selecting a method for hull construction, but there are some general guidelines. The hull size, not the overall model size should be the determining factor. Based on personal experience, I suggest using the guide below.

GUIDE TO METHOD SELECTION

Size	Solid	Lam.	Built-up	P-O-F	Comb.
small (up to 12″)	x	x	x		
medium (12″-18″)		x	x	x	x
large (18″-24″)			x	x	x
very large (24″ and up)				x	x

Most home-sized models will fall in the 12″-18″ category, where the selection is widest, but in all sizes you have some choice. To narrow down the choice, you must study the plans. Examine Fig. 4-11.

Look at the top view on your plans and observe the lifts at the ends of the hull. If they are round, making either the stern or the bow elliptical in shape, you can eliminate pure *plank-on-frame*. It will be necessary to build up a solid structure using *lamination* on the round end, though the central body of the hull can be plank-on-frame. Measure the beam (widest point) from the longitudinal centerline to the side. If it exceeds 3″, eliminate *laminated*. Sheet balsa in widths greater than 3″ is expensive and hard to find.

Now study the side view, and especially the cutaway. If the main deck is largely flat, with little rise at the ends (see Fig. 4-12), *built-up* may be the answer. But if the main deck rises sharply, eliminate *built-up*. It's hard to make long, gradual curves from solid material.

Finally, take a look at the body plan. The characteristic of *deadrise* is controlling here. It applies to the flatness of the bottom. Ships are marked by sharp deadrise or low deadrise, as shown in Fig. 4-13. In a vessel with sharp deadrise, the bottom angles up from the keel, making the ship's underside a V. Some low-deadrise ships are flat-bottomed (clippers, for example), others are round-bottomed. If your ship has sharp deadrise, use the *plank-on-frame* method, even if one or both ends are rounded.

The overriding concerns in selecting a method for hull building are ease of construction and the model's finished appearance. Choose the method you'll find most comfortable, but keep your final goal in mind. If the ship has a gun deck covered by upper decks and you want open gunports, use the *plank-on-frame* or combination techniques. If you want open cargo and personnel hatches with visible finished space below decks, choose either *plank-on-frame* or *built-up*.

CHANGING SCALE

Chapters 2 and 3 referred to the need to change scale. This is necessary when the plans are of a different scale than the ship, or when the various plans for one ship are drawn in more than one scale. For example, some of the reconstruction drafts for the frigate *Constellation* are drawn to 1/4″ scale, but the

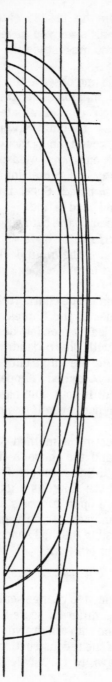

HULL WITH ROUND LINES

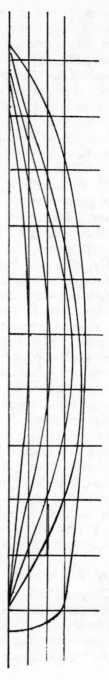

HULL WITH SHARP LINES

Fig. 4-11. Round vs. sharp lines.

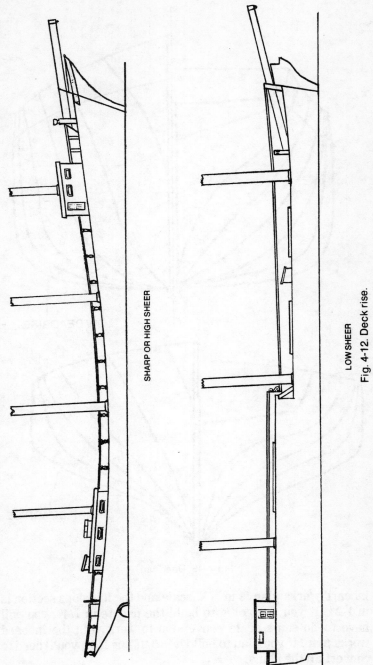

SHARP OR HIGH SHEER

LOW SHEER

Fig. 4-12. Deck rise.

61

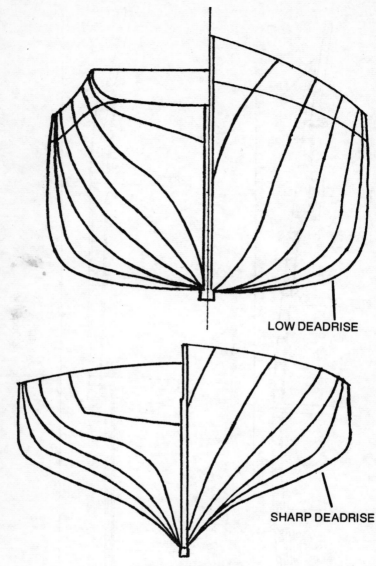

LOW DEADRISE

SHARP DEADRISE

Fig. 4-13. Deadrise.

inboard works plan is in 1/5″ scale and the midships section is in 1/2″. If you are going to build the frigate in 1/4″, you will have to do some scale conversion to work with the inboard works plan. If you plan to build it in 3/16″ or 1/8″, you'll need to convert all the plans.

It is *not* necessary to redraw the entire set of plans. In fact, you may be able to get by without redrawing anything. In most cases, you will only need to measure on the plan and convert the measurement to your scale.

An easy way out of the scale-conversion problem is to have the drawings themselves changed. You can take them to a blueprint service and have them blown up, or reduced to bring them to the new scale. For instance, if the drawings are in 1/4" scale and you intend to build in 3/16", tell the service to reduce them 25%. You can use the conversion table which follows to determine the percentage of change. There is usually a per-square-foot charge for this service. There is usually, too, some sacrifice of quality in the result, and light or tattered plans may not come out in satisfactory condition.

You can easily work directly from the original drawings, however, by changing scale each time you make a measurement. To do this, use the conversion table which follows.

Table of Scale Conversion Factors

from	to 1/8"	to 3/16"	to 1/4"
1/16"	2.0	3.0	4.0
1/12"	1.5	2.25	3.0
3/32"	1.33	2.0	2.67
1/8"	1.0	1.5	2.0
5/32"	0.8	1.2	1.6
3/16"	0.67	1.0	1.33
1/5"	0.625	0.94	1.25
7/32"	0.57	0.86	1.14
1/4"	0.5	0.75	1.0

The equation for converting a measurement in one scale to that of another scale is:

$D_2 = D_1 \times F$ where
D_1 = Dimension in the "from-scale"
D_2 = Dimension in the "to-scale"
F = Conversion factor between scales

Example: A yardarm is 6" long in 3/16" scale. Find its length in 1/8" scale.

F = .67 (from table)
$D_2 = 6" \times .67 = 4.02 = 4"$

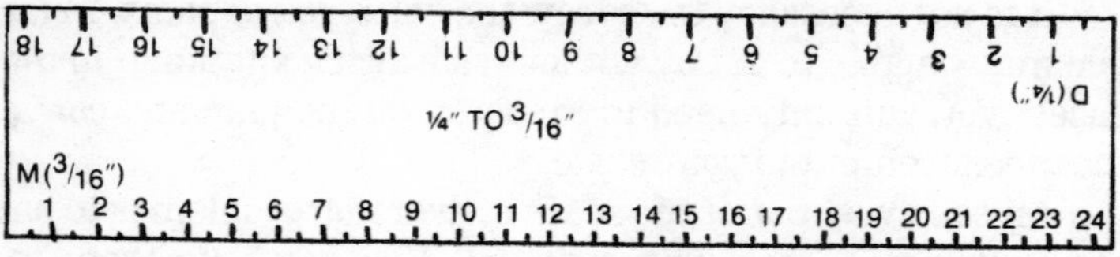

Fig. 4-14. "Home made" scale conversion ruler. "M" is the scale of the model, and "D" is the scale of the drawing.

It's easiest to make measurements in the metric system and then multiply by the scale conversion factor. Scales are expressed in fractional inches, but fractions themselves are harder to work with than metric measurements. If, for example, a hatch will be 1″ wide on the draft. You are building in 3/16″ scale. Measuring the hatch in metric, you read 25 mm. The conversion factor for 1/4″ to 3/16″, according to the conversion table, is .75. So $25 \times .75 = 18.75$ mm, or about 19 mm. That is the hatch size in 3/16″ scale. If you are a doubter, draw a line 19 mm long and measure it in inches. The length is 3/4″, or 12/16″. In 3/16″ scale, 12/16″ represents 4′, which is the size of the hatch.

If the metric system makes you nervous, you can buy rulers with inches in tenths. Flowcharting templates and form-design rulers are usually graduated in tenths of an inch, and can be purchased at office supply stores. The same rules apply as for the metric example, thus saving the possible agonies of computing with fractions.

You can also make a simple tool for scale conversion as shown in Fig. 4-14. Take a piece of stiff paper—a 3″ × 5″ card, for example—and mark the opposite edges D and M. On the D edge, mark off and number the feet in the scale of the drawing, then divide the feet into halves. On the M edge, mark off the feet and half-feet in the model scale. Use the D edge to make your drawing measurements and the M edge to make the parts for the model, measuring in "feet."

Conversion of scales that are multiples of each other—3/32″ to 3/16″, for example, or 1/4″ to 1/8″—is easiest. Just double or halve any measurements, depending on which way you're converting. But for other conversions, like 5/32″ to 1/8″, use a decimal-based measuring system to avoid fractions.

Admittedly, scale conversion sounds a little scary in description, but it's very simple, especially if you use metric measurements. After you've made a few conversions, the process will become automatic. This simple little trick of making conversions, which seems too formidable, or simply doesn't occur to many people, will vastly expand your selection of possible models.

WORKING DRAWINGS

In the building of every ship model, it becomes necessary to make working drawings. These drawings are patterns for specific parts, taken from the drafts. The drawings include lifts for laminated hulls, sections for plank-on-frame vessels, stemposts, deckhouse sides, rudders, and any other parts that need to be worked out. The process of making working drawings is not difficult. You need not worry about fancy draftsmanship so long as you pay reasonable attention to accuracy.

There are several ways to make a working drawing, depending upon its intended use. All working drawings have reference points. Ships are all curves, and curves must always, even in higher math, be expressed in relation to some point of reference. This is why drafts invariably include the locations of sections, lifts, and buttocks. When making a working drawing, then, you should always choose two or more convenient references, draw them on your working plan, and make all measurements on the draft and on the working drawing in relation to these points.

Drawings may be made on paper or directly on the material, again depending on the application. To make lifts for a laminated hull, you score the plank itself to show the location of section lines, then using a ruler and if necessary a converting scale, you mark with an "X" the intersection of the lift with each section. Then join the X's, working in the curves, and you have a cutting plan right on the material. Fig. 5-4 shows a plank marked out in this manner.

On the other hand, to make frame patterns for a plank-on-frame hull, you have to trace on a piece of paper the section line from the body plan, or draw it relative to the lifts and the centerline. Then you must fashion several pieces of material to conform to the paper shape. Working drawings should always indicate what they represent: "Frame 5, aft side," "Lift B, starboard, top," etc.

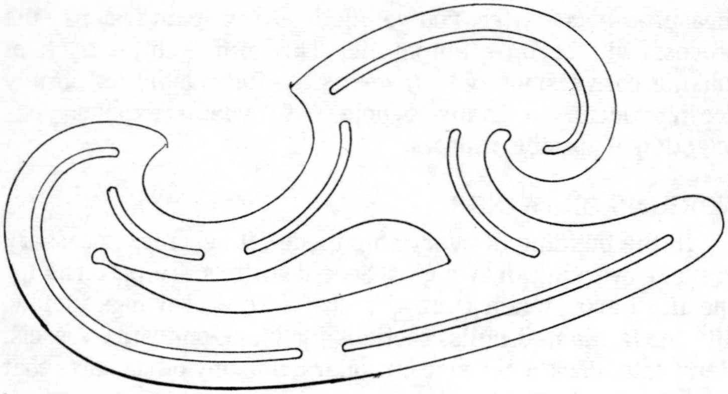

Fig. 4-15. A French curve.

The easiest way to make a working drawing is to trace it from the draft onto a piece of typing paper. Use masking tape to hold the sheet of paper in place. To transfer the drawing to a wood sheet, lay carbon paper with the carbon side down on the wood, then tape or pin the plan in place and run a sharp, hard-lead pencil over the cutting lines. Make certain the wood grain is running the right way, and that you label the part.

Because the hand does not readily reproduce a complex curve even with reference points, you would do well to invest in a set of *French curves*, (Fig. 4-15). These are transparent plastic forms with a multitude of curves, used by draftsmen and artists. I made most of the drawings you see in this book with a set of French curves purchased in an office-supply store for $1.75.

If you make your working drawings on paper, it's wise to keep them with the drafts and file everything away for future reference. You may want to build the same model again some day, or someone may borrow the plans from you. The working drawings will be a great timesaver.

Chapter 5

Constructing Laminated and Built-Up Hulls

Now that you have selected your ship, researched her, acquired the plans, read them, and chosen a hull-building method, it is time to begin construction.

Hull construction is the single most important step in creating a ship model. The hull is the largest part of the ship and it forms the foundation for everything that follows.

Hull construction will probably take considerably less time than you expect, so do a good, careful, deliberate job. Try not to make any mistakes, but if you do, remember that almost no mistake is irremediable. You can always fix things by using a little putty or by reworking a poorly-done part. If you rush through hull construction, the ship will look hurried and sloppy no matter how exquisite your details and rigging. Take your time and the ship is bound to come out well.

BUYING MATERIALS

Use balsa planks for the basic laminating material. Measure the distance between lifts on the body plan for the thickness of the planks. If you're building in a different scale, don't forget to convert the lift measurement.

Measure the breadth of the vessel at each lift, converting if necessary, to find the width of the layers. Balsa planks come in widths graduated by the inch (2″, 3″, 4″), but 4″ is the widest commonly found. Most hulls will be less than 4″ beam, so you could laminate with each layer as a single piece. There is a strong danger, though, that you will get single pieces out of alignment. Thus, the first (lowest) layer should be of one piece, and all the others of two pieces, divided along the centerline of the ship. To find the width of the planks you need to buy, divide the greatest breadth by two and round to the next-higher inch (e.g. greatest breadth = 4 3/8". 4 3/8" ÷ 2 = 2 3/16", rounded to 3" for width of planks).

You now know the thickness and width of the planks, so the only remaining question is how many to buy. For this you need to use a little ingenuity. Because the lift halves resemble elongated humps, it is often possible to get three pieces out of a plank that will seemingly produce only two.

Suppose, for example, that the laminated pieces are 17" long. It would seem that a 36" plank would produce two pieces, since 17" × 2 = 34". By careful piecing as shown in Fig. 5-1, however, you can get three. Thus, count the number of laminated pieces you'll need and divide by three for the number of planks. If the hull is less than 12" long, divide by four.

THE LAMINATING PROCESS

Begin with the bottom layer of the hull, to which the keel will be fixed. As mentioned earlier, this layer should be a single piece of wood. Cut one of the planks to the length of the hull at lift 1, making certain the cut is straight across the plank at exactly 90° to the sides, and set aside the unused balsa for later work.

Now score the plank for lift 1 exactly down the longitudinal center on the top and bottom, using a straightedge. Draw an arrow on the top, pointing toward the end that will be the bow. All work will now be done on the top only.

Referring to the plan, begin at the bow and work aft, marking the centerline to indicate the location of each section. Use a square or a protractor to score each section line perpendicular to the centerline, and mark section numbers in the wood.

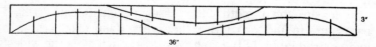

Fig. 5-1. Piecing lifts on a balsa plank to get three out of each plank.

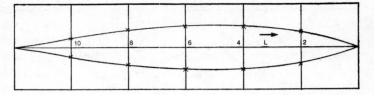

Fig. 5-2. Lift 1 prior to cutting it out.

Now return to the forwardmost section. On the lines plan (top view), measure along the section line from the centerline to the intersection with lift 1. Convert the measurement if necessary, and mark the intersection with an X on the balsa at section 1, measuring to the left from the centerline. (See Fig. 5-2.) Then measure and mark the same distance to the right of the centerline. Repeat this process—measuring, converting, and marking both sides—for each section of the hull.

When this step is finished, use a French curve to join the X's along each side in a smooth continuous curve. Extend the curve to the bow and stern ends of the centerline. The result should have the appearance of a finless fish, corresponding to the form of lift 1 on the drafts.

Cut out the piece along the curved sides. A jigsaw is best for this, because it cuts vertically, but you can use a sharp hobby knife. Words of caution on cutting thick stock with a knife: don't try to go all the way through on the first cut. Slit slightly into the wood on the first pass, to establish a path for the blade that conforms to the cutting line. Work two or three inches at a time, making several slices of successive depths until you get through.

Lay the wood on a flat cutting board of adequate size, but not the dining room table, because you will mar whatever is underneath. And take care to address the grain properly. The blade will tend to wander with the grain, so when cutting a curve make sure the grain is moving away from the curve and not into it. This will keep you from nicking the curve and wobbling down its length. (See Fig. 5-3.)

Laying out and cutting the rest of the laminated pieces is essentially the same procedure. Each plank will be marked according to the lift dimensions across its top. Instead of cutting a full layer, however, you will cut halves on either side of the centerline. Use the edge of the balsa as the centerline, score the section lines, and mark the distances by section from

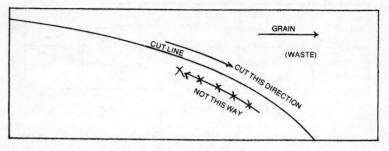

Fig. 5-3. Addressing the grain.

the centerline to the intersections with the lift being built, as shown in Fig. 5-4.

When you have cut out the lift half, use it as a pattern to trace its twin. Mark the lift number on every piece, and always draw an arrow pointing to the bow.

The side with the scored sections is always placed on top, since these lines will be used as references in assembling the hull. Extend at least one section line over the edge of the centerline and down to the bottom of the piece, making certain it is exactly vertical. This will serve as an alignment mark later.

If you are laminating a warship, beware of the characteristic known as *tumblehome*. It is also found on some older merchant vessels. Tumblehome occurs when a ship narrows upwards from a maximum breadth at the waterline. (See Fig. 5-5.)

Study the body plan of your ship. If your vessel has tumblehome, make **two** sets of lifts for the layer of maximum breadth. Because the layer immediately above will now be identical to the one of maximum breadth, its lift dimensions conform to the lift line it sits upon. Mark each succeeding layer according to the dimensions of the lift across its bottom, rather than to the dimensions of the lift above as you did on the bottom of the ship.

Assembly of the hull goes rapidly. Paint contact cement on the top of the lowest lift and on the bottoms and centerline edges of the second half lifts. When the cement becomes tacky, carefully set the marked half of lift 2 in place, making certain that the edge is placed exactly on the centerline for the entire length, and that the section scoring down the edge is precisely in alignment with the section line on the base lift. Press it down all over with your fingertips, working from amidships toward the ends. Then position the other half, getting the points of the bow and stern lined up with those on the installed half. Before pressing it down, squeeze the sides to make a firm bond along the centerline. NOTE: Before installing a piece, make certain it is correctly oriented with the bow to the front.

Amidships near the centerline of lift 2 on both sides, push a lill pin into the work to act as a nail and keep the joint from slipping. Use the end of a knife blade or some similar object to countersink the head of the pin.

Continue building upwards in a similar manner, always making sure the centerline and section reference marks line up.

Cement a strip of ordinary paper at least 1/2" wide along the centerline joint on every other layer, using contact cement. Leave the last inch or so of the centerline at each end uncovered so you don't lose your longitudinal reference, and mark the paper to show where the section reference lines up. The paper strip will keep the layer halves from coming apart when you drill for masts, and will generally strengthen the hull without adding any noticeable thickness.

When the lamination is completed, turn the hull upside down and cement a hardwood strip 1/8" thick and as wide as the keel along the scored centerline on the bottom. This false keel should fall about one half inch short of the bow.

Let the cement harden overnight, then use a knife to rough-shape the hull. (See Fig. 5-4C.) The inside angles, where one lift joins another, are the shaping guides. Slice down the stairsteps until these angles are nearly at the surface.

To finish the shaping, sand with coarse sandpaper until the lift lines disappear, then carefully sand with fine-grit paper to produce a satin surface. If in the rough-shaping you cut too deeply and can't smooth out the nick without destroying the curvature, fill it with liquid balsa or some other soft putty and sand the patch to conform to the hull lines.

The final step prior to installing bulwarks and deck beams is to cut off the false keel. Do it carefully, so you don't slice into the hull. If you get a couple of inches at one end free, you should be able to pull it right off.

BUILT-UP HULLS

Built-up hulls are essentially the same as laminated ones, except that they are partially or wholly hollow to provide for

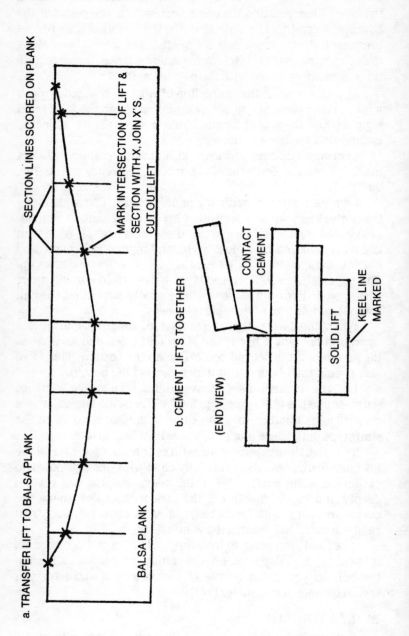

a. TRANSFER LIFT TO BALSA PLANK

SECTION LINES SCORED ON PLANK

MARK INTERSECTION OF LIFT & SECTION WITH X, JOIN X'S, CUT OUT LIFT

BALSA PLANK

b. CEMENT LIFTS TOGETHER

(END VIEW)

CONTACT CEMENT

SOLID LIFT

KEEL LINE MARKED

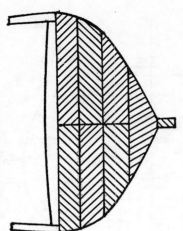

e. INSTALL KEEL, BULWARKS, AND DECK BEAMS

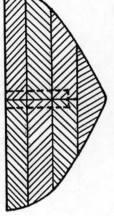

d. SAND SMOOTH, THEN CUT OFF FALSE KEEL AND DRILL FOR MASTS

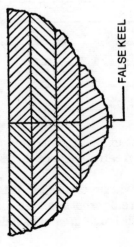

c. CEMENT ON FALSE KEEL (THIN STRIP). THEN ROUGH-SHAPE WITH KNIFE.

FALSE KEEL

Fig. 5-4. Laminating a hull.

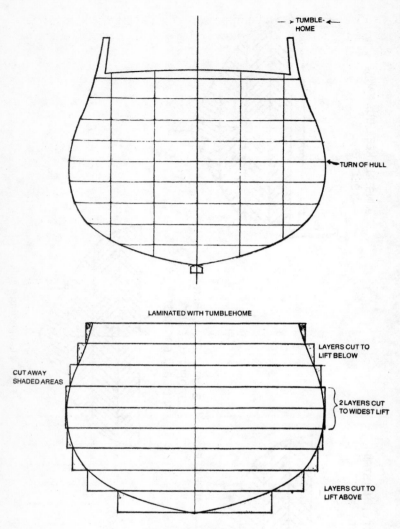

Fig. 5-5. Tumblehome.

cargo holds, open hatches, or cabins visible from outside the model. Such built-ins can greatly enhance a ship model's interest.

The subject of built-ins will be covered in detail in later chapters. Some guidelines are appropriate here, however, so that you can decide what built-in features to include, and how to engineer for them.

First, in order to be appreciated, a cabin or hold must be visible from outside the model. If a cabin has no hatch, don't waste time finishing it. The exception to this rule may be the captain's cabin, which ordinarily occupies the entire breadth of the stern. A broad gallery of windows across the stern may provide a suitable peephole into the cabin, but only if the windows are at least 1/4″ high and numerous. Also, there must be another source of illumination such as a skylight.

For a built-in to be visible, you generally need an opening at least 1/2 × 1/2″. This size will provide just a glimpse to give you the impression that there is an inside to the ship, and you have to do very little inside finishing to make an appealing feature for your model.

Assume, for example, that you want to be able to see down the main cargo hatch into the hold of the ship. (See Fig. 5-6.)

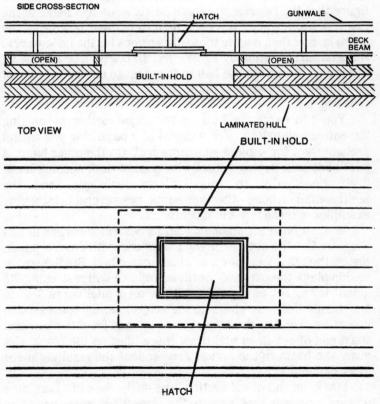

Fig. 5-6. Size of built-in in relation to opening.

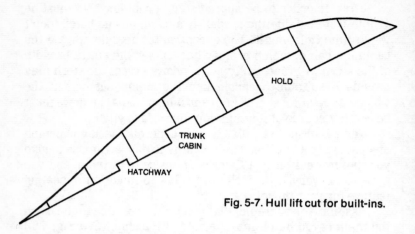

HOLD

TRUNK
CABIN

HATCHWAY

Fig. 5-7. Hull lift cut for built-ins.

Holds usually allowed for 6 feet of headroom, so you should figure that the interior deck will be six scale feet beneath the exterior deck. Check the deck plan to find out how large the hatch is, and then double those dimensions for the hollow area. If the hatch is 1″ wide by 1 1/2″ long, the hold will be 2″ wide by 3″ long, centered on the hatch. It is best to extend the size of the hollow area outward to the nearest buttocks and sections. (See Fig. 5-7.)

You can carry the built-up technique further by making the entire hull hollow. For a model of a large ship you should probably opt for a plank-on-frame hull. On the other hand, a pilot boat or a fishing vessel with a large deck opening lends itself beautifully to this built-up technique, and the Smithsonian, among other museums, has several outstanding examples of these types of models.

Make a base lift on one piece, as described earlier in this chapter. Cut the outline of each succeeding lift from a plank, just as though it were for a solid laminated hull. But then trace on this plank the curve of the lift on which it will rest, using the actual lower lift as a pattern. Draw a parallel curve 3/8″ to 1/2″ inside this line, closer to the centerline. Choose a section line at each end of the ship at least an inch from the bow and stern end-of-cut lines and draw these lines on the plank. Cut away the balsa in the hollow area so that the resulting piece looks like that in Fig. 5-8.

Mark the end-of-cut section lines on the base lift. Laminate upwards, always making sure the centerlines, represented by

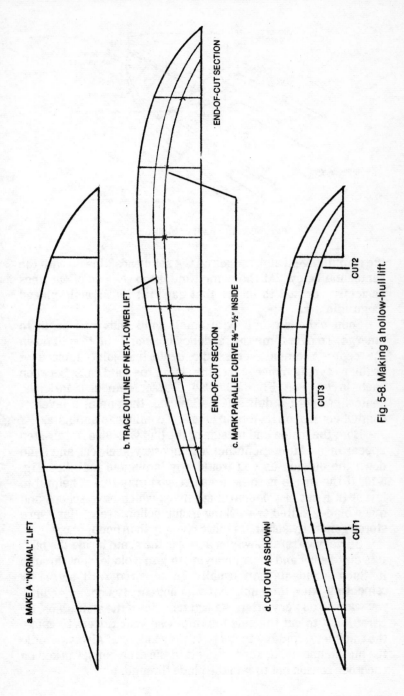

a. MAKE A "NORMAL" LIFT

b. TRACE OUTLINE OF NEXT-LOWER LIFT

END-OF-CUT SECTION

END-OF-CUT SECTION

c. MARK PARALLEL CURVE ⅜"—½" INSIDE

d. CUT OUT AS SHOWN!

CUT1

CUT3

CUT2

Fig. 5-8. Making a hollow-hull lift.

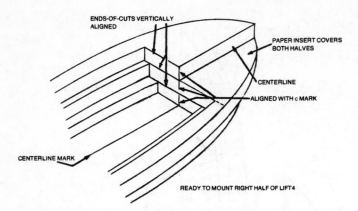

PAPER INSERT COVERS
BOTH HALVES

CENTERLINE

ALIGNED WITH c MARK

CENTERLINE MARK

READY TO MOUNT RIGHT HALF OF LIFT4

Fig. 5-9. Alignment of built-up lifts.

the remaining straight edges on the solid ends, line up with the centerline below. At the same time, keep the end-of-cut lines perfectly vertical to insure that each lift is correctly placed longitudinally.

Soon a hollow hull with small solid ends will begin to emerge. To overcome the tendency of such a hull to split down the center, cement across the centerline joint a piece of ordinary typing paper, cut to the size of the solid ends, between each layer. See Fig. 5-9. Use contact cement. Mark the centerline, with a dull soft-lead pencil, then paint a layer of contact cement on its top surface and continue to laminate.

Both the inside and outside of the hull will have a stair-step appearance. After mounting a temporary keel, cut and sand down the outside as you would any laminated hull. See Fig. 5-10. If the inside is to be finished, you may find it helpful to invest in a set of woodcarving knives which have scoops and other blades suited to working inside hollow areas. Hardware stores generally sell them more cheaply than hobby shops.

Be very careful how you address the grain inside the hull. It is quite easy and most annoying to jam a blade right through it. Such accidents can usually be repaired with putty by cementing back the hunk that was cut out; it's not something you want to do very often. As you trim down the stair steps, be careful not to cut the side too thin. Use your fingers to gauge the thickness, and try to keep it fairly uniform. Always cradle the hull in one hand, supporting it in the area being worked on (another reason not to jam the blade through!)

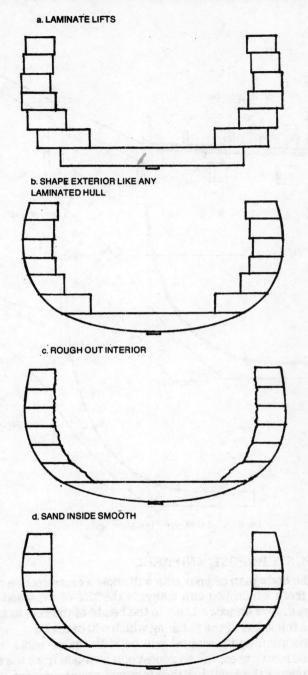

a. LAMINATE LIFTS

b. SHAPE EXTERIOR LIKE ANY LAMINATED HULL

c. ROUGH OUT INTERIOR

d. SAND INSIDE SMOOTH

Fig. 5-10. Shaping a built-up hollow hull. (Cross sectional view.)

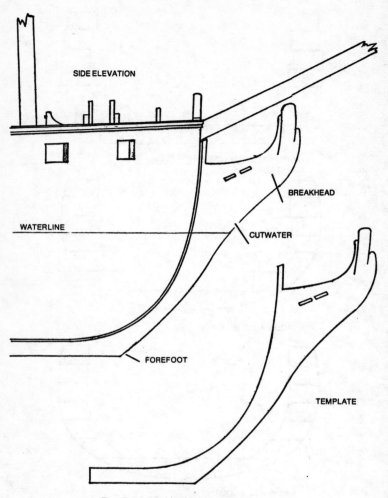

SIDE ELEVATION

BREAKHEAD

WATERLINE

CUTWATER

FOREFOOT

TEMPLATE

Fig. 5-11. Making the stem template.

STEM, STERNPOST, AND KEEL

The body plan of your ship will show a cross section of the keel, from which you can compute the size of the wood strip required. Add an extra 1/16″ to the height of the keel to adjust for the thickness of the planking which will be added.

The stem and sternpost will be of the same width as the keel. In most cases, the sternpost can be made from the same size strip as the keel, but the stem will require a piece whose dimensions will permit cutting a generous curve. Use basswood or a similar hard wood for all these parts—definitely not balsa.

Stem

As a first step, make a working drawing of the stem on a 3 × 5 card or some other stiff paper. Follow the curvature around under the bow and down the keel about 1/2". Cut out the drawing, taking care to make the curves smooth, since it will be used both as a template for preparing the hull and as a pattern for the stem. See Fig. 5-11.

Lay the hull upside down and hold the stem template in place. Using it as a guide, cut and sand the curve of the bow so that the template fits exactly in place. This may make it necessary to take some more off the sides of the bow in order to make the thickness of the cutwater uniform.

Lay the edge of a ruler on the keel line, as shown in Fig. 5-12, and use it to draw on the template a line that is an extension of the keel. Cut the template along this line, and save

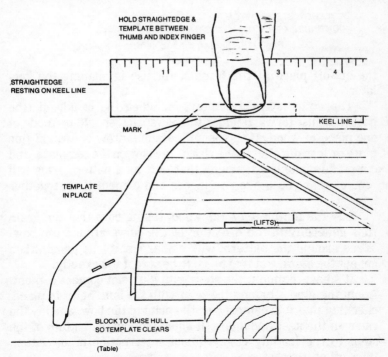

HOLD STRAIGHTEDGE & TEMPLATE BETWEEN THUMB AND INDEX FINGER

STRAIGHTEDGE RESTING ON KEEL LINE

MARK

KEEL LINE

TEMPLATE IN PLACE

(LIFTS)

BLOCK TO RAISE HULL SO TEMPLATE CLEARS

(Table)

Fig. 5-12. Making the stem template along the keel line.

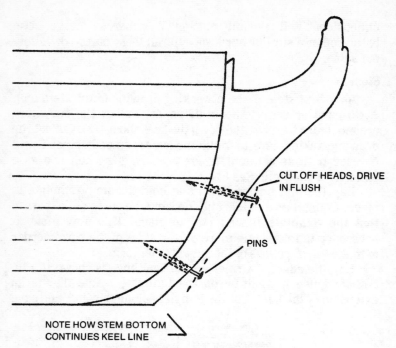

CUT OFF HEADS, DRIVE
IN FLUSH

PINS

NOTE HOW STEM BOTTOM
CONTINUES KEEL LINE

Fig. 5-13. Placing pins to secure the stem.

the cut-off piece at the forefoot for use in shaping the keel later.

The entire stem assembly, including the beakhead (the part that just forward under the bowsprit), should be made of one piece of wood. If this is not possible, draw a straight line more or less parallel to the rise of the bow on the template, and cut off the beakhead, saving that part as a pattern. This will require that you make two pieces and cement them together later.

Lay the template on the wood, taking care that the grain runs generally in the direction of the curve around the bow. Trace around the pattern, with a sharp, soft-lead pencil, then cut out the stem. Put it in place to be sure it fits exactly.

It's best to mount the stem with glue, not contact cement. Apply the glue all along the joint with the hull. Set it in place, checking that it is centered on the point of the bow, and lay the ruler on the keel line again. It should follow the bottom of the stem to the leading edge without interruption or deviation. Wipe off any excess glue.

When the bond has hardened, drill two pin holes from the leading edge into the hull, one near the forefoot and the other just below the start of the beakhead. (See Fig. 5-13.) Push lill pins into these holes, cut off the heads, and drive them in until flush with the leading edge. Put a drop of water into each hole to make the wood swell tight around the pins. Use putty to fill the holes. Finally, sand the leading edge to smoothness, taking care not to round the corners.

Sternpost

The sternpost mounts on the after-edge of the run, between the tip of the keel and the counter. It serves to stiffen the run, but primarily it is the fram member to which the rudder is attached. In most cases, the sternpost is not absolutely vertical. It slants aft from the end of the keel to the counter. In many ships, also, the sternpost tapers upwards, as in Fig. 5-14. Before beginning, study the side view of your vessel to determine the characteristic of the sternpost.

Cut the sternpost from a stick the same size as the keel. Make the piece slightly longer than the post will actually be.

The after-edge of the run may still be rough. If so, lay the post in place on the rudder and mark a line at the proper angle

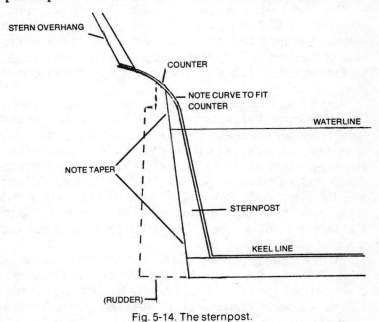

Fig. 5-14. The sternpost.

for the sternpost mounting. Cut down the run perfectly straight along this line, and sand it.

Next, mark and cut the sternpost to achieve the proper taper. Be careful of the grain; shave with it rather than into it. It will probably be necessary to whittle a curved or angled top into the post, to make it fit snugly against the overhang of the counter.

Set the sternpost in place, making sure there are no gaps in its joint with the hull. Then end of the sternpost will jut past the keel line. As you did with the stem template, lay a straightedge along the keel line and use it to draw an extension of the keel line on the sternpost.

Cut the post along this line, taking care to make the cut vertical through the wood. Mount it, using the same glue as you did on the stem.

When the joint has hardened, drill a pin hole from the trailing edge of the sternpost into the hull, halfway between the counter and the keel. Drive an ordinary sewing pin into the hull through this hole, after cutting off the head. Put a drop of water on the hole to swell the wood shut around the pin.

Keel

Cut the keel a couple of inches longer than seems necessary, so that when in place it will extend aft a half inch past the sternpost and forward an inch or so past the leading edge of the stem. If the hull and end posts are correctly made, the keel should lay flat, with no gaps, all the way from stem to stern.

Lay a straightedge against the sternpost, using it to draw a line of the correct angle on the keel (the after end of the keel should continue the angle of the sternpost's trailing edge). Cut along this line, then drill a pinhole vertically through the keel about two inches from each end. Set the keel in place, lining up the aft end with the sternpost trailing edge and the keel sides with the sides of the fore and aft posts. Holding it firmly in place, drive a sewing pin into the hull through each pinhole. For ease of removal, leave 1/4″ of the pin sticking out, and don't cut off the head.

Before making the stem, you were instructed to cut a piece off the bottom of the template at the forefoot. Lay this piece in place now on the keel, (Fig. 5-15), so that its leading edge follows a smooth continuation of the curve of the forefoot. Mark the curve on the keel with a sharp soft-lead pencil.

Pry out the pins and remove the keel. Whittle the forefoot of the keel around the mark, but make it slightly oversized, cutting to about 1/32" from the pencil line.

Apply liquid glue along the hull edge of the keel, including its joints with the end posts, and set it in place, using the pins as a guide to exact placement. With the glue still wet, adjust it

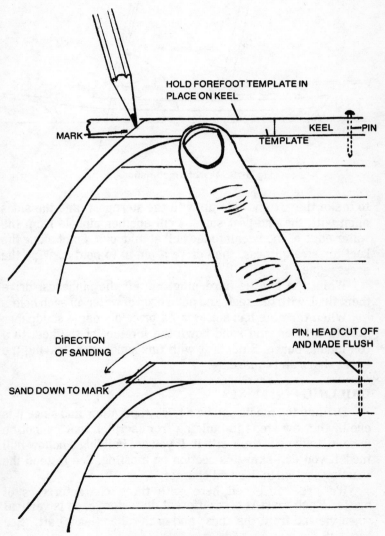

Fig. 5-15. Shaping the forefoot.

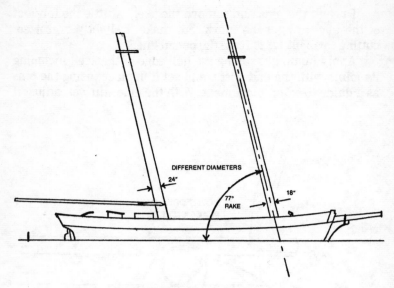

DIFFERENT DIAMETERS

24"

77°
RAKE

18"

Fig. 5-16. Mast characteristics.

to make the aft end line up with the sternpost, and the sides align with the end-post sides. Drill another pinhole from the water edge of the keel into the hull at midpoint. Sight along the keel for straightness, then drive a pin in to hold it. Wipe the excess glue.

While the glue is hardening, nip off the pinheads, drive them flush with the keel, and put a drop of water on each hole.

When the glue has set, wrap a piece of coarse sandpaper around a block and sand down the forefoot of the keel to a continuous curve. Smooth it with fine sandpaper, leaving the edges sharp and square.

DRILLING FOR MASTS

Drilling for masts can be a tricky operation, and since it is one of the few steps in building from scratch that cannot be undone, take your time with it. If you are building a hollow-hull model, you can skip this section on masting. See instead the masting section in the next chapter.

We are concerned here with three characteristics of masts: Each mast is of a different diameter; each is vertical when viewed from the ends; and each rakes (leans) aft. (See Fig. 6-16.)

The diameter problem is easily solved. Purists may differ on this, but in the vast majority of cases, dowels make perfectly suitable masts. They come in 36″ lengths, ranging from 1/8″ to about an inch, graduated by 1/16″ diameters. The mast diameters are almost always indicated on the plans somewhere, but if they are not, measure them on the drafts at the point where the masts enter the deck. If a diameter comes out to be an odd size, round it to the next higher multiple of 1/16″ to find the dowel size (e.g. 11/64″ rounds to 3/16″).

In studying your drafts, you will notice that the masts rake aft, from a slight angle in frigates to a wide angle in Baltimore clippers and pilot boats. The angle of rake may be the same for all masts, or it may increase as you work aft. In any case, it will usually be indicated on the drafts. If not, you can determine the angle of rake by measuring with a protractor laid on the waterline, as shown in Fig. 5-17.

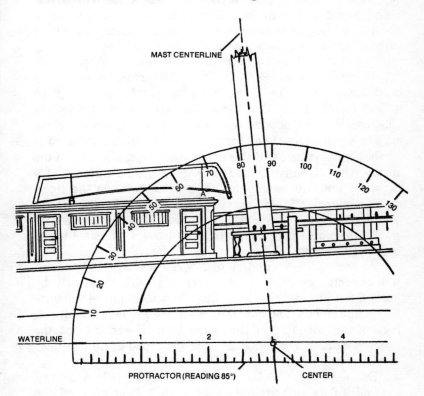

Fig. 5-17. Measuring the rake of the masts with a protractor.

The problem in drilling masts is one of precision. Viewed from either end, the mast, and thus the hole it sits in, must be perfectly vertical. Each hole must be exactly on the centerline so that the masts will line up. At the same time, the holes must be angled for the correct rake. This calls for some engineering ingenuity.

The easiest solution is to use a drill press. First, mark the mast centers on the centerline. Tilt the table at the angle of rake, and set the ship in its cradle on the table with the bow pointing downhill (see Chapter 7, Fig. 7-12 for instructions on making a temporary cradle). Drill carefully for each mast, using a bit corresponding to the diameter of that mast. The holes should penetrate at least 1 1/2″, but in no case come closer than 1/4″ to the surface of the underside.

If you don't have a drill press, you can probably borrow one without much trouble. If you don't have a friend to borrow from, check with your local high school shop teacher. Some communities have facilities such as visual arts centers that let citizens use heavy shop machinery for a small fee. You may even be able to prevail on a carpentry or machine shop.

If you cannot locate an available drill press, you can make a drilling jig from a thick balsa plank. Use a piece 1″ × 2″ × 12″ long. Cut the plank into two 6″ pieces. At intervals of 1½″ on one of the pieces, use a protractor to measure the angle of rake for each mast. From edge to edge on the 2″ side, represent this angle and one parallel to it at the distance of the mast diameter (Fig. 5-18). Cut a groove at a depth of one-half each mast's diameter between the lines, using a sharp knife and carving tools. Do this for each mast, (remember—the diameters vary) then use the grooves as guides to mark the other board. The grooves will slant in the opposite direction.

As you cut the second set of grooves, also to a depth of half the diameter of each mast, check the work frequently by putting the grooved sides together. You should have a square hole slanting down at the joint. When the grooves are all cut, cement the two halves of the jig together. When combined, the grooves will form openings as wide and broad as the diameter of each mast.

Draw a line across the jig centered on each hole, and bring the ends of the line around on the sides 1/2″ or so. Find and mark the mast centers along the centerline of the hull. From

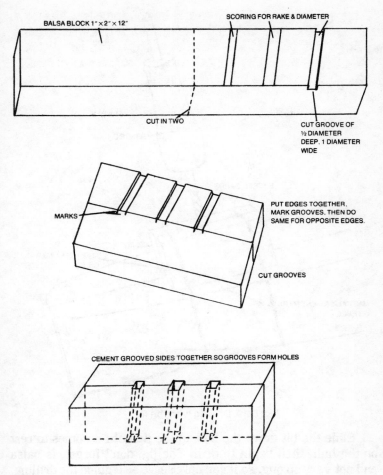

BALSA BLOCK 1" × 2" × 12"

SCORING FOR RAKE & DIAMETER

CUT IN TWO

CUT GROOVE OF
½ DIAMETER
DEEP. 1 DIAMETER
WIDE

MARKS

PUT EDGES TOGETHER.
MARK GROOVES. THEN DO
SAME FOR OPPOSITE EDGES.

CUT GROOVES

CEMENT GROOVED SIDES TOGETHER SO GROOVES FORM HOLES

Fig. 5-18. Making a mast drilling jig.

these marks, draw lines perpendicular to the centerline to the edges of the lift, as shown in Fig. 5-19.

To align for drilling, rest the jig on the hull. Line up the jig centerline on the hull's, and align the side marks on the jig with the mast lines drawn on the lift. Secure the jig with a couple of rubber bands around the whole works.

Before drilling: Make sure you have the right-diameter hole in the jig lined up with the mast location, that the hole is raked aft and not forward, and that the right bit will be used. It is best to drill with a manual bit and brace, but if you are proficient with an electric drill you can use it.

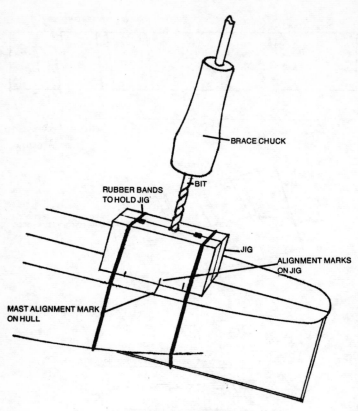

BRACE CHUCK

BIT

RUBBER BANDS
TO HOLD JIG

JIG

ALIGNMENT MARKS
ON JIG

MAST ALIGNMENT MARK
ON HULL

Fig. 5-19. Drilling with the jig.

Slide the bit down the hole in the jig until it comes to rest on the hull, then begin to drill. The jig, don't forget, is balsa and not very strong, so it can only serve as a guide for drilling. Don't depend on it for a support. It will be necessary to move and realign the jig for each mast, using the hole that corresponds to that mast's diameter.

FALSE MASTS

A *false mast* is an unfinished dowel that will be replaced later by the actual mast. It should be inserted after the holes are drilled. It will serve at this point as a means of checking the alignment of the mast holes, and later as a reference in laying the deck.

Buy dowels of the correct mast diameters. They tend to bow, so choose the dowels carefully, sighting down their length until you find the straightest ones. You can buy dowels in most hardware stores, but hobby shops usually have a better selection of the small diameters needed for ship modeling.

To make false masts, cut a piece 10″ to 12″ long from each diameter. The easiest way to cut a dowel is to mark the cut with a pencil, then press down a sharp heavy-duty blade on the mark and roll the dowel under the blade by moving the knife to and fro, always pushing down hard. As the cut deepens, lift the blade and rotate the dowel now and then to make the cut of a uniform depth all the way around. Break the dowel gently when the cut is quite deep, then shave the end smooth.

The dowel will slip into its hole more easily, and with less risk of damage to the hole's sides, if you chamfer the end slightly. To do this, cut all the way around with the knife, making the end a blunt point by slicing off the rim.

Hold the hull in one hand, supporting it under the mast hole, and with the other hand gently force the mast into place by pushing and twisting simultaneously. If you encounter a great deal of resistance, check to make sure it's the right mast for that hole. If it is, pull it out and sharpen the point slightly for the last 1/2″ or so, then try again. *Do not lubricate the mast* with anything. Lubrication will cause the hull to swell around the mast.

When all the masts are installed, sight down the ship's length. You know you have proper alignment if the other masts disappear behind the closest one.

Check the rake of each mast with a protractor. Should one of the masts be out of alignment, you can rout the hole by inserting the bit all the way. While turning the bit, twist the hull in the direction opposite the mistake. Keep routing and reinserting the mast until the problem is resolved. An other way to correct the error is to shave the inserted part of the mast on the leaning side until it becomes loose enough to straighten. Neither method, however, is as satisfactory as doing a good job of drilling in the first place.

THE BOWSPRIT

The *bowsprit* is the shortest and stoutest of the spars extending forward from the bow. There are a great many types of bowsprits, depending on the size of the vessel, the era, the intended use of the ship, the weather she was designed for, and the builder's preference.

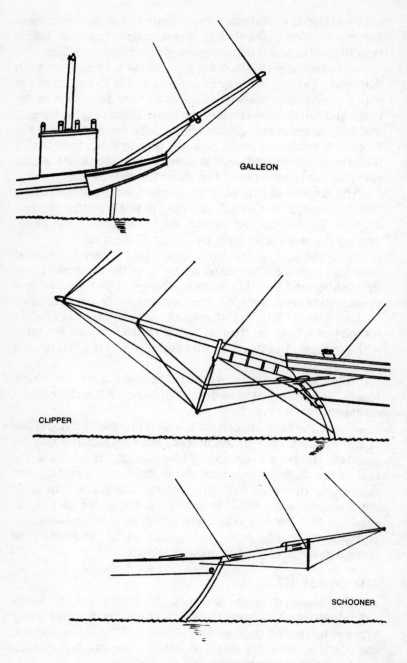

GALLEON

CLIPPER

SCHOONER

Fig. 5-20. Examples of bowsprits.

Note in Fig. 5-20 that all bowsprits share the common feature of an upward slant. This slant is called the *steeve,* and it is important to the appearance of the model. A bowsprit with the wrong steeve will make the ship appear droopy or haughty, so take care to get it right. Steeve is measured in degrees with reference to the waterline.

At this stage, it is necessary to shape and install the actual bowsprit. The finishing and detailing of the spar, however, can be left until later.

There are two basic types of sprits, round and square. The round sprit can be a dowel. Figure its diameter as you did for the masts. Square sprit can be made from a balsa or hardwood strip with the appropriate side measurements. Cut the sprit at least an inch longer than it measures on the plans.

Many sprits are square at the outboard end and the end where they enter the hull, but are round in between. These are represented on plans as shown in Fig. 5-21. To make such a sprit, use a square balsa plank. Measure and mark on each squared edge the point where the square part ends. Note that the square tapers into the round. Cut diagonally away from the square on one edge, at both ends, then carefully shave the intervening edge. Do this on all four sides, making the central portion an octagon with all eight edges straight and equidistant from each other.

Some bowsprits are octagonal and will be complete at this point. For those that are not octagonal, however, use fine sandpaper wrapped around your index finger, and sand the edges until the sprit is round. Be careful not to sand the squared edges at the ends.

Bowsprit mountings vary. If yours lies atop the foredeck, you will have to wait until the deck is laid to mount the sprit. In most cases, however, the sprit enters the hull below deck level, or partially through the foredeck. For adequate support, the sprit should be at least an inch into the hull, and held by a mortise.

A round sprit to be mounted in a mortise needs to be squared to a tenon before you cut into the hull. Measure from the outboard end of the sprit to the point of entry into the hull and mark this point on the dowel. Add another inch and cut the sprit from the dowel, then shave that last inch square. Dowels are usually very hard wood, but not difficult to square if you follow the directions in Fig. 5-22.

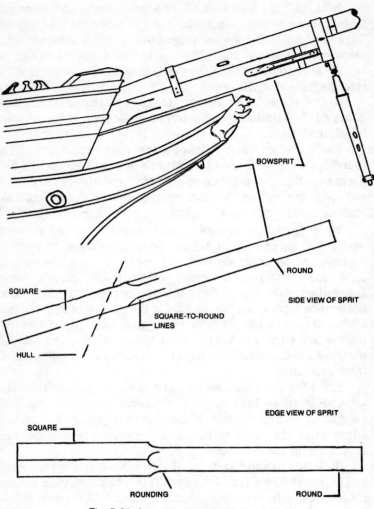

BOWSPRIT

SQUARE

ROUND

SIDE VIEW OF SPRIT

SQUARE-TO-ROUND
LINES

HULL

EDGE VIEW OF SPRIT

SQUARE

ROUNDING

ROUND

Fig. 5-21. A square-to-round bowsprit.

As you cut the mortise, you will occasionally need to check the steeve to make sure it is right. To do this, make a pattern from a blank sheet of paper. Place a protractor on the lower left corner and mark the angle of steeve. Draw a line from the corner through the mark and across the sheet, then cut along this line with scissors.

Measure the width of the bowsprit tenon and mark this measurement on the top lift, centered on the centerline. Draw two parallel lines aft from the prow a couple of inches, and then draw a perpendicular line about 1 1/2″ back from the prow. This "box" will serve as the boundaries of the mortise.

With a sharp knife, cut deeply along the mortise boundaries. Use a narrow chisel or similar woodcarving knife to cut the mortise, eyeballing the angle of steeve but making it perhaps a bit shallower than the final steeve will be. Cut down as far as necessary (you'll need to refer to the lift lines on the plan), stopping occasionally to put the sprit in place. Set the steeve pattern on its edge behind the sprit and make adjustments to bring the sprit parallel to the cut of the pattern. (See Fig. 5-23.)

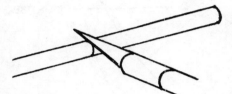

MARK END OF SQUARE. CUT SLIGHTLY BY ROLLING DOWEL WITH KNIFE BLADE.

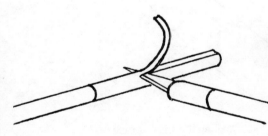

SHAVE A FLAT SURFACE ON ONE SIDE, END TO GROOVE.

 TURN OVER AND SHAVE OPPOSITE SIDE.

 SHAVE REMAINING TWO FACES.

 SHAVE ALL FACES DOWN UNIFORMLY, MAKING CORNERS SQUARE AND CONTINUING SIDES OF DOWEL.

Fig. 5-22. Squaring part of a dowel.

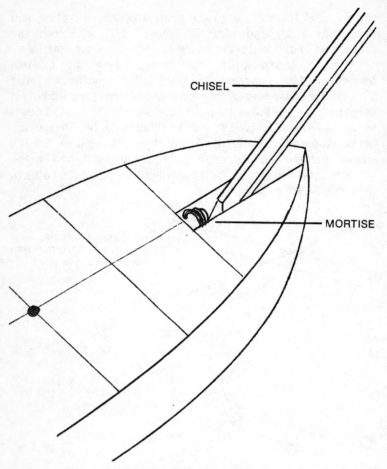

CHISEL

MORTISE

Fig. 5-23. Making the sprit mortise.

When the depth and angle of the mortise are correct, you can mount the sprit. If the mortise is too large, and the tenon is not gripped enough by the mortise to hold it securely, wedge the tenon in place with slivers of scrap wood. As you do so, make sure the steeve is correct and the sprit is pointing straight ahead, not angling to the side. Put a few drops of glue on the joint to fix the sprit in its tenon.

The basic hull is now completed. Since the next chapter deals with the alternative method of plank-on-frame hull construction, you can skip to Chapter 7 for instructions on completing the hull.

Chapter 6

Plank-On-Frame
and Combination Hulls

Plank-on-frame construction comes the closest of any modeling technique to the methods employed on real ships. The section lines on the hull body plan are made into ribs and mounted on a keelson (a timber above the keel that runs the length of the ship), the same way frames of wooden ships were mounted. A thin sheathing is applied to the framework, and planking is installed atop the sheathing.

The combination method uses a partially laminated hull as the foundation, with the lamination used preferably as high as the waterline. The rest of the hull is then built up with frames taken from the body plan. See Fig. 6-1.

The selection of methods should be tempered by considerations of the hull characteristics. Large models may be relatively expensive if the combination method is used. On the other hand, frame hulls tend to develop a twist and generally take longer to build than combination hulls.

The combination method, as mentioned earlier, is something I developed on my own, and this perhaps explains my preference for it. I have not seen such a method in any other literature on the subject of model ship building, and yet it is really quite simple and combines the best elements of laminated and plank-on-frame techniques, at the same time eliminating many of the problems of both. The *Hancock* model, shown under construction in this chapter and elsewhere in the book, was built using the combination technique.

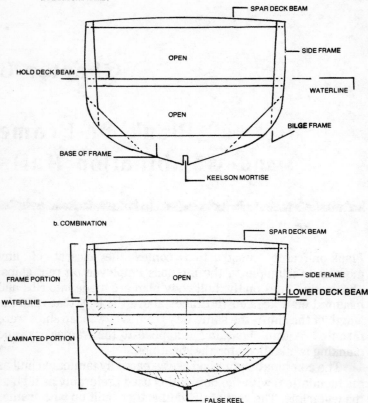

a. PLANK-ON-FRAME

SPAR DECK BEAM

SIDE FRAME

OPEN

HOLD DECK BEAM

WATERLINE

OPEN

BILGE FRAME

BASE OF FRAME

KEELSON MORTISE

b. COMBINATION

SPAR DECK BEAM

FRAME PORTION

OPEN

SIDE FRAME

LOWER DECK BEAM

WATERLINE

LAMINATED PORTION

FALSE KEEL

Fig. 6-1. Sections of the same hull in plank-on-frame and combination arrangements.

THE PLANK-ON-FRAME HULL

Small models do not readily lend themselves to either of these techniques, as was explained in Chapter 4. The combination technique is, in my opinion, ideal for the medium-sized model that most people want for their homes. For big models, plank-on-frame is the only way to go.

Keelson

The *keelson* is the backbone of a real ship, and also of a plank-on-frame model. This timber lies inside the ship, directly above the keel, and runs from the forefoot to the sternpost. All the frames fasten to it.

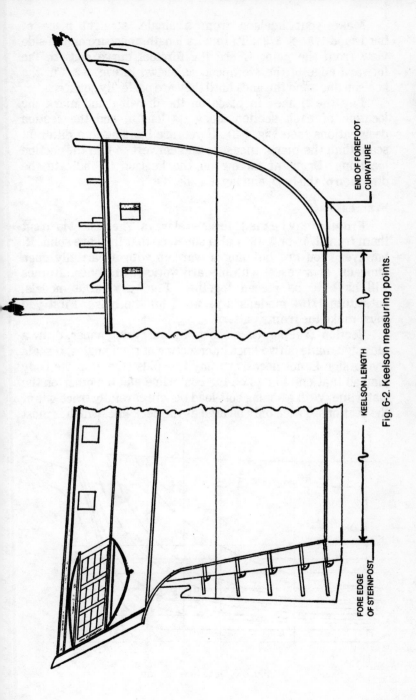

Fig. 6-2. Keelson measuring points.

END OF FOREFOOT CURVATURE

KEELSON LENGTH

FORE EDGE OF STERNPOST

Make your keelson from a single, straight piece of hardwood 1/8″ × 3/8″. To find its length, measure on the side view from the point where the forefoot curve ends to the forward edge of the sternpost, as shown in Fig. 6-2. Cut the keelson and sand the ends until they are perfectly squared.

Lay the timber in place on the drawing and mark the location of each section along its length, and the section designations (see Fig. 6-3). If you are building to a different scale than the plans, measure and convert to find the section locations. Draw an arrow on the keelson to indicate the direction of the bow, and lay it aside.

Frames

Frames may be made in several ways. The easiest is to cut them from 1/8″ or 3/16″ balsa sheet, so that they are solid. If, however, you are building a warship with a partially open gundeck, or a vessel with inboard works, some of the frames will have to be pieced together. For very large models, substitute 1/16″ modeler's plywood for the balsa. First you must make the frame pattern.

Section Tracing. On a sheet of plain typing paper, draw a plus sign made of two lines intersecting at right angles. If scale conversion is not necessary, lay this plus sign atop the body plan so that one line is on the centerline and the other on the waterline. With a sharp, soft-lead pencil, carefully trace one of the sections. Trace only as high as the deck line, which is most

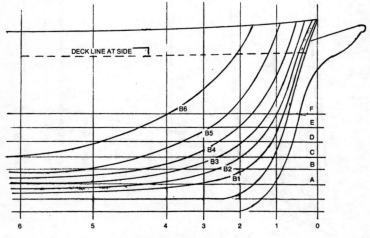

Fig. 6-3. Deck line on plan.

accurately measured on the side view (shown in Fig. 6-3). The deck line is usually designated by a dotted line marked "deck line at side" or "underside of deck at side." Since half-sections are shown on body plans, trace only to one side of the centerline, and mark the intersection with the deck line.

Scale Conversion. If scale conversion is necessary, it will not be possible to trace the sections lines. Figure 6-4 shows a step-by-step method for converting scale and making a plan for a frame (in this case, Frame 5). First, draw a grid of the lifts and buttocks in the proper scale. If the body plan is in 1/4" scale and the ship is in 3/11", the distance between reference lines will be .75 on the draft, according to the conversion table in Chapter 4. It may be necessary to add lifts to the body plan, continuing them at the same uniform distance as those put in by the draftsman.

Next, measure the distance, lift by lift, from the centerline to the section line. Convert the scale, and mark the distance on the appropriate lift on your grid. When all intersections are marked from the keel to the deck (*not* to the top of the bulwarks), join the marks with a curve.

Pattern Construction. Once the curve is drawn, by either the trace or conversion method, draw a line perpendicular to the centerline, passing through the section's deckline mark. (Use a protractor or square.) On the centerline, make a mark 1/8" above this deck line, then use a French curve to draw a long gradual curve from the centerline to the section line (see Fig. 6-5). This curve represents a deck beam that will stand when the hull is built.

At the very bottom point of the frame, measure 1/4" up along the centerline. At that point draw a short line perpendicular to the centerline. Also draw a line parallel to the centerline and 1/16" from it, intersecting with the first line. (See Fig. 6-5.) The space between these lines will form the mortise or notch for mounting the frame on the keelson.

Now fold the drawing along the centerline. Crease it sharply, exactly on the line. Cut out the pattern along the curved deck beam line and section line, using sharp scissors. Then cut out the mounting notch by cutting along the short lines just to the point where they intersect. When you unfold the paper you will have a complete frame pattern. Mark the frame number on the waterline near the edge. Repeat the procedure for each section line.

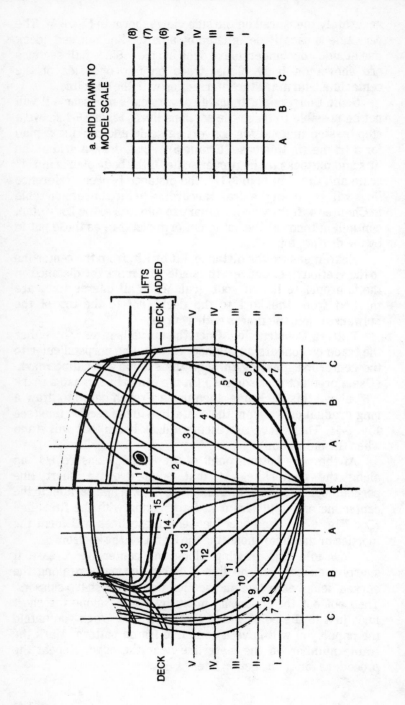

DECK

LIFTS
ADDED

— DECK

V
IV
III
II
I

(8)
(7)
(6)
V
IV
III
II
I

a. GRID DRAWN TO
MODEL SCALE

A   B   C

102

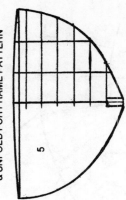

d. FOLD ON c, CUT TO SHAPE,
& UNFOLD FOR FRAME PATTERN

5

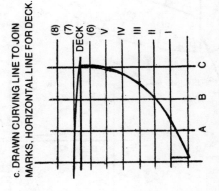

c. DRAWN CURVING LINE TO JOIN
MARKS, HORIZONTAL LINE FOR DECK.

(8)
(7)
DECK
(6)
V
IV
III
II
I

C   B   A

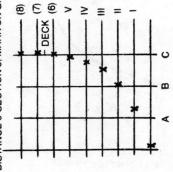

B. ON EACH LIFT, MEASURE & CONVERT
DISTANCE c-SECTION 5, MARK ON GRID

(8)
(7)
DECK
(6)
V
IV
III
II
I

C   B   A

Fig. 6-4. Changing scale and making a working drawing of Frame 5.

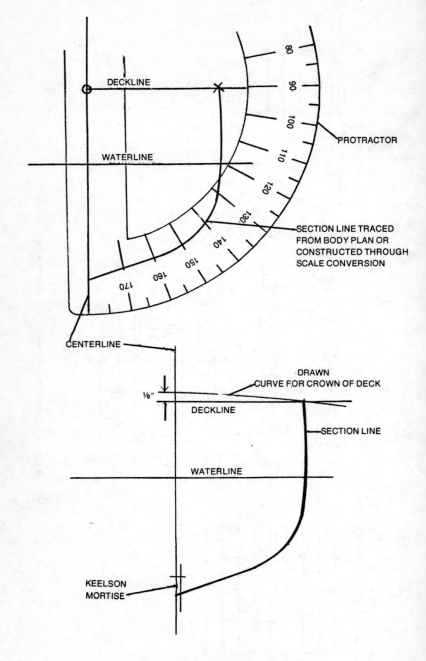

DECKLINE

WATERLINE

PROTRACTOR

80
90
100
110
120
130
140
150
160
170

SECTION LINE TRACED
FROM BODY PLAN OR
CONSTRUCTED THROUGH
SCALE CONVERSION

CENTERLINE

DRAWN
CURVE FOR CROWN OF DECK

1/8"

DECKLINE

SECTION LINE

WATERLINE

KEELSON
MORTISE

Fig. 6-5. Making a frame pattern.

104

The frame pattern may now be used to make a solid frame.

Frame Cutting. Pin the pattern to the balsa (or fasten it to plywood with a couple of pieces of tape), and trace around the edges with a soft pencil. Mark the locations of the waterline and centerline outside the pattern and remove the pattern from the material. Mark the frame number inside the outline. Draw the centerline and waterline on the frame, and check the mortise to be sure it is exactly 1/8″ × 1/4″ and centered on ghe centerline. Then carefully cut out the frame.

Pieced Frames

Pieced frames are used when the deck is open or inboard works are visible. As their name suggests, such frames are made by assembling several pieces.

The design of the frame depends upon what will be inside it. The outside must conform to the section line that the body plan provides. But for the inside, you're pretty much on your own. Pay attention to the thickness of the ship's side, especially if it is a warship that will have open gunports.

The sides of warships actually ran about 12″ to 18″, but in a model you can get by with 24″ sides. In 1/8″ scale, this means your side should not exceed 1/4″ in thickness. You'll probably want to plank inside, so deduct 1/32″ for that. Outside you will have 1/32″ sheathing and 1/32″ planking, so subtract another 1/16″. The frame member, then, can be only 5/32″ thick measuring across the breadth of the ship, and that's not very much. In most merchant vessels, the side thickness is not as critical as this.

In most cases, a pieced frame will support two decks, and occasionally three. The top deck beam should have a crown matching the crowns of the solid frames—1/8″ higher in the center than on the sides. It's not difficult to carve this curve into the beam before mounting. Lower decks, however, need not have a crown. Any roundness of these decks will not be noticeable. If the vertical spacing between decks is not given on the plans, assume there are six or seven scale feet separating them.

Use the frame pattern to work out your piecing plan. Figure 6-6 shows a typical piecing layout. If possible, make the frame solid, up to the waterline, and piece it only above that point. If the arrangement of decks prevents this, you will have to make a fully pieced frame.

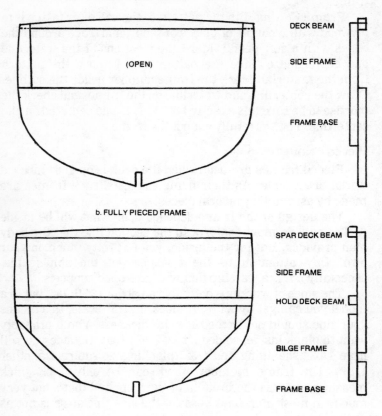

a. "TYPICAL" FRAME

DECK BEAM

SIDE FRAME

(OPEN)

FRAME BASE

b. FULLY PIECED FRAME

SPAR DECK BEAM

SIDE FRAME

HOLD DECK BEAM

BILGE FRAME

FRAME BASE

Fig. 6-6. Pieced frame layouts.

Despite its appearance on paper, a pieced frame is not flat. The pieces must overlap fore-and-aft for the sake of strength. Thus, where pieces join, make one of the pieces at least 1/4″ longer than it appears on the plan, and be sure that the joint portion conforms to the lines of the piece it joins. Figure 6-7 shows this arrangement.

Make the frame from the bottom upward. First, cut the base piece and make sure the slot fits snugly on the keelson. Next, carve the pieces above. Make both pieces identical, so that the frame will be perfectly symmetrical. The best material for this is 1/8″ hardwood strip.

All the side pieces should be carved first. Assemble them in their proper positions by laying them on the pattern, without glue. Last to be cut are the deck beams, which should reach almost, but not quite, to the outboard edges of the frame. Lay them in place, and check the whole works against the plan to be sure everything is correct.

Remove all pieces except the base. On it, mount the first side pieces using glue, not contact cement. It may be necessary to lay a piece of 1/8″ stock under these pieces to support them as they dry. Be sure they line up correctly with the plan.

Assemble all the side pieces first, mounting similar pieces on both sides at the same time. Mount the deck beams last. The glue may cement the pattern to the frame. If this happens, cut it off with a knife after the frame bonds are thoroughly set. Always mark the section number on the frame and mark the waterline.

Frames

After you have made all the frames that mount directly on the keelson, it is time to build the skeleton of your hull. It is also time to confront the annoying twist problem.

Twist is not a result of sloppy workmanship, but rather a natural phenomenon arising from the assembly of many parts into a long structure. Each frame is imperceptibly out of alignment with its neighbor, but when you multiply these tiny imperfections by fifteen or twenty frames, they produce a noticeable flaw.

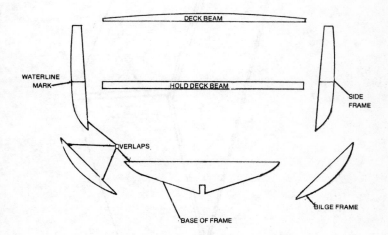

Fig. 6-7. Exploded view of fully pieced frame.

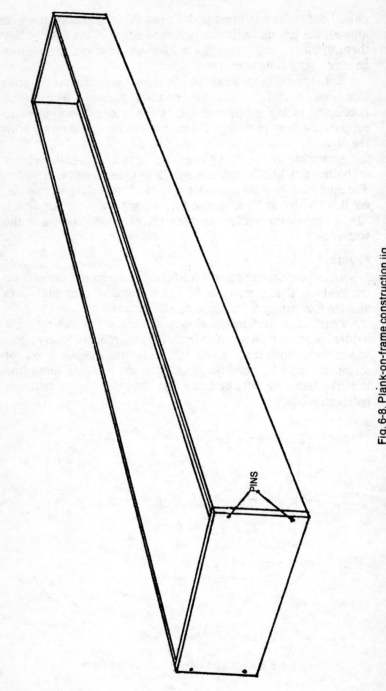

PINS

Fig. 6-8. Plank-on-frame construction jig.

This problem is most easily dealt with by constructing the frame in a jig. Make the jig from 1/4″ balsa plank. It should be at least 2″ wider and longer than the hull, and 1/2″ deeper than the distance from keel to waterline. Thus, for example, if the hull is 22″ long, 5″ beam, and 2″ draft, make a 24″ × 7″ open-top box of 1/4″ × 3″ balsa as shown in Fig. 6-8. Always make sure this jig is resting on a flat surface while the hull is under construction inside it. When the frame is completed, you will be able to dismantle the jig and use the balsa for other things.

Before beginning construction of the frame, you will need to make wide beams. Count the frames and cut that number of pieces of 1/8″ × 1/8″ balsa strip. Make each strip at least an inch longer than the width of the jig. Mark the center of each strip. Glue these strips on the marked-up side of each hull frame. The guide beams should rest above the waterline, and their center mark should be aligned with the frame centerline. If you have pieced frames, cement the guide beams atop the waterline marks on the side pieces or, if the frame has a solid base up to the waterline, cement the beams directly on the top edge of the base. See Fig. 6-9.

Turn over all the frames. Using the guide beam ends extending outboard as a reference, mark the waterline on the reverse sides (that is, on the lower edge of the beam). For each frame except those at the ends of the hull, cut 1/4″ × 1/4″ strip balsa into a beam that reaches almost from one edge of the frame to the other. Cement it in place, with its lower edge on the waterline.

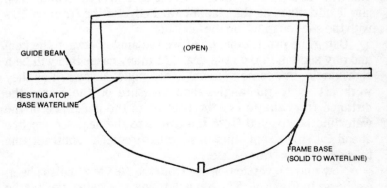

Fig. 6-9. Guide beam.

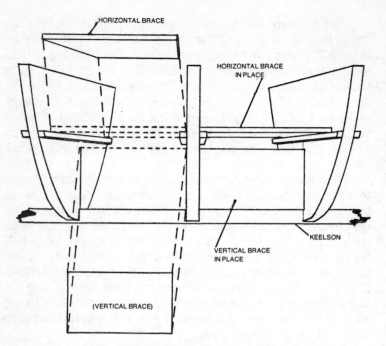

Fig. 6-10. Vertical and horizontal frame braces.

Now you're ready to begin mounting the frames on the keelson. You will need a 1/8″ × 3″ balsa sheet, a tube of glue, a sharp knife, and a protractor.

Start by mounting the frame closest to the stern. The guide beam should be positioned on the forward face. Squeeze some glue into the mounting mortise at the bottom of the frame, then slip it into place so that the forward edge of the frame aligns with the section mark on the keelson.

Using the protractor, measure the angle between the keel and any section line on the draft. In many cases this will be a right angle, but some vessels' keels angle downward as they work aft. Note the angle, then measure on the frame the distance from the top of the keelson to the underside of the waterline beam, and from the frame to the next section line ahead of it. From this last measurement, subtract the thickness of the frame base.

Now make a vertical brace from the 1/8″ × 3″ balsa sheet, as shown in Fig. 6-10. The top will follow the waterline and the sides will join the frames, so make these parts at right angles to each other. The aft edge should be the length of the distance from the keelson. The angle at the bottom is the same as the angle between the keel and the section line. The bottom edge is as long as the distance to the aft side of the next frame. Glue this brace to the top of the keelson and the forward face of the frame.

Next, mount the forward-most frame with the guide beam facing aft, and make a vertical brace for it. This brace will be glued to the after face of the frame, so do not deduct the frame thickness from the section-to-section measurement along the keelson top.

Before the glue has completely hardened, set the framework into the jig. Make sure all four guide beams' ends are resting on the jig. (See Fig. 6-11.)

When the glue hardens, begin mounting frames from the bow aft. Use a vertical brace between every other pair of frames (between #1 and #2, between #3 and #4, etc.). Between every set of frames, mount a horizontal brace, which is merely a rectangle of 1/8″ balsa 3″ wide and long enough to fit snugly between the frames. Glue this brace atop the waterline beams, as shown in Fig. 6-10.

Now mount the deck beams. Remember that these beams should have a crown matching the crown of the frames, 1/8″ higher in the center than the sides. Carve this curve into the beam. Then locate the widest frame. Forward of this frame, the deck beams should be mounted on the aft face of each succeeding frame; abaft the widest frame, reverse this procedure and mount the deck beam on the forward face of each frame. (Refer back to Fig. 6-6.) This procedure will prevent the planking (added later) from bulging out because of the beam ends.

Mount each frame with its fore face on the section mark on the keelson top, then put in the horizontal brace, and finally check to be sure both ends of the guide beam are on the jig. You may find it best to cement the beams to the jig so that the frames will not be accidentally knocked out of place before the glue sets.

This work will progress with surprising speed. When I built the six-foot *Bear* model, for example, it took only two or three evenings to mount all the frames on the keelson. The *Flying Fish* I built took one evening to frame.

Pieced frames may take a bit longer than solid ones, since the bracing has to be tailored to the frames. If you have only

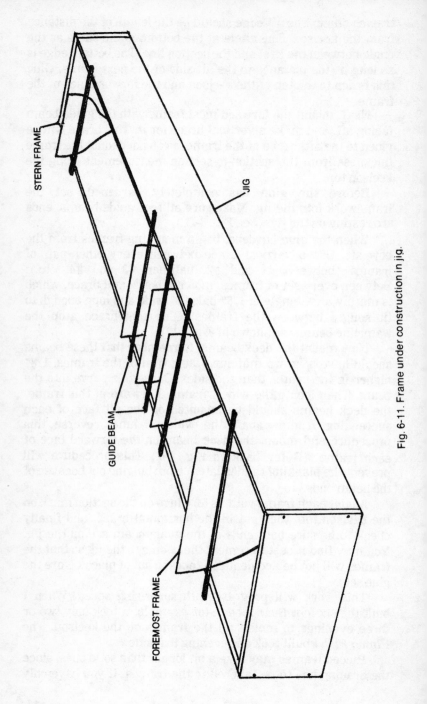

Fig. 6-11. Frame under construction in jig.

STERN FRAME

JIG

GUIDE BEAM

FOREMOST FRAME

112

three or four pieced frames in a row, you can eliminate the vertical bracing, but horizontal bracing must always be provided somehow to keep the frames from flopping around. One way to stabilize the frames is to lay a lower deck if the frames have one. Cut a piece of 1/32" balsa sheet to fit the deck beams, cement it in place, and then lay a deck of 1/32" × 1/8" hardwood strips running fore and aft. Use contact cement for the decking.

Another way is to mount a temporary horizontal brace. Cement small blocks of balsa on the waterline marks at the sides, then cut a piece of 1/8" × 3" sheet to fit and glue it in place. Later, after the hull is planked, tear out these temporary braces and the mounting blocks.

After all the frames are in place, take a sharp knife and carefully cut off all the guide beams flush with the frame edges. If the guide beams are glued to the jig, leave the end frames until last.

Bow and Stern

I have built framed bows and sterns on several models, and this experience leads me to recommend that you refrain from doing so. For a first effort, you should also avoid a framed stern. Instead, build up solid ends of balsa using the laminated technique. It takes a bit of carpentry, but the results are much more satisfactory than those framed ends yield.

The idea in solid ends is to provide a generous surface for holding the planking in place. Usually the planking is curved quite sharply at the ends, and it has a tendency to pull loose unless there is a surface to cling to. Also, solid ends are easy to shape correctly, thus achieving an accurate portrayal of the real ship's ends. If possible, build out from the last frame, and take the solid part from the keel all the way to the deck. I suggest, before you start, that you review Chapter 5.

The Solid Bow. Begin by tracing on the side view of the ship. If the plan has a complete cutaway view (inboard works), it is ideal for this purpose; if not, use the hull side elevation, but deduct the stempost and keel. You need only the form of the hull itself. Trace the shape of the bow from the foremost section forward, from forefoot to deck level, and draw in the location of the section line with a straightedge. If you are converting scale, it's easiest to do this drawing on graph paper, plotting the points and then joining them with French curves.

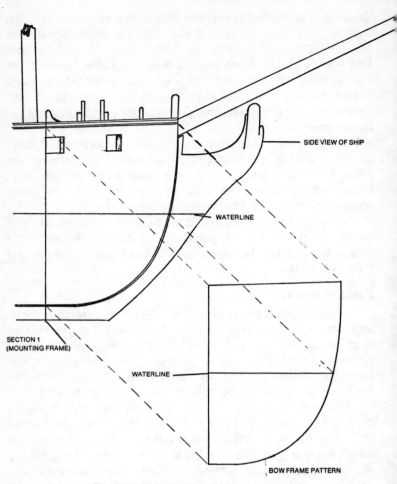

SIDE VIEW OF SHIP

WATERLINE

SECTION 1
(MOUNTING FRAME)

WATERLINE

BOW FRAME PATTERN

Fig. 6-12. Making the bow frame pattern.

Cut out the pattern and hold it in place against the model, aligning the pattern top with the top of the frame. (See Fig. 6-12.) Mark and cut from the pattern the place occupied by the keelson. Use the pattern as a template to mark the outline on a sheet of 1/8″ balsa, then cut out the piece. We'll call this piece the bow frame.

First, test the fit of the bow frame by setting it in place. Trim and adjust it, as necessary, to make a firm joint with the frame and keelson. When you are satistied, lay it in place on the side view plan and transfer the lift lines onto it. Draw the

114

lift lines on both sides. If the lifts do not go all the way up to deck level, draw "hypothetical" lines at the same interval as the real lifts. Mark the waterline with and X so you know which it is, and lay the bow frame aside. (See Fig. 6-13.)

On the lines plan of the hull, find and trace the shape of the waterline forward from the section line representing the frame on which the solid bow will be mounted to the stem. We'll call this foremost frame the mounting frame. Mark the centerline and mounting frame locations on the drawing and cut it out (See Fig. 6-14). Draw a line parallel to the centerline and 1/16″ toward the center of the drawing. When you trim off this border you have the pattern for the waterline bow lifts.

Make this lift and all the others of balsa sheet the same thickness as the distance between the lift lines. For ease in working the wood, always have the grain running fore and aft.

Use the lift pattern as a template to mark two identical pieces on the balsa. Cut them out carefully, addressing the grain properly so the cuts are smooth curves (see Chapter 5 for advice on cutting thick balsa).

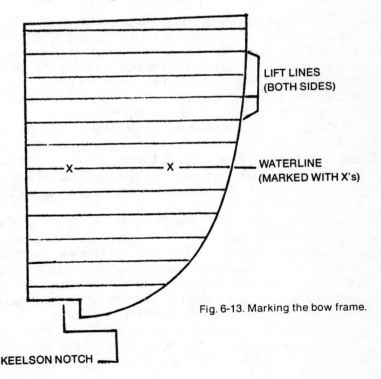

LIFT LINES
(BOTH SIDES)

WATERLINE
(MARKED WITH X's)

Fig. 6-13. Marking the bow frame.

KEELSON NOTCH

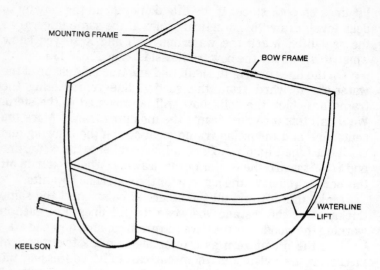

Fig. 6-14. Starting the solid bow.

When these lifts are cut out, you are ready to mount the bow. Fasten the bow frame to the keelson and mounting frame with glue. This piece should make a flush joint with the keelson and be perfectly vertical. In the absence of a reference line on the mounting frame, measure from each top corner of the frame to the joint with the bow frame. The measurements will be equal if the bow frame is vertical. See Fig. 6-14.

Using glue, mount the waterline lifts on each side. The top of the lift must follow the waterlines scored on the mounting and bow frames. Turn the hull framework over to let the cement harden. If the bow frame touches the table, put a book or a block of wood under the second or third transverse section frame to hold it up.

To make other lifts, use the same technique as you employed for the waterline lift. The lifts should be made in descending order from the waterline. In this way, working with the hull upside down, you can stack them toward the keel. Cement each lift to its neighbor, to the bow frame, and to the mounting frame with contact cement. When you have laminated down to the keel, turn the hull right side up.

Most ship plans do not show hull lines above the waterline. If yours does, you can continue to laminate the lifts upward to deck level. If not, it is fairly easy to obtain the lift lines.

On the body plan bow view, draw in lift lines as shown in Fig. 6-15 at the same interval as the lines below the waterline. Continue them upward to deck level or just below it. Draw in the same lines on the side view.

Lay out a right angle on a piece of paper, representing the bow frame and mounting frame. Draw in the section lines measuring forward from the mounting frame along the centerline.

Now, on the side view, measure the length of the first lift above the waterline from the mounting frame to the after-edge of the stem. Convert if necessary, and mark this distance on the centerline of the pattern. Next, on the body plan, measure the distance along the same lift from the centerline to the first

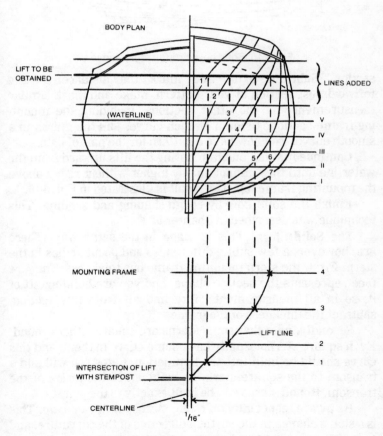

Fig. 6-15. Obtaining lift from body plan.

117

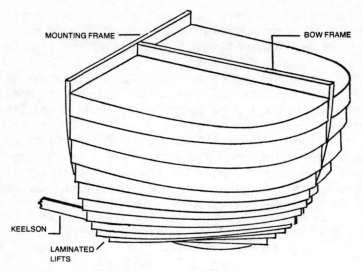

BOW FRAME

KEELSON

LAMINATED
LIFTS

Fig. 6-16. Solid bow's rough appearance.

section. Subtract 1/16″ and mark the distance on the forwardmost section of your pattern. Make and mark similar measurements on the other sections, including the mounting-frame section. Using a French curve, join the marks in a smooth curve. You now have a pattern for the pair of lists.

Continue making and laminating the lifts upward from the waterline until they cannot go any higher without rising above the mounting frame top. The result is illustrated in Fig. 6-16.

Finish the solid bow by rough-shaping and sanding. This technique was described in Chapter 5.

The Solid Stern. This is made in the same way. There are, however, a few subtle differences and peculiarities in the stern. First, the stern mounting frame has thickness. The *fore* face represents the section shape, and you are building aft of it, so in all measurements, fore and aft from this section, subtract the thickness of the frame.

Secondly, note that some sterns are square, others round. Even square sterns usually have some curve in them, and this curve should be built into the lamination. Later you will add a transom to the square stern, so build out to the *inside* of the transom. Round sterns can be built exactly to the plans.

Be aware, especially on round sterns, of the *knuckle*. This is a sharp change in the vertical direction of the curvature, and is usually marked by a molding, as shown in Fig. 6-17. Since

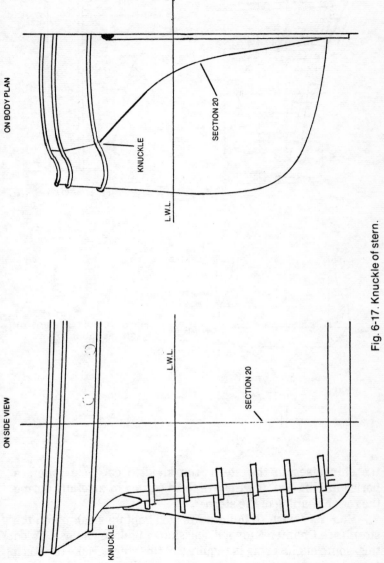

ON BODY PLAN

KNUCKLE

SECTION 20

L.W.L.

ON SIDE VIEW

L.W.L.

SECTION 20

KNUCKLE

Fig. 6-17. Knuckle of stern.

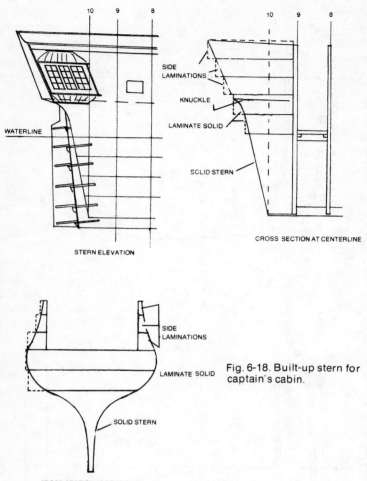

STERN ELEVATION

WATERLINE

10 9 8

10 9 8

SIDE
LAMINATIONS

KNUCKLE

LAMINATE SOLID

SOLID STERN

CROSS SECTION AT CENTERLINE

SIDE
LAMINATIONS

LAMINATE SOLID

SOLID STERN

Fig. 6-18. Built-up stern for
captain's cabin.

CROSS-SECTION AT SECTION 10

the ship rises in the stern, the knuckle does not follow a horizontal lift line. It will have to be carved in carefully during the rough shaping of the stern.

You may wish to build a finished captain's cabin into the stern (see Chapter 5 for a discussion of built-in cabins). To do this, some engineering is required at this stage. Make the stern frame extend upward only to the level of the cabin deck. Laminate solid lifts up to this point. See Fig. 6-18.

The cabin will be open astern, with the stern mounting frame as its forward bulkhead, so all you have to make is the sides. For this, you have two choices: either make partial frames as you would for a combination hull (to be described next in this chapter), or use the built-up technique discussed in the last chapter. I suggest the frames, since the stern planking on a square-stern vessel is seldom difficult or strained.

If you do select the built-up method, refer to Fig. 5-5 in Chapter 5 and the accompanying text dealing with tumble-home. Cut the side pieces so that their outsides follow the lift lines and their insides make a smooth vertical wall. These pieces should have at least 1/4" breadth as a joint with their neighbors above and below.

On the top solid lift, draw a line on each side representing the inside wall. Laminate upward, keeping the inside walls vertical and in alignment with these lines. Make mortises in the top built-up lifts at the very stern and glue a 1/8" × 1/8" hardwood beam athwart the lifts to provide strength.

Such a stern will have an upside-down staircase appearance at the transom joints (see Fig. 6-19.) After you have given the exterior a finished shape, turn the hull upside down, resting on blocks, and trim down the stairsteps to a straight line at the correct slant of the transom. Don't forget the outboard curve of the transom; put a little angle in these surfaces to provide a good joint for it.

THE COMBINATION HULL

This method was developed primarily as a means of overcoming the inherent twist problems in plank-on-frame hulls, while still retaining some of the benefits of plank-on-frame construction. Drawing "b" in Fig. 6-1 shows a cross section of a combination hull.

The combination method is easy and quick, and most models lend themselves readily to it. Using the laminated technique, you build up a solid hull to the waterline and drill mast holes in the proper places.

I use the waterline because this is the most readily apparent vertical reference in the hull, but in truth any lift line may be used as the point of demarcation. If you plan inboard works below the waterline, either select some lower lift as the top of the laminations, or else use cutouts in the lift planks as described in Chapter 5 under *Built-up Hulls*.

The partially laminated hull will look something like an aircraft carrier once it is shaped. Upon this base, build up the

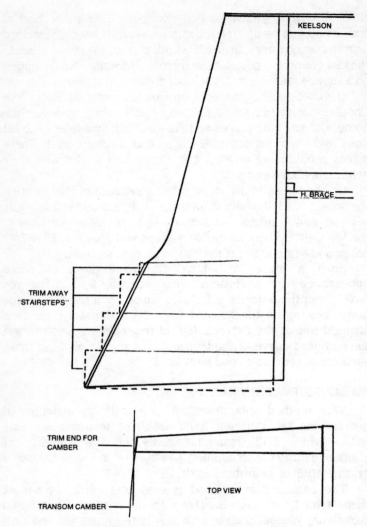

KEELSON

H. BRACE

TRIM AWAY
"STAIRSTEPS"

TRIM END FOR
CAMBER

TOP VIEW

TRANSOM CAMBER

Fig. 6-19. Trimming the stern for the transom.

solid bow or stern. Figure 6-20 shows a photo of the *Hancock* model with the solid bow in place.

The previous description of solid bows can serve as a guide, but there is one important difference between building up on a laminated base and putting a solid bow or stern on a plank-on-frame: On a combination hull you have no mounting frame.

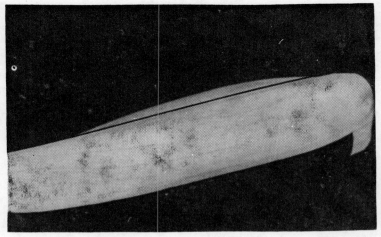

Fig. 6-20. The laminated portion of the Hancock model's combination hull, turned upside down. Note the solid bow.

As a reference in making the lifts, it is usually best to select the first section line intersecting the keel. Make all the lifts to foredeck level end at this line (which should be drawn on the top of the waterline lift), and then align them vertically as you build up. For shaping and sanding later, it is a good idea to make a solid hardwood *former* representing the shape of this section from waterline to deck, and cement it to the aft side of the built-up bow, as shown in Fig. 6-21.

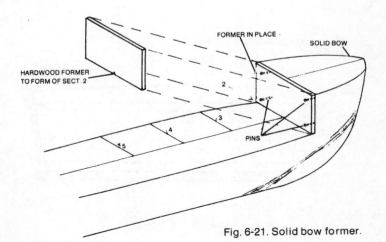

Fig. 6-21. Solid bow former.

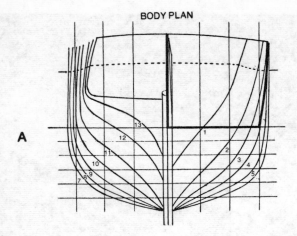

BODY PLAN

PATTERN 4

DARK LINE INDICATES
TRACING OF PATTERN

FRAME PIECES ASSEMBLED
ON PATTERN

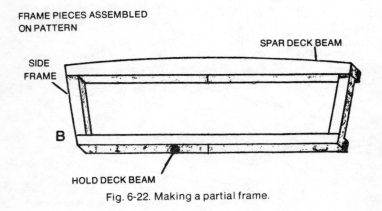

SPAR DECK BEAM

SIDE
FRAME

B

HOLD DECK BEAM

Fig. 6-22. Making a partial frame.

Balsa sometimes tends to slip and usually bonds rather poorly, so to keep the built-up bow strong, drive a lill pin through each lift, countersinking the head. Place these pins far enough from the centerline that you won't encounter them later as you chisel out the sprit mortise.

Once the laminated part is done and the hull resembles that in Fig. 6-20, it is time to make the partial frames. This is done just as described in the frame-making section earlier in this chapter, except that the frames extend up to the deck line only from the waterline. See Fig. 6-22.

You can fasten the frames to the laminated hull base with mortise and tenon joints similar to those used for timberheads as discussed in Chapter 5. In this case, the bottoms of the side frames will extend downward, overlapping the waterline by 1/2" or so.

Usually, though, you can mount the frames right atop the base. Lay the side frames on the pattern and glue the deck beam across the top and another beam across the bottom, where it will rest directly on the hull base. If there is to be a deck down there, pay attention to the thickness of the lower beam. If necessary, add a third beam above the lowest one to support the deck, or you may have to shave down the lower beam to keep it six or seven scale feet beneath the upper deck. (See Fig. 6-22B.)

In the lower beam, drill two vertical pinholes about a half-inch on either side of the centerline. Glue the frame in place, so that the side frames are flush with the sides of the laminated hull, and then push lill pins through these holes to fix the frame more securely.

Unless the frames are unusually tall, vertical braces such as those used in pure plank-on-frame hulls are not necessary. You will probably never need horizontal braces, since the joints with the laminated portion of the hull perform this function. If vertical braces are necessary, make them from 1/8" balsa sheet and later, after the hull is planked, cut them out.

It's easiest to mount each frame as soon as it is made and the glue is set. You will not need guide beams or a building jig as you would for a fully framed hull.

Work fore to aft, framing as far astern as you can while still resting the frames on the laminated base, or up to the solid stern if you have built one.

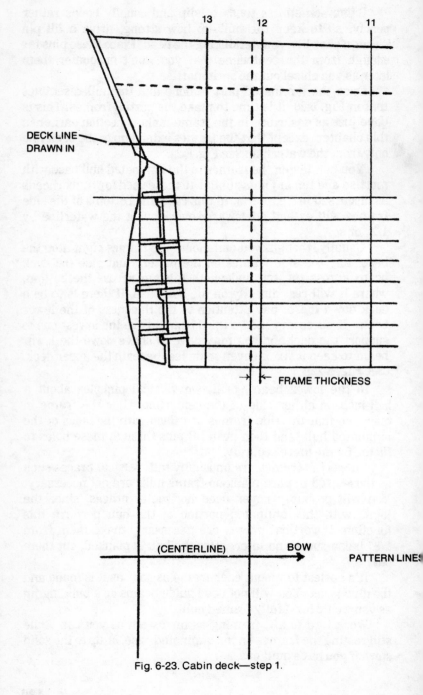

Fig. 6-23. Cabin deck—step 1.

The Framed Stern

A framed stern for a finished captain's cabin will require a little ingenious carpentry. Make all fore-and-aft measurements from the section line representing the aft-most frame, and deduct the thickness of the frame itself.

From 1/8" hardwood sheet, cut a solid piece representing the shape of the deck that extends into the cabin. This can often be found on the lines plan. If not, you can make a good approximation by estimating the position of the deck and using the three projections on the draft as follows:

1. Draw the cabin deck line on the side view and measure from the section of the mounting frame to the transom fore side. Subtract the thickness of the frame. This gives the length of the deck. On a piece of paper, draw two parallel lines as far apart as the length of the deck and bisect both with a perpendicular line. (See Fig. 6-23).

2. On the body plan, draw in the estimated deck line and measure from the centerline to the intersection of this line with the mounting frame section. On one of the lines of the working drawing, mark this distance in both directions from the centerline. (See Fig. 6-24.)

3. Again on the body plan, measure the distance from the centerline to the point where the deckline meets the transom. On the other line on the working drawing, mark this distance in both directions from the centerline. Join the marks to form a quadrangle. (See Fig. 6-25.)

4. On the lines plan (top view), draw a line perpendicular to the centerline, passing through the corners of the transom. Measure aft from this line to the center of the transom. This gives the camber, or curvature, of the transom. On the bisecting line of the working drawing, mark this distance astern of the transom line, and use a French curve to draw the curve in. Join the marks on the parallel lines to obtain the deck shape. Use scissors to cut out the cabin deck pattern, and transfer the pattern to 1/8" sheet hardwood. (See Fig. 6-26.)

On the stern mounting frame, mark the deck level, and measure the distance from the top of the lamination to this point. Cut balsa of this thickness using the deck piece as a

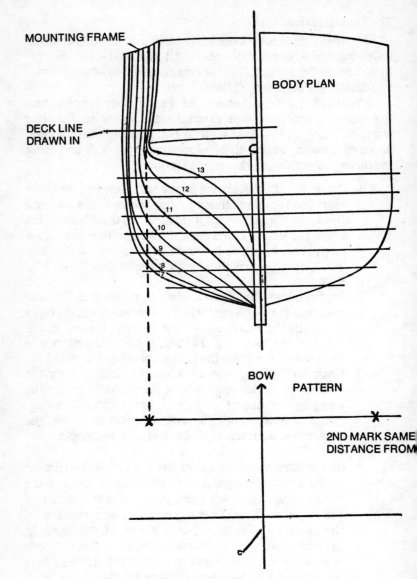

MOUNTING FRAME

BODY PLAN

DECK LINE
DRAWN IN

13
12
11
10
9
8
7

BOW
PATTERN

2ND MARK SAME
DISTANCE FROM

c

Fig. 6-24. Cabin deck—step 2.

pattern. (See Fig. 6-27.) Cement the balsa in place, overhanging the stern, and cement the hardwood deck atop it. Sand
down the edges of the balsa until they blend into the laminated
base to form the counter.

On the side elevation plan, trace the quadrangle formed by the cabin deck, the transom, the quarterdeck, and the mounting frame section. Deduct the thickness of the mounting frame from the foreside of this quadrangle, and use this pattern to cut two 1/16″ balsa pieces which will form the cabin sidewalls.

At the top aft corner of each sidewall, cut a 1/8″ × 1/8″ notch to serve as a beam mortise. On the inside faces of both pieces, cement 1/8″ × 1/8″ hardwood strips flush with the fore, bottom, and transom edges. Glue the sidewalls in place.

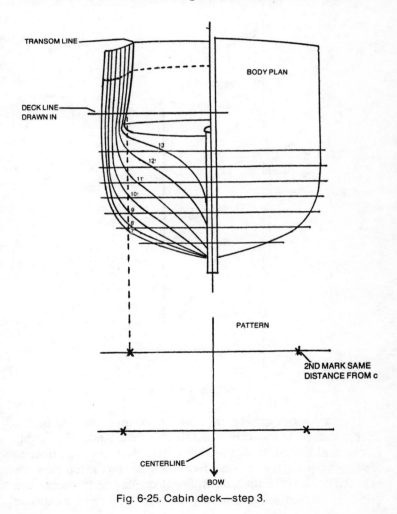

Fig. 6-25. Cabin deck—step 3.

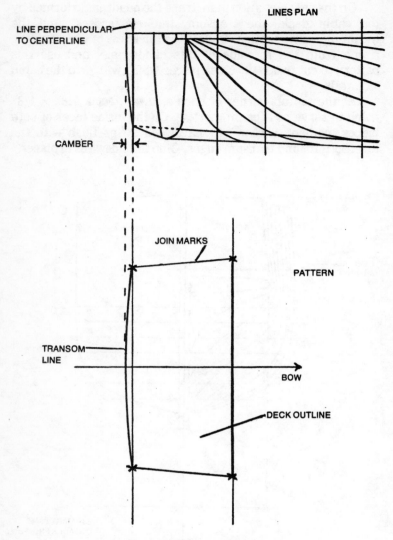

LINES PLAN

LINE PERPENDICULAR TO CENTERLINE

CAMBER

JOIN MARKS

PATTERN

TRANSOM LINE

BOW

DECK OUTLINE

Fig. 6-26. Cabin deck—step 4.

To make the quarterdeck and transom mounting beam, first measure the camber of the transom. Add 1/8″ to this figure find the width of the beam (for example, if camber is 1/8″, you need a 1/4″ beam). Next measure on the top view the breadth of the quarterdeck where it meets the transom, and add 1/8″ to find the beam length. Cut a 1/8″ thick hardwood

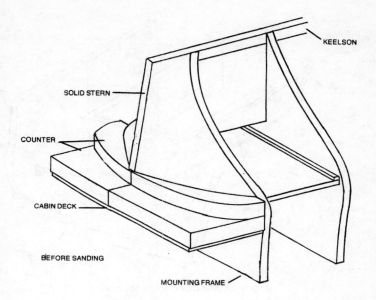

KEELSON

SOLID STERN

COUNTER

CABIN DECK

BEFORE SANDING

MOUNTING FRAME

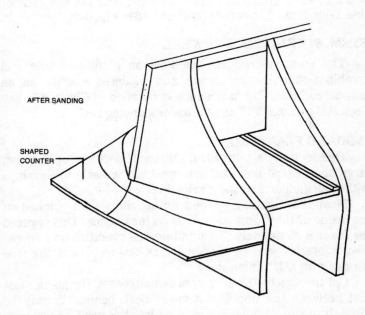

AFTER SANDING

SHAPED
COUNTER

Fig. 6-27. Counter and cabin deck in place.

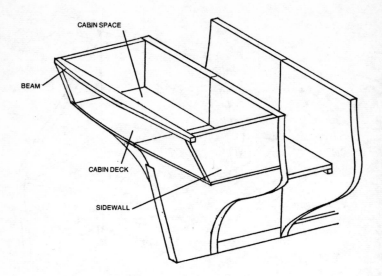

Fig. 6-28. Stern cabin framework.

beam, draw in the camber with a French curve leaving 1/8" of width at each end, and shave down the beam to the camber line. Glue it into the corner mortises. (See Fig. 6-28.)

STEM, STERNPOST, AND KEEL

The stem, sternpost, and keel on plank-on-frame and combination hulls are made and mounted exactly as on laminated hulls. The procedure is detailed in Chapter 5. See Figs. 5-11 through 5-15 and the accompanying text.

INBOARD PLANKING

This section pertains to all ship models with an open waist, large open cargo hatches, and most particularly to warships with open gunports on the gun deck.

Most 19th Century wooden sailing ships were planked on the inside of the frame as well as on the outside. This covered the frames completely. To simulate this condition on a model whose interior will be visible, plank the insides of the side frames with 1/32" balsa sheet.

Cut the sheet to size, or approximately so. The plank must rest between the upper and lower deck beams. It may be difficult to slip a long piece of wood into this area, so you may find it necessary to cut the sheet into shorter pieces. If so, hold it in place outboard and carefully cut it so that the butts meet on a frame.

After slipping the sheet inside the frames, hold it in place and make sure it forms a nice smooth line. If it does not, your side frames are uneven and it will be necessary either to shave down the insides of the offenders or to shim out those that are too narrow with balsa scraps. Then mount the inside plank, using either glue or contact cement, as shown in Fig. 6-29.

Plank both sides of the interior, but do not install the deck. For a merchant ship, paint the interior dirty white or light gray. On a warship, paint it dark red in conformance with the international naval practice of the time; it kept the gunners from being distracted by spattered blood.

GUNPORTS

Gunports should now be pierced in frigates and other warship models. Some merchantmen up until the early 1800s also carried guns in the upper hold, and these may be pierced the same as warships.

Unfold the side-view draft on a table and rest the hull above it with the sections lined up. Using dividers, find the distance to one edge of an amidships gunport from the *fore* side of the nearest frame. (See Fig. 6-30.) Transfer this measurement to the corresponding place on the hull, pricking the *outboard* side of the interior planking with the divider point. Next measure the distance from the frame to the other edge of the gunport. Remember to convert it necessary.

Using a scrap of strip wood and a sharp, hard-lead pencil, score the locations of the two pricks, making sure the two lines are vertical (parallel to the adjacent frames).

Next, measure the distance from the lower edge of the gunport to the gun deck beams, which is usually indicated by a dotted line on the drafts. Cut a piece of strip wood to this width to act as a guide.

If you have done a good job of planking the interior, the bottom edge of the planking should follow the deckline. Place the guide with one edge flush with the lower edge of the interior planking and mark the lower sill of the gunport.

Use the dividers to measure and prick the location of the upper sill. Place the guide on the prick, parallel to the upper edge of the planking, and mark the sill to complete the outline of the gunport, as shown in Fig. 6-30.

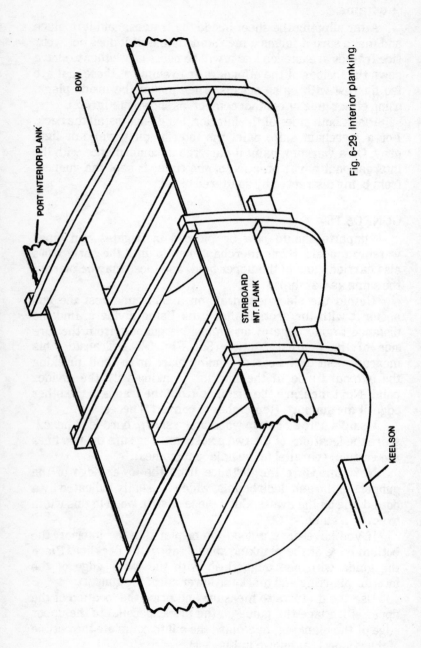

Fig. 6-29. Interior planking.

Repeat these operations for each gunport on both sides of the model. The process goes quickly after a few ports, so take heart if the first one or two seem time-consuming.

Don't bother with the foremost port on each side of the bow, nor with the ports covered by the quarter galleries astern. When all the other gunports are scored, cut them out. Use a new X-acto #10 or equivalent blade. Carefully cut the vertical sides first, making several progressively deeper slices until the tip of the blade goes through the balsa, then cut along

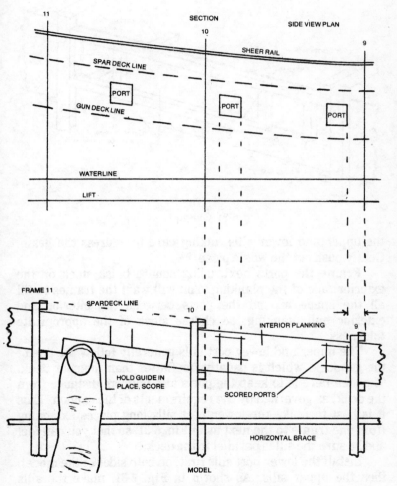

Fig. 6-30. Marking gunports.

135

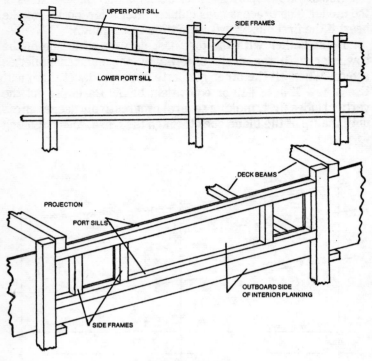

Fig. 6-31. Gunport framing.

the upper and lower sills, taking care to address the grain. Gently push out the waste piece.

Frame the ports next, using square balsa stock on the exterior face of the planking. You will want the frames to fill all the space around the ports between the interior and exterior hull planking, so choose stock of the appropriate thickness.

The upper and lower port sills generally follow the line of the gundeck, which is usually far flatter than the spar deck. The idea here is to keep the ports at a uniform distance from the deck, as governed by the requirements of the cannon. Thus it is best to make the lower port sills long pieces extending from one frame to the next as in Fig. 6-31, so that you can feel and be sure the sill is parallel to the deck.

Install the lower port sills first, on both sides of the model, then the upper sills. As shown in Fig. 6-31, make the sills parallel along the tops and bottoms of the cutouts, and once they are firmly cemented, trim away any excess or irregularities from the cutouts so that they form a smooth surface with the sills.

Finally, install the side frames of the ports. Each piece should be cut individually. Hold the stock in place, score the cut line with the knife, then lay it down and slice it off. Mount each piece before going on to the next, so they don't get mixed up. It probably won't take more than an hour to frame all the ports on a fair-sized frigate.

THE BOWSPRIT

The bowsprit, like the stem, sternpost, and keel, is mounted on a plank-on-frame or combination hull with a solid bow just as it is done on a laminated hull. Details are provided in Chapter 5, Figs. 5-21 through 5-25.

If instead of a solid bow you have carried the frames forward to the forepeak, you can mount the bowsprit by drilling or cutting a hole at the right place in the first frame and making a smaller hole where the butt of the sprit meets the second frame. The smaller hole will serve as a mortise; cut a tenon to fit it on the butt of the bowsprit. Mount and glue the sprit in place, and wedge it securely in the first frame with some hardwood scraps, as illustrated in Fig. 6-32.

If the bow frames are not solid, and the sprit passes through them without touching, make a set of hardwood knightheads (see glossary) mounted between the upper and lower deck beams to clamp the sprit in place.

Framed bows in general are very tricky and should only be undertaken by experienced modelers. I don't know of any really good reason to undertake to construct one.

THE MASTING

The masting of the ship should now be accommodated. The determination of mast diameters and the role of the false mast were detailed in Chapter 5, and illustrated in Figs. 5-16 and 5-17.

If you have constructed a combination hull, you should already have drilled the mast holes, so it remains only to cut and mount the false masts. The procedure is the same as that used on a laminated vessel, and is detailed in Chapter 5.

With plank-on-frame hulls, false masts fulfill the same functions, but the mounting of masts is different. Except on

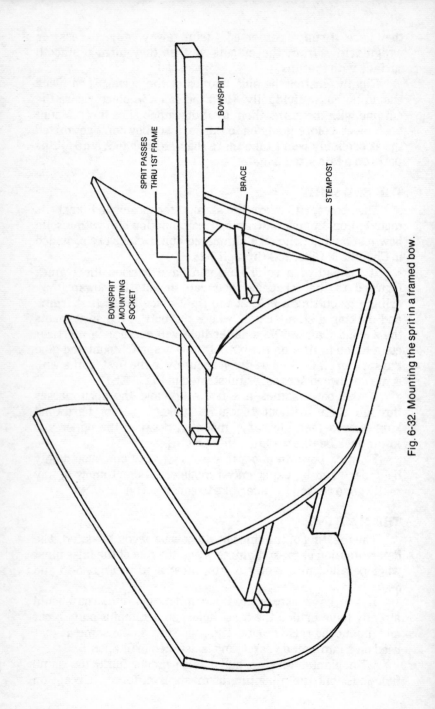

BOWSPRIT

SPRIT PASSES
THRU 1ST FRAME

BRACE

STEMPOST

BOWSPRIT
MOUNTING
SOCKET

Fig. 6-32. Mounting the sprit in a framed bow.

extremely deep-vee hulls (sharp deadrise), the masts should be carried all the way to the top of the keelson, where they are secured by a socket.

To prepare for masting, first establish where the masts are and cut away the vertical frame braces. Next, locate where the masts must pass through the horizontal frame braces and cut a hole centered on this spot that is large enough to permit the dowel to pass but still touches it on all sides. If the dowel squeaks a little and offers a bit of resistance, that's fine. Just be sure the hole is exactly centered on the centerline of the ship and is also longitudinally precise, since this affects the uprightness and rake of the mast.

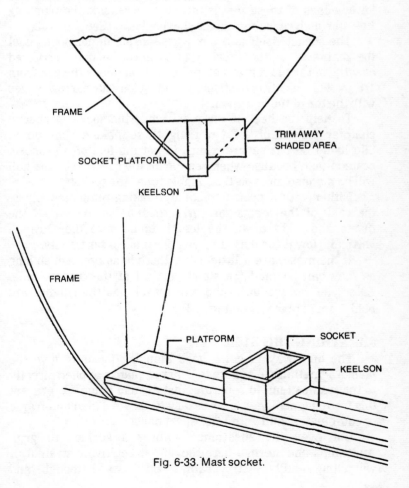

Fig. 6-33. Mast socket.

On the top of the keelson, mark the exact center of the mast as determined relative to the section lines. On a hull with sharp deadrise, and for the mizzen masts of most ships, the dowel may be too large to permit the planking to be added later without causing a bulge. In this case, cement directly atop the keelson a vertical extender made of the same stock as the keelson and mark its point of intersection with the centerline of the mast.

On either side of the keelson (or extender) and flush with its top, cement a piece of 1/4" square balsa stock long enough to reach from frame to frame. This will provide a level platform 5/8" wide to accommodate the mast socket. The lower edges of these pieces may extend outside the planking line, in which case they can be shaved down. (See Fig. 6-33.)

The socket itself is a box whose inside dimensions equal the diameter of the mast it is to accommodate, centered exactly on the mast mark atop the keelson. Make the box from 1/8" × 1/4" hardwood strips, standing on the narrow edges with the top of the box open.

To help the heel of the mast enter the socket properly, chamfer the end of the dowel slightly to make a blunt point. Slip it in and out several times to get the feel of a properly seated mast, because when you mount the real masts, the hull will be planked and you'll be unable to see the sockets.

Either with a protractor or by making templates, check the rake of the masts for correctness. Also, mount all the masts and sight down the length to be sure they are all vertical. Now is the only time you can make adjustments.

If the masts are a little loose, there is no problem so long as they can be made to stand vertical at the correct rake. Later you can wedge in the real masts, and the rigging will hold them in place. (See Fig. 6-34.)

SHEATHING THE HULL

The only way to get a good planking job is to give the planks something to adhere to. Narrow planks applied directly to the frames tend to separate, distort, and bulge. To prevent this from happening, it's necessary to sheath a plank-on-frame or combination hull with 1/32" sheet balsa.

But even the sheathing requires a surface to grip. Amidships and stern, where the ship is relatively straight, it will cling readily to the frames. Up forward, though, and

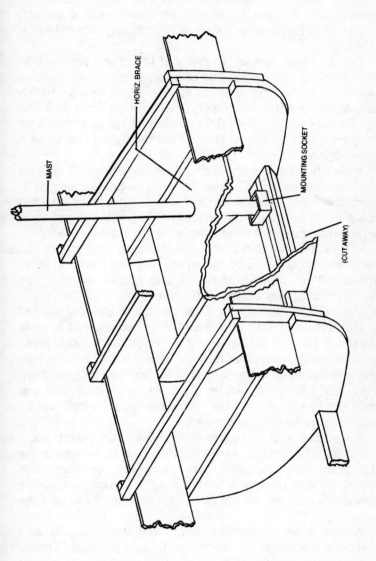

Fig. 6-34. Mast mounted in a plank-on-frame hull.

sometimes on the run and the counter, the lines of the hull are very curvy and the only thing the sheathing has to fasten to is the sharp corners of the frame sides.

Sight along the planking lines of your hull. Wherever it appears that the sheathing will encounter only a corner, cement to the frame edge a strip of 1/32" balsa cut to the width of the edge.

Cut the balsa across the grain. If the frame edge is 1/8" wide, measure 1/8" on the end of a balsa sheet, press a ruler down hard on the strip to be cut off, and carefully slice with a sharp knife. The strip will emerge in one piece if you do it this way. Be very careful with it, because it will have virtually no strength. It will, however, follow even the tightest curve on a frame edge.

Attach it to the frame edge with contact cement. The balsa may separate on tight bends, but that is fine so long as it covers the edge. Give the cement a little time to set up, then sand a bevel into the balsa corresponding to the direction of the planking using fine sandpaper wrapped around a block.

One of the nice things about sheathing is that you can be sloppy and no one will be the wiser. You can have irregular gaps of 1/8" or more in the sheathing without affecting the integrity of the planking that will cover it.

Use 1/32" balsa sheet in strips about 3/4" wide for most of the hull. Down around the turn of the bilge you will have to slim them down to half that width. Ideally, each strip should run all the way from stem to stern. If that's not possible, butt them amidships on a frame edge. Stagger vertically adjacent strips' butts between two or more frames, rather like you would lay bricks. Sheath the entire combination hull just as though it were a plank-on-frame hull.

Sloppiness in sheathing is okay to a certain extent, but a good start is important. Apply the first strip to the tops of the frames, running its upper edge along the deck line. Use contact cement to mount it and all other strips, but before applying the cement cut the fore edge to lay snugly against the stem.

As you plank downward toward the keel, you will soon observe a tendency for the strips to arch upward. This is caused by the greater bulk of the hull amidships. To correct this, makes silver planks as described in Fig. 7-9 of Chapter 7.

To round the bilge, turn the hull upside down for better access to the bottom. Try to bring the strips parallel to the

Plate 1. Model form for Hancock. This is a combination hull with a solid bow.

143

keel, so that you end up with a strip about 1/2″ wide meeting the keel along its entire length.

Sheath one side completely, then sheath the other. The tension gives the balsa surprising strength, but it is still fragile and needs careful handling. Sand the seams on curving places very lightly with fine sandpaper.

If you have gunports, you will have to find and cut them in the outer sheathing. Lay the hull on its side with the deck beams facing you. Hold a lill pin with needlenose pliers, and from the inside of the hull poke the pin through all four corners of each gunport. Turn the hull over and do the same thing on the other side. The pinholes will serve as cutting guides. Cut a little inside them, push out the waste, then shave the balsa sheathing to bring it flush with the port frames. On the sides of the ports, a fingernail file is ideal for this job.

And now sit back. Suddenly your skeleton has fleshed out into a real ship. Not very seaworthy yet, perhaps, but her lines are there in all their grace and beauty.

Chapter 7

Completing the Hull

~~~~~~~~~~~~~~~~~~~~~~~~~~~~~~~~~~

The first step toward completion of the ship's foundation is
building the *bulwarks*. These are the "fences" surrounding the
decks. On many 19th Century vessels, the bulwarks make a
single sweeping line the entire length of the vessel, ignoring
the levels of the decks within. Thus, if the vessel has raised
decks at the ends, the bulwarks are often flush with the
decking at the ends and so high on the main deck that a man on
deck cannot see over them.

For safety, such ships usually carry fancy railings around
the quarterdeck, and occasionally on the foredeck as well. Our
concern here is with the bulwarks themselves, and we will
defer the railings until Chapter 9.

BULWARKS

Ordinarily the bulwarks are supported by timberheads,
which are extensions of the frames. The tops of every second
or third frame are continued above the deck level, and to them
are fixed planks somewhat thinner than those of the hull. On
warships, the bulwarks are planked inside and out, so that the
timberheads are hidden. On merchantmen, the planking
usually carried only to the outside, leaving the timberheads
exposed. When this is the case, a plank called the *ceiling* is
fixed along the tops of the timberheads just below the railing to
control the sloshing of water on deck. You can determine

which type of bulwark your ship has by studying the inboard profile.

On both plank-on-frame and laminated hulls, the timberheads are made by cutting and cementing short wooden pieces to the hull so that they extend to the appropriate height above the deck level. Care must be taken to insure that they follow the proper vertical curvature of the section, or else you may have a sudden and unsightly angle in the exterior of the ship where the bulwark begins.

In plank-on-frame hulls, cement the timberheads to the inside of the hull sheathing. In laminated hulls, it is necessary to cut notches in the hull for anchoring the timberheads, as shown in Fig. 7-1. In both cases, figure that the timberhead must have as much length anchoring it as it has above the deck level.

Make the timberheads from hardwood, not from balsa. The curvature of the planking will exert some pressure on them and during the detailing of the hull and the rigging you will occasionally bump them, which means they must be fairly strong. The size of the timberheads will be governed to some extent by the thickness of the bulwark as required by the plans. Use stock no thinner than 3/32", unless the scale of the ship is tiny. If the piece must be curved to conform to the lines of the section, use a thicker piece and carve it down to the same thickness as the straight timberheads, working in the curvature. This may also be a requirement on the anchoring end of the timberhead.

It's easy to make the timberheads, since the majority will be straight. Mark the lengths on a piece of straight stock, using the knife blade to make indentations precisely where the cut will occur. Then before cutting them, go back and very lightly, but visibly, score them at the midpoint to indicate where they meet the deckline.

You can probably get by with one working (load-bearing) timberhead at each section line or frame member of the hull. "Cosmetic" timberheads (those not actually bearing the bulwarks) may be added after the planking has been applied. If your vessel has a round bow or stern, it will probably be necessary to build up solid bulwarks, which we will discuss later in this chapter.

On a laminated hull, mark the location of each timberhead with a lead pencil. Cut one timberhead from the marked stock to be used as a template for notching the hull. Hold the timberhead vertically, with the midpoint mark lined up with the deckline. If some timberheads have different anchoring lengths, adjust the position of the template piece accordingly. Using the non-cutting edge of a knife blade, mark the balsa hull around the timberhead.

Once all the outlines of the mortises are made, cut them out carefully with a sharp-pointed blade. Cut only as deeply as necessary to make the timberhead flush with the surface of the hull, and try to make the interior of the mortise smooth so that it will present a good surface for cementing.

Cut off the timberheads from the straight stock as you need them. Bevel the tops of slanting timberheads so that they will present a level surface. You can use contact cement to install them, but if the mortises are tight you may have problems working the timberheads into them. It works just as well to cement the pieces in place using liquid glue.

For plank-on-frame and combination hull, the installation of timberheads is easy. Either to the fore or aft side of each frame member, paint some contact cement on the inside of the balsa sheathing. Cut off the timberheads from the stock, paint cement on the anchor end, and when tacky, press them in place, making certain the midpoint mark is flush with the top of the sheathing. See Fig. 7-2.

Solid bulwarks are required where the curvature of the topside is too tight to plank easily. It's best to make them from thin balsa, laminating upward and offsetting sucessive layers to accommodate the vertical curvature of the hull section. If the curve is really tight, make each layer in sections to make the grain more or less follow the curvature, and overlap the ends of the sections so that they do not occur at the same place in succeeding layers (make a masonry pattern, as shown in Fig. 7-3).

Make the pieces a little too wide, not exactly to the indicated width. If the bow (or the stern), sweeps upward, build up higher to create the necessary height. When it is all built up, smooth the stairstep top with a knife, bringing it to the same height as the timberheads. Shave the bulwarks inside and out until they are smooth and of the proper thickness. Sand lightly.

DECK BEAMS

The decks of ships, like paved roads, are constructed higher in the center than on the edges, in order to provide a

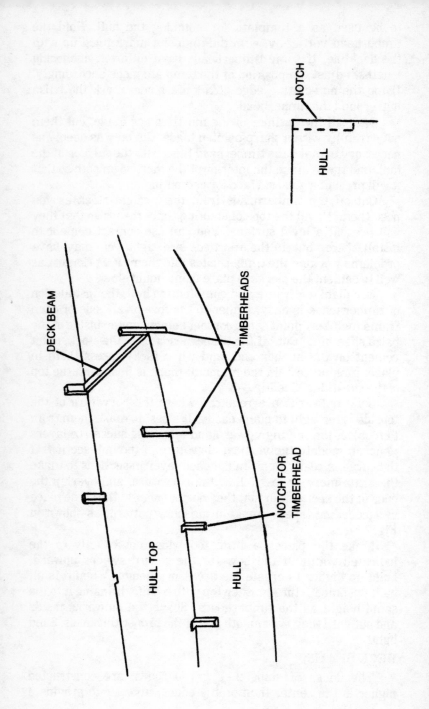

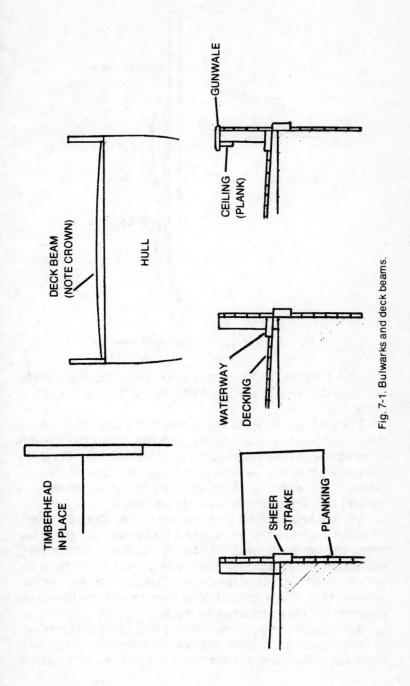

Fig. 7-1. Bulwarks and deck beams.

GUNWALE

CEILING (PLANK)

WATERWAY

DECKING

DECK BEAM (NOTE CROWN)

HULL

TIMBERHEAD IN PLACE

SHEER STRAKE

PLANKING

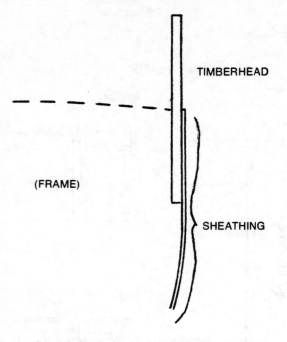

Fig. 7-2. Timberhead on plank-on-frame hull.

run-off for water. This crown is achieved by shaving a slight arch into the deck beams, as discussed earlier and illustrated in Fig. 7-4.

The deck beams should be spaced at the same intervals as the weight-bearing timberheads, fastened across the breadth of the ship with their ends touching the timberheads. Cut them from straight stock, preferably 1/4″ × 1/8″. Use dividers to measure the exact distance between the timberheads and transfer the measurement to the straight stock.

Using a long gradual curve on one of your French curves, mark the crown on the beam with a lead pencil. The top of the crown should occur in the center of the beam, with a very gradual curve to each end. Figure on making a 1/8″ drop for each 3″ on either side of the crown. Carefully shave away the waste with a sharp knife, taking care to address the grain properly. Cut the beam from the stock.

Admidships the beam may rest directly atop the balsa. As you work toward the ends, however, the distance of the deck above the lamination will increase due to the sheer. To adjust

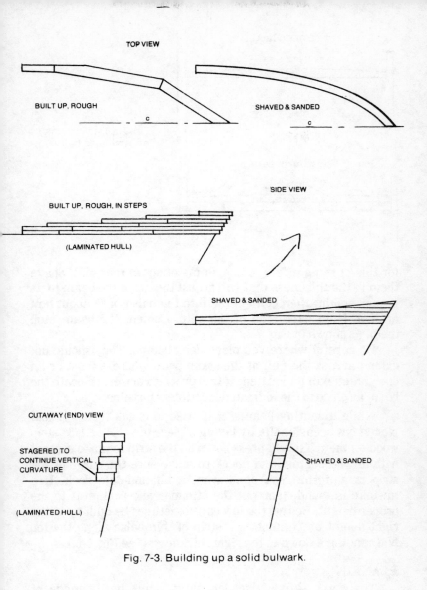

TOP VIEW

BUILT UP, ROUGH

SHAVED & SANDED

c

c

SIDE VIEW

BUILT UP, ROUGH, IN STEPS

(LAMINATED HULL)

SHAVED & SANDED

CUTAWAY (END) VIEW

STAGERED TO
CONTINUE VERTICAL
CURVATURE

SHAVED & SANDED

(LAMINATED HULL)

Fig. 7-3. Building up a solid bulwark.

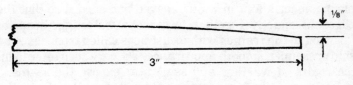

1/8"

3"

Fig. 7-4. Crown of deck beam.

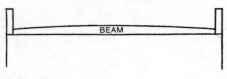

DIRECTLY ON HULL.

BEAM

Fig. 7-5. Deck beams on laminated hull.

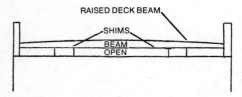

RAISED DECK BEAM

SHIMS

BEAM
OPEN

for this curving effect, make shims of scrap material. Shave them to the thickness that will adjust the top of the beam to its proper height, then cement them to the balsa base about half an inch from each side of the ship. Cement the beam atop them, as shown in Fig. 7-5.

Be careful where you place deck beams. They should not extend across the hull at the same point where a mast or an open hatch will be located. If this problem arises, relocate the beam as close to the indicated location as possible.

While mounting beams, it is wise to check their vertical placement occasionally by laying a piece of 1/16″ × 1/8″ strip wood on them. Gently press down on the strip to make contact with all the beams, and check to make sure the curve of the strip is uniform. You don't want a hill-and-dale deck. If a mistake is found, tear out the offender and realign it to the proper height. Beams too low can sometimes be built up to the right height by cementing a strip of thin balsa along the top and sanding it down to the right thickness. (See Fig. 7-6.)

PLANKING

The outer skin of wooden ships is ordinarily made of planks about a foot in width, shaved and sanded so that their edges fit exactly together to make a watertight bond, and fastened to the frames with locust pegs called trunnels. A new ship presents a smooth appearance, but very soon after launch the rigors of weather and sea water expose the seams. To create this realistic aspect in a model, it should be planked.

152

Planking the Hull

The best planking material is 1/32" basswood strip. Select a width that corresponds to a foot in scale for the hull, and 9" in scale for the bulwarks.

In most cases, the strips will not be long enough to run all the way from the forefoot to the sternpost, just as real planks were rarely long enough to extend from bow to stern. Stagger the location of the butts (the joints where planks meet end to end) all along the hull, making certain they do not occur in the same area in any group of three (see Fig. 7-7). Likewise, avoid butts on the flare of the bow and on the tight closing curves on the stern, because the ends will tend to pop loose with time.

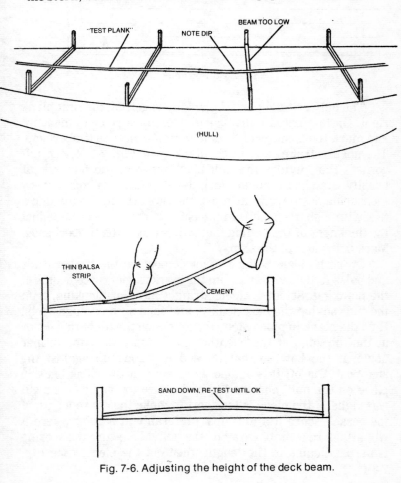

Fig. 7-6. Adjusting the height of the deck beam.

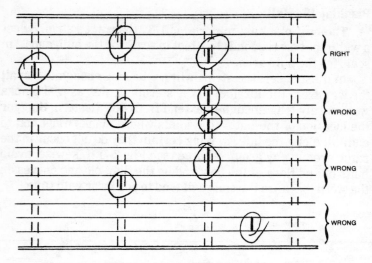

Fig. 7-7. Butting deck planks.

The only critical part of planking is getting the first plank right. On laminated hulls, use dividers or a ruler to measure and mark the position of the *sheer strake* on each timberhead. The sheer strake is a thick plank (see Fig. 7-1, lower left corner) that divides the hull planking from the bulwark. It usually stands at about deck level. Mark its location by measuring down from the top of the timberhead and making a tick with a sharp pencil. In measuring, don't forget to deduct the thickness of the railing that will lay atop the timberheads. Mark both sides of the ship.

On both sides, point contact cement on the timberheads and balsa hull downward from the marks about three widths of the planking. Select a clear, straight piece of planking, trim the ends so that they are square, and sand off any rough spots. Hold the plank in place along the marks on the timberheads, or at the top edge of the sheathing, and mark it at the proper angle at the bow so that its end will snug up against the stempost. Cut off this angled piece and put the plank back in place on the hull, checking to make sure the angle of the cut was right. If the piece is too short to make the entire length of the vessel, score it amidships, preferably at a point where it will attach to a timberhead or the hull. Make sure the scoring is perpendicular to the length, then cut the piece. (See Fig. 7-8.)

Use this plank as a pattern to make its twin for the opposite side. Paint contact cement on what will be the inner sides of each plank, and on the end face of the angled end. When the planks are ready, press the angled end of one into place against the stempost, then, slowly and carefully, making sure you align the top with each mark, press along the length. The sweep should be smooth and graceful, not at all wobbly. Install the opposite piece in the same manner.

Now take a fresh strip and trim the end square. Lay it in place butted against the installed plank and mark the angle of the stern transom. Take the piece away and cut it there. Paint on contact cement and lay it aside to dry while you repeat this process on the other side. When the piece is dry, install it as you did the forward plank, making certain that the butt is firmly in contact and continues the sweep of the planksheer without any wobbles or other interruptions.

From here on, the planking is quite simple and fast. Cut each piece for the angle of the stem or stern as you did the planksheer. Make the butts occur at random intervals, avoiding clusters. When installing a plank, keep it constantly in contact with the plank above. Since the distance from planksheer to keel is much greater around the belly of the ship than at the ends, it will be necessary to make a very sharp-pointed plank from time to time to mount on the belly. Do this each time the planking begins to *hog* or arch upward.

To make such a *sliver plank*, lay a fresh plank or a long remnant in place on the belly, in the center of the arch, so that it is parallel with the planks a few widths above. (See Fig. 7-9.) The center of the piece should make contact for a distance with the installed plank, then ride up and over it. Mark where the

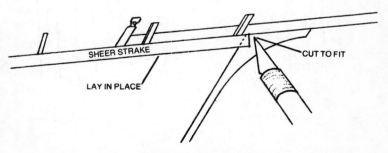

Fig. 7-8. The sheer strake.

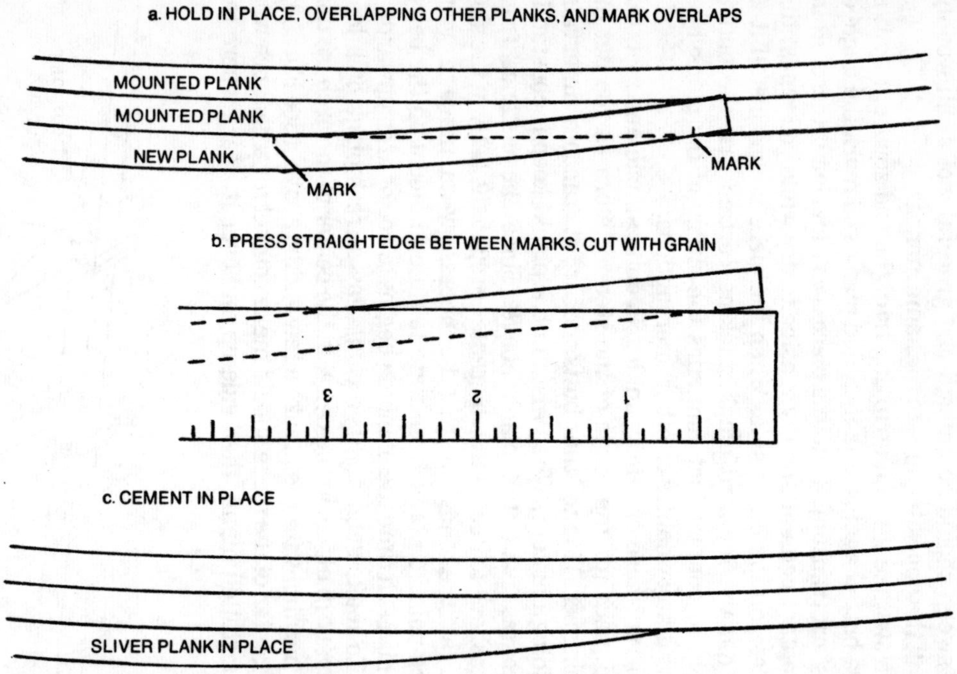

a. HOLD IN PLACE, OVERLAPPING OTHER PLANKS, AND MARK OVERLAPS

MOUNTED PLANK

MOUNTED PLANK

NEW PLANK

MARK

MARK

b. PRESS STRAIGHTEDGE BETWEEN MARKS, CUT WITH GRAIN

c. CEMENT IN PLACE

SLIVER PLANK IN PLACE

Fig. 7-9. Making a sliver plank.

overlap begins and where the lower edge of the new plank intersects with the edge of the installed plank, lay the piece on a flat cutting board, and using a straightedge, slice it along a straight line between these two marks. It will probably be necessary to do this on both the fore and aft ends. Try it out in place, and if necessary, round the beginning of the cut a little to make a tight seam. Then, before you forget exactly where it goes, coat it with contact cement and install it.

It's best to do a few planks on one side, then switch to the other, so that the planking proceeds more or less at the same rate along both sides. With a plank-on-frame hull, this is especially important, since the hull can develop a slight twist or bow if all the planking is installed on one side before the other is begun. This advice is given from the vantage of bitter experience.

Inevitably, even the most painstaking craftsman will occasionally create a gap in the plank seams. Sliver planks are especially prone to gapping. Use plastic balsa or a similar soft sanding putty to fill in the gaps. Put in a little too much, then use an old dull knife blade to work it down and make a shallow continuation of the seam. It will look different, patched, and sloppy, but as long as the smoothness of the planking is maintained, don't worry. The discoloration will vanish with a coat of paint.

Even if you plan to copper your hull below the waterline, you should maintain "artistic integrity" in the planking that will be covered. I did not do so in one clipper, and the sloppy planking job does not stand up well under scrutiny, even through the copper.

As you approach the keel, try to bring the planking parallel to it, using sliver planks. Don't be dismayed if the last plank does not fit exactly between the installed planking and the keel. Even on real ships, this piece presented problems unique enough to give it a special name: the *garboard strake*. The only way to make a garboard strake on a model is by patient fitting.

Cut a strip from a sheet of 1/32″ balsa, as wide as a normal planking strip. It will be quite flexible, more so than the other planks. Turn the ship with the keel up and lay the piece in place as best you can, with the edge against the last installed plank. Then, trimming carefully with a new blade, slice away at the edge facing the keel, working inch by inch along the keel

Fig. 7-10. The round stern of the Flying Fish model. Note the knuckle at the upper and lower moldings, the preventer chain, and the planking of the counter.

until each inch fits exactly into place. When it's right, cement it where it belongs and do the other side. It only takes about five minutes on each side.

Planking the bulwarks is easy and fast. Work upward from the sheer strake, making butts only on timberheads where both ends have something to fasten to. On clippers and other sharp-bowed vessels, you may have to indulge in some fancy trial-and-error knifework to get around the bowsprit. The bulwark planking should be firmly in contact with the spar all the way around. If you have too much width in the very top plank, so that it extends above the timberheads, use a straightedge to trim off the excess along the edge of the plank. Check frequently as you trim; the top edge of this plank should correspond exactly to the tops of the timberheads.

At the bow, there will likely be more planking required because of the upward sweep. Build up as the timberhead tops rise, using the same sliver plank idea found on the belly.

Carefully check over the entire planking job for gaps in the seams. Repair any you find. Also, make sure all the butts are firm and sticking tight. If any pop out, apply a new coat of contact cement and reglue them.

Planking a Round Stern

Round sterns on real, as well as model ships, present some peculiar construction problems. In Chapter 6, we presented a way of building up a solid round stern. Here, we will discuss a method for planking such a stern.

Round sterns are generally rounded from above, but from the side, they present series of straight-line surfaces, as seen in the photo of the *Flying Fish* in Fig. 7-10. This minimizes the amount of bending and piecing necessary to plank the stern. At a point near the start of the roundness, the horizontal planking of the hull ends, and the vertical planking of the stern begins.

When planking a model with such a stern, establish a demarcation point by drawing a line in the same relative position on both sides of the solid stern, perhaps an inch before the turn. Bring the horizontal hull planking to this point exactly, keeping all ends vertical and squared on the line. (See Fig. 7-11.) When the hull is planked, turn the ship over with the keel up.

Use 1/32" balsa sheet to plank the stern. Cut pieces the same width as the hull planks, and long enough to cover from

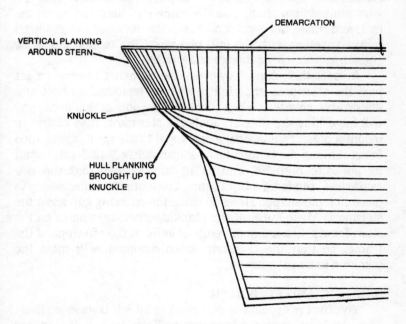

DEMARCATION

VERTICAL PLANKING
AROUND STERN

KNUCKLE

HULL PLANKING
BROUGHT UP TO
KNUCKLE

Fig. 7-11. Planking a round stern.

the knuckle to the gunwale. Begin by installing a few straight vertical planks, the first against the ends of the hull planks. When the stern begins to curve, cut pieces slightly wider at the top than at the bottom.

Try to keep the seams perfectly vertical, as seen from a vantage straight out from the stern at that point. The balsa is flexible enough that it will easily conform to the curvature of the stern. Keep the knuckle edges straight and on the line, since they will later be used as guides for mounting the stern moldings. The center seam on the stern should occur on the centerline of the ship and be vertical.

Planking Square-Stern Vessels

Many pre-1800 square-stern vessels, and a few thereafter, carry a counter under the stern. A counter is a flat or concave surface as seen from the side, extending out abaft the sternpost with the planking of the hull ending at its lower edge and the transom joined to its upper edge.

You should have framed in the counter or structured your laminations to accommodate it as described in earlier chapters, so the only job now is to plank the counter. This is a very simple operation. Use the same size planking as on the hull, and make the ends conform to the curvature as required by the meeting with the hull planking. The corner should be smooth and sharp, as though watertight.

In post-1800 ships, however, the planking sweeps on aft past the sternpost and right up to the transom, without any discernible counter. When planking the hull in this area, you will have to make a seam abaft the sternpost. It is easiest to mount a plank on one side, attaching it to the stern frame, then to cut it along the centerline as shown in Fig. 7-12. Next, install its opposite number, cutting in such a way that the two centerline cuts form a tight seam. Sometimes it is necessary to piece in a pie-shaped sliver to fill in the planking gap abaft the sternpost. Make sure all the planking that terminates on the stern frame has a smooth edge exactly at the after end of the frame, so that the transom, when mounted, will meet the planking in a neat corner.

SANDING AND FINISHING

The first prerequisite of a good paint job is good sanding. The planking seams add much realism to a hull, but the roughness of the planks, especially on the curves, should be worked down to a smooth satiny texture.

Use a medium-grade sandpaper for the first sanding. Cut it into pieces about 3″ × 5″ to keep it to a manageable size. It's a good idea to sand outdoors, where the fine dust won't collect on furniture and clog the atmosphere.

Sand small areas, using your fingers instead of a block to press the sandpaper against the work. In rough areas, move the paper across the planking until the roughness vanishes, then sand with the grain to remove any scoring.

Be careful to sand *up to* the keel, stempost, and sternpost, without sanding these parts themselves. The edges of the keel

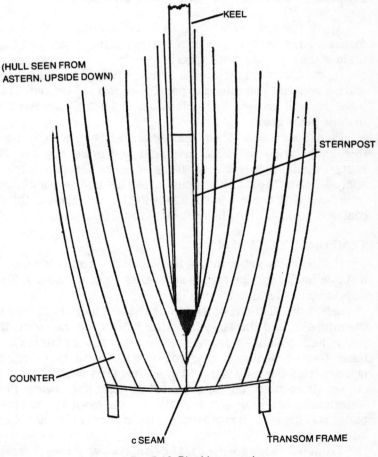

Fig. 7-12. Planking counter.

and posts should remain sharp and not become rounded. When the hull has been completely sanded, repeat the sanding with fine grade paper, bringing it to a silky feel.

Use a good-quality flat-finish modeler's paint to finish the hull. The vast majority of sailing ships have black hulls, but there are exceptions, and some hulls are multi-colored. Ordinarily, these multi-hued hulls have moldings dividing the colors, and the divisions follow the planking seams. This makes it quite easy to find and adhere to a paint line.

Paint from the bulwarks downward, from end to end without jumping around. If the hull is multi-colored, do all of one color at a time. Never put fresh paint over half-dried paint, not even at the edges, because it will show later as a rough spot.

Apply the paint sparingly. Thick paint, with globs, never makes a good finish as two or more thin coats. Brush *with* the grain of the planking, not across it.

Paint at least an inch below where you think the waterline will be, whether you intend to paint or copper the bottom. The waterline will not follow the planking, so don't blindly adhere to some plank seam.

Paint one side, then the other. After the coat has thoroughly dried (at least overnight and preferably for 24 hours), sand it lightly all over using very fine sandpaper, then apply a second coat. This should bring the hull to a uniform color, but if it doesn't, sand again lightly and apply a third coat, and so on until the hull's color is consistent.

TEMPORARY CRADLE

It's too early yet to mount the hull permanently, but since a stable holder for the ship is soon going to be necessary, it's time to build a temporary cradle.

Select two sections of the hull, one about halfway between the midpoint and the bow, the other halfway to the stern. If you've built a plank-on-frame hull, you can use the patterns for these frames again. If not, you'll have to lift the section outlines from the body plan and make frame patterns.

On these patterns, select a lift at least 1/4″ below the waterline of the ship, and mark it. Use the same lift on both patterns. This lift will represent the top of the cradle. (See Fig. 7-13.)

From a 3″ wide sheet of 1/4″ balsa, cut two pieces at least an inch wider than the frames. Fold one of the frame patterns along the marked lift line, and lay the pattern so this fold breaks over the top edge of the piece and is approximately centered along the edge. Using the pattern edges as a guide, mark out the shape of the section on the wood, only make the marks about 1/8″ out from the edges. Repeat this process for the other side and then cut along the lines. You will be retaining the portion of wood *outside* the outline for the cradle, not the inner portion, as you did in making a hull frame.

Now measure the distance between the sections used for shaping the cradle and add 1/2″. From the balsa plank, cut two rectangles of this length and as high as the cradles. Cement these rectangles to the side edges of the cradles to make a sort of box. (Again, see Fig. 7-13.) For added strength, push two or three lill pins through the rectangle sides into the cradle.

After the cradle joints have had time to dry, set the hull in place, making sure it's headed in the right direction. The cradles should hold the hull without gripping it or rubbing as it is moved in and out. If necessary, shave down the cradle's curves, but be certain that any adjustments are made on both sides to keep the hull level. If the cradle is too large, letting the hull rock from side to side, build it up by cementing on layers of flannel or felt in the same relative places on both sides.

As a final test of the cradle's levelness, lay a long piece of strip wood across the bulwarks and measure the distances of the ends from the table. If it is level, both distances should be the same.

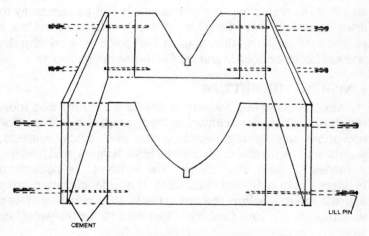

Fig. 7-13. A temporary cradle.

MARKING THE WATERLINE

In marking the waterline of the ship it is necessary that the cradle be absolutely level. This simple operation is critical to the appearance of the model.

Find the position of the waterline by measuring down amidships from the top of the hull planking on the side view of the hull. Convert the scale, if necessary, and make a pencil mark on the hull.

Set the cradle and hull in the center of a large table (with the tablecloth removed) or on a smooth tiled floor. Adjacent to the mark on the hull make a pile of books, boards, or other firm, flat objects. Use a long, soft-lead pencil, laying it atop the stack and extending it to the ship. Adjust the stack until the pencil, when firmly pressed down, touches the mark. See Fig. 7-14.

If possible, get someone to help you by gently pressing down on the deck beams amidships to hold the hull in place. Then, moving the stack of books and pencil as a unit, slowly draw the waterline all the way around the ship. Be especially careful not to let the pencil slip or be forced downward on the curves of the bow and stern.

On a black hull, the waterline mark will show up as a reflective line, so you will need plenty of ambient light to see it. Before you proceed, sight along the waterline from both ends of the ship to make sure it is level and straight.

Some painted-bottom ships carry a distinctive colored stripe at the waterline. If yours is one, it will be necessary to draw a second waterline 1/8″ above the first, to act as a painting guide. To do this, place a 1/8″ piece of wood atop the stack of books or boards and repeat the marking process.

FINISHING THE BOTTOM

Most ocean-going vessels of the 19th Century and most warships of earlier centuries had copper bottoms. The exceptions are fishing vessels, some pilot boats, coasters, yachts, and incidental craft such as hoys, luggers, and tenders. A modelers' plan will tell you the color of the bottom; a builders' plan will not (although the side elevation may indicate plates below the waterline). In general, you can assume that any 19th Century vessel over 90′ on the waterline will carry copper.

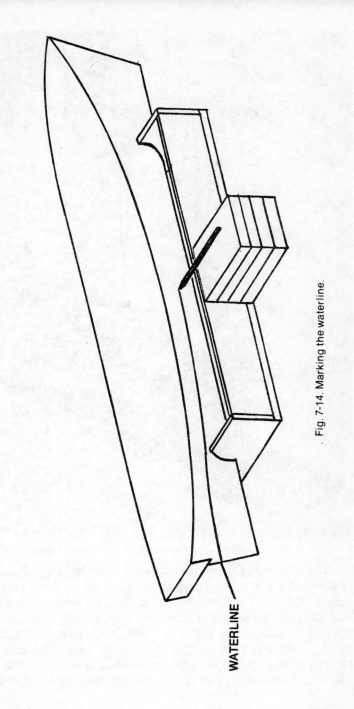

WATERLINE

Fig. 7-14. Marking the waterline.

Fig. 7-15. The kit-built Sultana model. (Courtesy Model Shipways, Inc.)

The purpose of a copper bottom is to inhibit the collection of barnacles and other clinging mollusks and to keep marine borers out of the timbers. With lesser success, but at considerably lower cost, tallow was occasionally used to coat the ship's underwater parts up until about 1800. This tallow usually resulted in a sort of dirty gray color that can be painted on the bottom, as seen in the kit-built *Sultana* model in Fig. 7-15 (*Sultana* was an American built British naval vessel of 1767). Tallow went out of vogue for anything but small craft in the early 1800's.

Painting The Bottom

If your ship needs a painted bottom, first paint a half-inch wide stripe along the waterline. Use a small, good-quality hair brush. Lay the hull on its side and paint from one end to the other, taking great care to keep the upper edge of the stripe exactly on the waterline mark.

Don't try to use masking tape on the edge, because the irregularity of the planking and its seams will provide plenty of opportunities for capillary action to carry the paint up where it doesn't belong. Besides, you can't correctly mask on the curves of the ends. Just take your time and apply the paint sparingly.

When the stripe has dried, paint the rest of the bottom on that side, using a larger brush. Apply as many coats as necessary to bring the finish to uniformity. When the last coat is dry, turn the hull around and paint the other side in the same manner.

If a waterline stripe is needed, paint it last. Use a very thin artists' brush such as a 000 sable bristle.

To give your ship a more realistic appearance, you can foul the bottom to simulate the collection of mosses and other marine junk all ships carry. When the hull paint is at least 48 hours old, make a turpentine wash by mixing a small amount of dark green plastic modelers' dope with turnpentine in an old cereal bowl. Combine about 10 parts of turpentine to one part of dope, stirring with a wood scrap. It will not blend to dilute the dope. Dip a wadded paper towel in the mixture, getting it wet with the turpentine and picking up some green, but not much. Smear it on the hull, working from waterline to keel in a random pattern to create smeary blotches.

Make a black turpentine wash the same way. Apply it all over the bottom, more heavily on the green blotches. Although rather alarming in the process, the result will be a very realistic-looking underside for your ship.

Coppering the Bottom

A copper bottom can be painted on, using a metallic paint such as plastic dope. To prepare the surface, first apply a coat of white gesso, then put on several coats of copper or bronze dope.

Such a bottom, however, is not nearly as satisfying as a suit of real copper. Ordinarily, ships carry plates of thin copper 18" × 48" applied over the planking and timbers below the waterline. A model so treated becomes strikingly handsome and infinitely more realistic than one with a painted copper bottom.

It's best to use .002" copper foil for the plates. This can be purchased in some hobby shops. Model Shipways sells it in 6" × 12" sheets.

To prepare the copper, unroll it and cut it into four smaller sheets each 3" × 6". Work out the wrinkles by laying it on a smooth place and rubbing the creases with a small piece of hardwood. Then fill a frying pan with cold water. If you have a gas stove, hold the copper flat over the flame with a pair of pliers, and when it is red hot in some places, immerse it in the water. If your stove is not gas, heat the copper with a blowtorch or use a disposable cigarette lighter with the flame as high as you can get it. This heating and quenching will cause the copper to darken and discolor to many hues, which is the desirable effect.

Now lay out the copper sheet on a flat surface. Measure from the same side along both shorter edges, using a sharp hard-lead pencil to make a dent in the copper every 18" in scale. Use a straightedge to draw parallel lines down the length with the marks as a guide (see Fig. 7-16).

Next, measure from the same side along the long edges, marking every fourth scale foot, and draw lines joining these dents. The result should be a grid with each rectangle 18" × 4" in scale. Hold the sheet with the short edge toward you, and carefully cut into the copper from this edge, about three plates deep along each line, using a pair of sharp shears. This will make a fringe along the short edge.

Lay the hull upside down and paint contact cement on the edge and side of the keel and sternpost for about 2", and over about two square inches of the run. Paint the three rows of plates at the fringed end of the copper with contact cement. When the cement is tacky, cut across the fringe on the scoring closest to the edge, letting the plates fall without touching each other. (See Fig. 7-17.)

Begin by plating the sternpost to the waterline and the keel edge as far as the cement goes. The direction of plating is *always* toward the waterline and the bow, so apply the

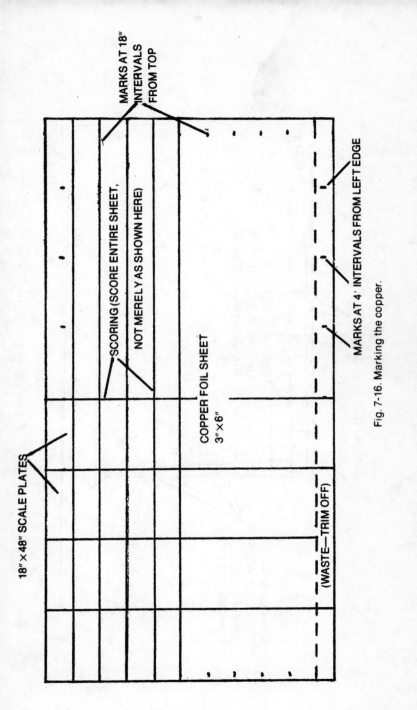

MARKS AT 18" INTERVALS FROM TOP

SCORING (SCORE ENTIRE SHEET, NOT MERELY AS SHOWN HERE)

18" × 48" SCALE PLATES

COPPER FOIL SHEET 3" × 6"

(WASTE—TRIM OFF)

MARKS AT 4' INTERVALS FROM LEFT EDGE

Fig. 7-16. Marking the copper.

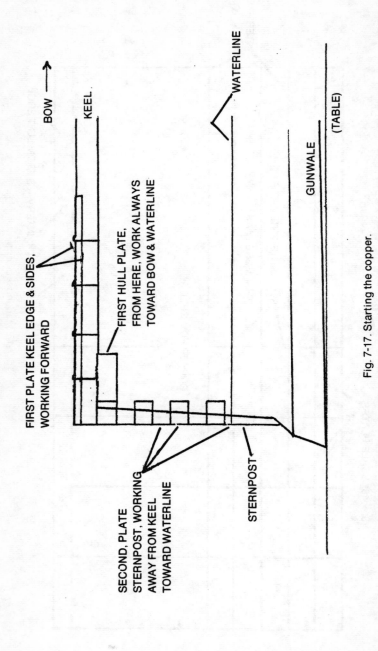

BOW →

KEEL

FIRST PLATE KEEL EDGE & SIDES, WORKING FORWARD

FIRST HULL PLATE, FROM HERE, WORK ALWAYS TOWARD BOW & WATERLINE

WATERLINE

SECOND, PLATE STERNPOST, WORKING AWAY FROM KEEL TOWARD WATERLINE

STERNPOST

GUNWALE

(TABLE)

Fig. 7-17. Starting the copper.

after-most plate first, then the next, and so on toward the bow. Each new plate should very slightly overlap its neighbors below and astern. Bend the edges over onto the keel's sides. When you have reached the end of the cement on the edge, do a row on the side of the keel. If the plate is wider than the keel's side, let it bend onto the planking. Press each plate firmly in place.

Now start on the planking, always working toward the waterline and the bow. Apply about four plates in a row, then start a new row of three, then two, and finally one. Make each new plate's edges slightly overlap its neighbors', and offset the plates in a brickwork pattern, as shown in Fig. 7-18.

The coppering job goes with surprising speed. It's a good idea each time you cut off a row of plates to deepen the fringe and paint cement on the next row, so that it can get tacky while you work. You should also apply cement to the hull a couple of dozen plates ahead. This way the plates and the hull will be ready when you get to them and you won't have to interrupt your work for cement to cure.

Never work closer to the bow near the waterline than at the keel. In fact, it's a good idea to work in a diagonal pattern, with the row closest to the keel a half-plate longer than the next row, which is a half-plate longer than the third, and so

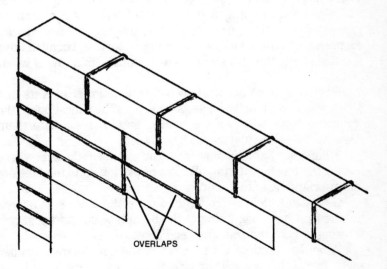

OVERLAPS

Fig. 7-18. Plate overlap.

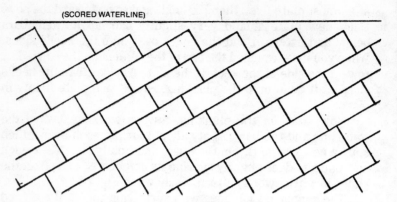

Fig. 7-19. Edge of plating fore and aft.

forth. The reason for this will soon become clear as you plate; as the belly of the ship begins to swell, it takes more rows of copper to reach from keel to waterline.

This phenomenon is easy to contend with. Make all rows parallel to the keel. It is not necessary to make "sliver" rows as in planking. The rows near the waterline will eventually curve downward and back up.

Carry the copper up to, but not over, the waterline. (See Fig. 7-19.) As the rows of plates begin to curve, you will have to add new rows angling away from the waterline, causing a jagged edge. This is fine, so long as the hull is covered with copper up to two scale feet from the waterline, because later you will girdle the hull along the waterline with a row of wider plates.

Continue on toward the bow in this manner, always staying farthest ahead along the keel. As you pass the widest point, the waterline rows will begin curving upward. Terminate them near the waterline just as you began them.

When you reach the bow, stop the plating of the keel where it joins the forefoot. Bring all rows of plating up to the forefoot and overlapping onto it a little.

Now turn the hull around and plate the other side as you did the first half, beginning at the bottom of the sternpost and working toward the waterline and forward.

When the plating has reached to the bow, mark a copper sheet for plates 2′ × 4′ in scale. Cut one piece 2′ × 8′ in scale, and cement it around the sternpost at the waterline. You can apply contact cement onto copper plates already in place. Work forward from the sternpost, mounting the plates with the edge directly on the waterline and the other edge on the installed copper. See Fig. 7-20.

The last step is plating the stem post itself. Make plates four feet long in scale and wide enough to cover the edge and both sides of the stem. Work around the curve of the forefoot toward the waterline. The waterline plate will take a little trimming to make it follow the line.

The copper will pick up fingerprints and mar from handling, so it's a good idea (though not necessary) to spray a coat of flat clear dope or varnish on it. After applying this protective coat, you may wish to "contaminate" the copper to simulate a dirty bottom. The section on painted bottoms provides hints on how to make a realistically fouled underside.

Rudders

On most wooden vessels the rudder is made of several vertical planks whose narrow edges are joined and held together by stout steel bands. On the fore edge of the rudder, directly beneath each band, a notch is cut to permit a round steel pin called a pintle to extend downward a few inches. When the rudder is mounted on the ship, these pintles slide into the gudgeon strops, which are steel bends fixed to the hull and wrapped around the sternpost. Thus the pintle and gudgeon strops both bear the weight of the rudder and act as hinges for it. (See Fig. 7-21.)

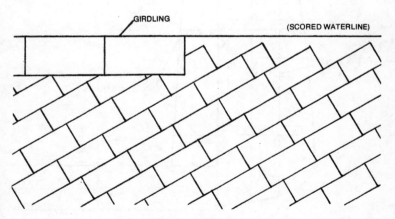

Fig. 7-20. Girdling.

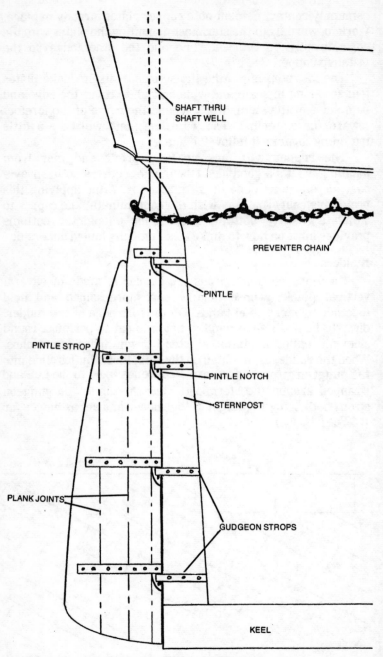

Fig. 7-21. Anatomy of a rudder.

174

Gravity generally holds the rudder in place. This arrangement is satisfactory except in heavy following seas when a wave is apt to sweep up under the counter and lift the rudder. After a few such experiences, seamen invented the *preventer chain*. It prevents the potentially disastrous loss of the rudder. Although the rudder might be lifted off its gudgeons, the preventer chain keeps it from washing away in the storm. This chain is attached by an eyebolt to the top after part of the rudder, then loosely draped to several eyebolts under the quarters.

On small craft the rudder is often carried completely outboard, with the shaft extending up over the taffrail to be joined with a tiller. (See Fig. 7-22.) Pre-1830, larger vessels usually embellished on this theme only slightly, by bringing the shaft up through a well in the overhanging stern. This arrangement requires a sizeable fan-shaped opening in the counter to permit the rudder shaft to swing. Following seas are thus presented with an invitation to invade the ship.

Beginning around 1830, a more watertight arrangement came into use, and survives to this day. The leading edge of the rudder, instead of extending straight upward to become the shaft, terminates at the top of the rudder blade. To this is fixed a round shaft whose center is on a line with the pintles. In this way, the shaft merely rotates rather than swings to turn the rudder, so a watertight sleeve can be used where the shaft enters the counter.

It is usually easiest to make a model rudder from one piece. Use a hardwood plank of the same thickness as the keelson. Transfer the rudder's outline from the drawing to the plank. Pay close attention to the type of shaft up top. If it is a continuation of the leading edge, make sure you extend the piece upward far enough to enter the hull 1/4″ (or stick above the taffrail, depending on the type). If it has an offset round shaft, make a small mounting notch one-half the shaft diameter deep, and perhaps 1/4″ long at the top leading edge of the rudder blade. See Fig. 7-23.

After you cut out the rudder, use an ice pick and a straightedge to score the plank joints. Shave and sand the leading edge to roundness, and then cut notches for the pintles. The pintle strops can be made by cutting narrow strips from card stock. Draw guidelines on the rudder at right angles to the leading edge at the top of each pintle notch. Use contact cement to mount the strops. They should begin at the trailing

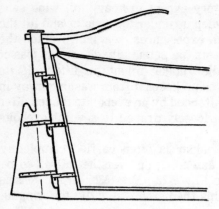

OUTBOARD SWING RUDDER

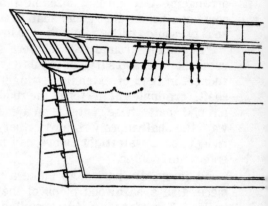

INBOARD SWING RUDDER

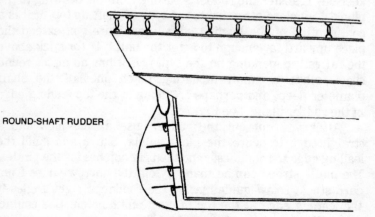

ROUND-SHAFT RUDDER

Fig. 7-22. Rudder types.

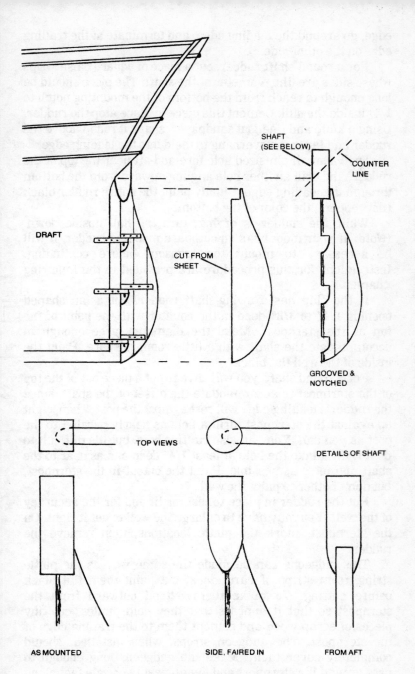

DRAFT

SHAFT
(SEE BELOW)

COUNTER
LINE

CUT FROM
SHEET

GROOVED &
NOTCHED

TOP VIEWS

DETAILS OF SHAFT

AS MOUNTED

SIDE, FAIRED IN

FROM AFT

Fig. 7-23. Making a rudder.

edge, go around the leading edge, and terminate at the trailing edge on the other side.

For a round-shaft rudder, cut a piece of square balsa strips whose sides are the diameter of the shaft. The piece should be long enough to reach from the bottom of the mounting notch to 1/4" inside the hull. Cement this piece in place atop the rudder. Using a knife and fine-grit sandpaper, shape it round above the rudder and taper the overhang to meld into the leading edge.

Drill a small pin-sized hole fore-and-aft near the top of the rudder, and drill another hole angling upward from the bottom through the leading edge. Finally paint the entire rudder black (not copper), the color of the bottom.

While the rudder is drying, turn the hull upside down. (*Note*: If your model has an outboard-mounted rudder, it will be necessary to mount the transom before continuing. Instructions for this procedure are provided in the following chapter.)

If the ship has a swing-shaft rudder, cut a fan shaped opening 1/4" to 3/8" deep in the counter with the point of the fan at the sternpost. Make the diameter large enough to accommodate the shaft with a little room to spare. Paint the inside of the well flat black.

For a round shaft, you will have to cut a piece out of the top of the sternpost to accommodate the offset of the shaft, since the rudder's leading edge will rest against the post. Then, right up against the sternpost, drill a hole as nearly parallel to the post as you can. You can also cut this hole, but it's difficult to do it right. Make the hole at least 1/4" deep and as near to the shaft diameter as possible. Paint the cutout in the sternpost, but don't bother to paint the well.

Put the rudder in place to test for fit and for the accuracy of the well. You may have to enlarge the well to get it right. On the sternpost, mark the pintle locations, then remove the rudder.

The gudgeons can be made the same way as the pintle strips, from strips of card stock, but paint them flat black before cutting. To make them extend outward from the sternpost so that it appears that they hold pintles, cut tiny pieces of scrap wood and cement them to the trailing edge of the sternpost. The gudgeon strops, when installed, should completely cover them. Make the gudgeons long enough to pass around the sternpost and lay at least two scale feet along the hull.

You can now mount the rudder. Turn the hull upside down and put the rudder in place. (See Fig. 7-24.) In the hole slanting up from the rudder's underside, insert an ordinary sewing pin.

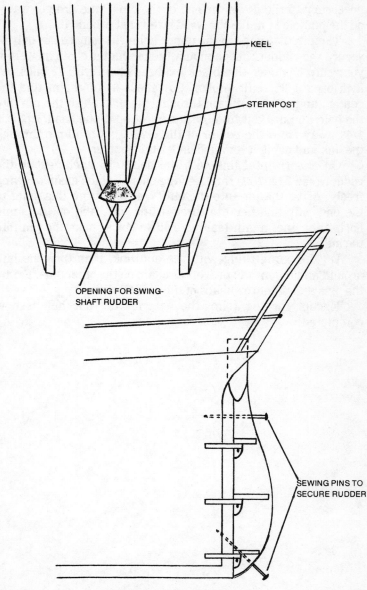

KEEL

STERNPOST

OPENING FOR SWING-SHAFT RUDDER

SEWING PINS TO SECURE RUDDER

Fig. 7-24. Mounting the rudder.

Check to make sure the rudder is properly placed. Gently tap on the pinhead with pliers or a tack hammer, driving it into the sternpost at least 1/4″. With wire cutters, snip off the pin close to the rudder, then drive it until flush with the wood. It may be necessary to file down the end of the pin. Put a drop of water on the pinhole to make the wood swell shut around it.

The pin that goes in the upper hole will be used not only to secure the rudder, but to mount the preventer chain as well, if your ship has one. Use black oxidized chain with 22 links per inch on a 1/8″ scale model. Cut about 6″ of chain, find the center, and stick a lill pin through the link. Push the pin into the hole and drive it into the sternpost up to the head. About 1 1/4″ away from the center of the chain, put a lill pin through the link and bring it forward under the quarter.

On a horizontal line with the point of attachment to the rudder (see Fig. 7-21), and leaving enough slack chain to swing freely, drive the pin into the hull. Halfway from this point to the end, slip another pin through the link, and on the same horizontal line, again leaving a little slack, push the pin into the hull.

Do the same thing with the end link, then turn the hull around and mount the preventer chain on the other side. Prime the pins and paint the heads of the pins flat black.

Except for the trim, the exterior of your hull is now completed.

Chapter 8

Hull Trim

Your hull has now progressed through several stages of evolution—from lines on paper, to pieces of wood, to a rough form, to a recognizable ship. All that remains to be done is the addition of the trim.

Hull trim is treated here in a rather broad sense, including not only functional and decorative touches, but such necessities as the transom.

Depending upon the complexity and era of the model, the trim can take anywhere from a couple of hours to complete to incredible periods of time. This is why, in the earlier chapters dealing with the selection of a model, you were encouraged to avoid elaborately festooned vessels if this is your first ship.

Museums are filled with awesomely decorated models that took years and years of skilled patience to decorate. You can also, however, find multitudes of lovely, simply-adorned vessels that give you almost as much pleasure in modeling and take much less time.

WALES AND STRAKES

Wales and *strakes* are long moldings that generally extend the entire length of the hull. There is a minor technical distinction between them, but from the standpoint of appearance, and for modeling purposes, they are considered to be identical.

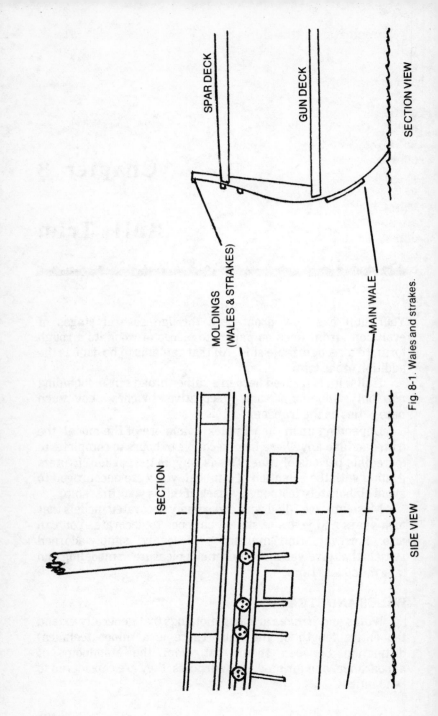

Fig. 8-1. Wales and strakes.

SPAR DECK

GUN DECK

SECTION VIEW

MOLDINGS (WALES & STRAKES)

MAIN WALE

SECTION

SIDE VIEW

Examination of the ship's plans, especially the side view, will tell you where to place the wales and strakes. They are generally found where the planking changes thickness, such as along the seam of the hull and bulwark planking. (See Fig. 8-1.) For decorative purposes, a wale can often occur at the top of the bulwark, just below, or fastened directly to the gunwale railing. Other common places for a wale are along the upper and lower port sills on warships, or about halfway between the bulwarks and the waterline on merchantmen.

Wales may be either squared or rounded in cross section, as shown in Fig. 8-2. Study sectional views of the hull or bulwarks to determine the shape of your ship's wales. If they are squared, use hardwood strips of the appropriate dimensions for the long curves amidships, and balsa strips of the same size on tight curves forward and aft. Rounded wales can be made from half-round if you can find it at your hobby shop (check the model railroad department). Failing that, you can buy plastic tubing and split it, or you can sand the outboard edges off the square stock to make the moldings.

The round stern, whose problems seem to have no end, can break moldings. The easiest way out is to cut strips of sheet plastic and apply them as the stern wales. This is the only substance that can make the sharp curves without breaking.

Always paint the wales before you install them. They usually constrast with the hull color: white on black, for

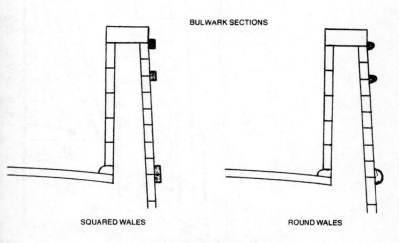

BULWARK SECTIONS

SQUARED WALES   ROUND WALES

Fig. 8-2. Squared and round wales.

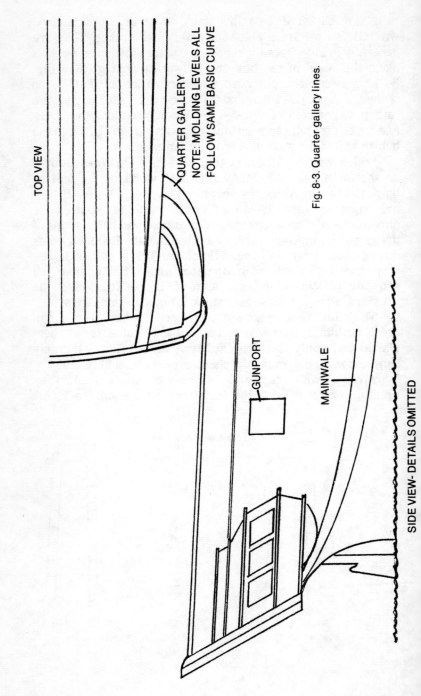

TOP VIEW

QUARTER GALLERY
NOTE: MOLDING LEVELS ALL
FOLLOW SAME BASIC CURVE

Fig. 8-3. Quarter gallery lines.

GUNPORT

MAINWALE

SIDE VIEW- DETAILS OMITTED

184

example. Almost without exception, the wales follow the planksheer, so run a bead of contact cement along the appropriate plank seam, coat the bonding side of the wale, and press it in place. If you have to butt two strips to make a very long continuous wale, do it amidships and preferably where the *channels* (protruding planks for attaching the mainmast shrouds) will later be mounted.

The main wale is a broad plank that follows the greatest breadth of each section along the hull. It is usually twice the width of a normal plank and generally protrudes about 1/32″ on a model of up to 3/16″ scale, 1/16″ on a larger scale. Its purpose is to keep the sides of the ship from scarring while at moorings. Paint it to match the hull and cement it atop the hull planks, following the seams for proper sheer.

QUARTER GALLERIES

Quarter galleries are fancy structures on either side of the stern. They are normally found only on large warships, where they seem to have been used as a mark of importance. Ostensibly the quarter galleries had the purpose of providing a relatively safe point of observation for important passengers during engagements, but in actual practice they were used as privies for the captain, commodore, and high-ranking passengers occupying the great cabin. And of course, they had a decorative function, which is of primary interest on a model.

As seen from above, a quarter gallery has the form of one-fourth of an ellipse, sweeping out abaft the stern-most gunport and terminating in the transom. From the side, all vertical lines (fore edge, window frames, etc.) are parallel to the transom, which means that the form of the quarter gallery at the moldings above and below the windows is the same, but offset. This is an important characteristic in modeling the galleries. See Fig. 8-3.

To find the basic shape of the quarter gallery (the form of the upper and lower section at the window lines), make a working drawing of the stern as described in Figs. 6-23 through 6-26. In this case, however, carry the transom curve outboard and mark in the outside of the hull planking.

Working from the top view of the quarter galleries, usually found on the deck plan and the side view drawing, mark the form of the curve at several reference points and draw it in, using a French curve. This will give you a template as illustrated in Fig. 8-4.

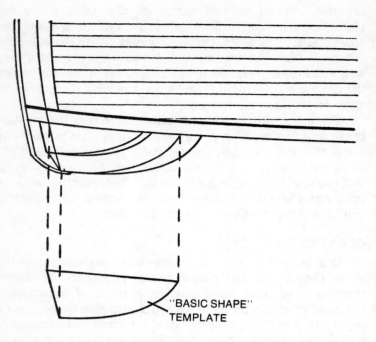

Fig. 8-4. Basic shape of quarter gallery.

Cut out the template and use it to trace and cut four identical pieces (formers) from a sheet of hardwood or modelers' plywood. These formers should be the same thickness as the moldings above and below the windows. Orient the grain fore-and-aft.

On most ships, the window moldings occur along the same lines as the wales of the hull. Prepare the hull by cutting away the wales at the stern where these four formers will be mounted.

Rough in the galleries one at a time, saving the fancy work on both for later. Start by gluing the lower former in place along the wale line, horizontally as viewed from the stern, with its aft edge corresponding to the curve of the transom. Use a lot of glue, but be careful to apply it evenly.

Fashion a block of balsa to fit between the upper and lower formers with the grain fore-and-aft. It must be the width measured vertically (not parallel to the transom) between the window-section moldings, and it must be large enough to overhang both formers on all sides while joining flat with the hull planking. Atop it, mount the upper former set abaft the lower former to correspond with the transom line. See Fig. 8-5.

Carefully shave down the balsa and then sand it so that a straight line is achieved from any given point on one former to the corresponding point on the other. Take care not to mar the hull sides during this step.

Quarter galleries usually have additional moldings covering knuckles a foot or so from the window-section moldings. These follow the same elliptical shape as the main formers, but are smaller. Make the lower former first, since it is larger than the top former. From the template for the basic formers, deduct along the curve about 1/16" of width at the transom and the amount of length indicated by the side view. Use this template to cut two hardwood formers, one for each gallery.

From sheet balsa, the thickness of the distance between the two lower formers, cut a block slightly larger than the lower main former. Cement it in place on the underside of the former, then cement on its underside the new former. Carve and sand the balsa to form straight beveled lines between the formers.

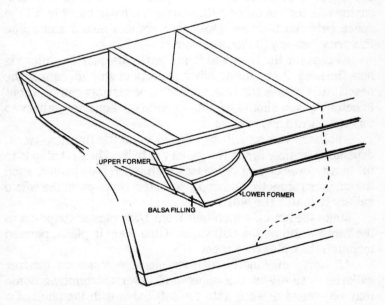

Fig. 8-5. Quarter gallery with roughed-in main section.

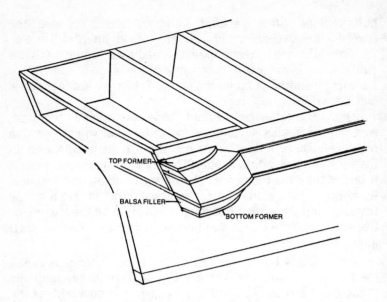

TOP FORMER

BALSA FILLER

BOTTOM FORMER

Fig. 8-6. Quarter gallery—finished shape.

Reduce the template now to the size of the former above the upper main former. Cut a pair of hardwood formers, saving one for the other galley. Rough a balsa block to fill the space between the two upper formers and mount and shape this area just as you did the lower.

Except for the trim and fancy work, the quarter gallery is now finished. As in many other aspects of ship modeling, the description makes the task appear to be terribly complex, but in actuality you should be able to build up a quarter gallery to this stage in an hour or two.

Another evening will be needed to do the finishing work, depending on how fancy the gallery is to be. The first step is to fill in any cracks and crevasses with a soft wood filler, sand the surfaces smooth, and apply a sealer. Next, paint the whole gallery to match the hull.

Make the knuckle moldings from 1/32" plastic strips cut to the same width as the hull wales. Glue them in place, painted to match the wales they meet.

All sorts of fanciful decorations are found on quarter galleries, usually at the upper and lower extremities. Some may be etched directly into the soft balsa with the point of a lead pencil. Before you try it, do two things: paint the etched areas with gesso, and try working details into a scrap of balsa to get the feel of it. It's best to use a medium-lead pencil with a slightly rounded tip on the lead. After etching on the finished work, paint these areas with a gold leaf dope. Great artistry is of course nice for this, but with a little patience anyone can come up with very good decorative effects.

Some decorations don't lend themselves to etching. Carved gilt ropes, for example, can be simulated by gluing on gold lame thread or waxed unbleached cuttyhunk impregnated with gold leaf dope. Gold scrolls can be obtained by cutting up cigar bands, soup can labels, cigarette packages that carry gilt printing, and other products of the garbage can. Stars, eagles, and other common devices can be gotten from scrap too, or you can buy them in hobby shops and from parts markers. Examples appear in Fig. 8-7.

Last to be made are the windows. Lay a piece of card stock on the gallery, following its curvature and, by rubbing a pencil on it, trace the upper and lower window-section moldings. Cut the card to fit exactly between these moldings and come exactly to the hull planking forward and the transom aft. Make sure it fits before proceeding.

Paint the card to match the hull. When the paint has dried, mark the outlines of the window frames with a sharp soft-lead

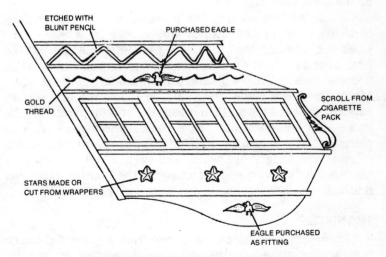

Fig. 8-7. Some decorations on a quarter gallery.

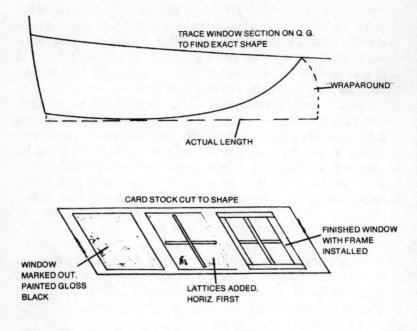

Fig. 8-8. Quarter gallery window section.

pencil. These lines will show up if you place a lamp to reflect off the card. (See Fig. 8-8.)

Inside the window outlines, paint the card with high-gloss black dope. Make the frames and lattices from white card stock cut into narrow strips. It's best to mount the lattices first, pressing them carefully into the gloss paint after it has become tacky. This will make them adhere without glue. Mount the cross piece first, parallel to the top and bottom edges of the card stock, then mount the upright parallel to the ends. After the paint has dried, cement the frames on, side pieces first. Be extremely sparing in the use of contact cement to avoid the danger of spoiling the work. Finally install the window section with contact cement. The quarter gallery is finished.

TRANSOMS

Transoms run the entire gamut from a plain flat board bearing the vessel's name and port of registry, to lavishly festooned examples of national profligacy.

In general, merchantmen were simply decorated across the stern and became almost austere as the 19th Century progressed, while at the same time warships, especially the big ones, became showplaces for man's tendency to glorify the essentially dirty business of war. This is especially true of the British, who always kept hundreds of sculptors busy on transom work. But Americans were guilty of it to a certain extent, too.

Whether simple or garish, a transom is best made off the ship and mounted only when it is complete. The choice of materials is a matter of personal preference, but one thing to keep in mind is the camber of the transom; it has to be flexible enough to bend around the stern.

With the exception of some whalers and 1830-era packets, the transoms of most ships are slanted aft from the sternpost, yet the drawings generally show them as seen from directly aft. This means you are dealing with a parallax; the vertical dimensions appear shorter than they actually are. On a flat or slightly curved transom, you can easily correct this problem by computing a factor to be applied to all vertical measurements. As shown in Fig. 8-9, measure the apparent height of the transom on the body plan or transom detail view, then measure the transom's actual height on the side view. Divide the actual by the apparent.

Let's say, for example, that the apparent height is 40 mm, and the actual is 50 mm. The verical factor, then, will be:

$$\frac{\text{Actual}}{\text{Apparent}} = \frac{50}{40} = 1.25$$

To show how this factor is used, suppose you now measure a window on the transom plan and find its apparent height is 12 mm. To determine its actual height, multiply by the vertical factor, so that :

Actual height × Apparent x factor = 12 × 1.25 = 15 mm

Rounded Transoms

With a few notable exceptions, such as the *Constellation*, the transoms of round-stern vessels are usually very simple. In fact, there is no transom per se, since the stern is essentially

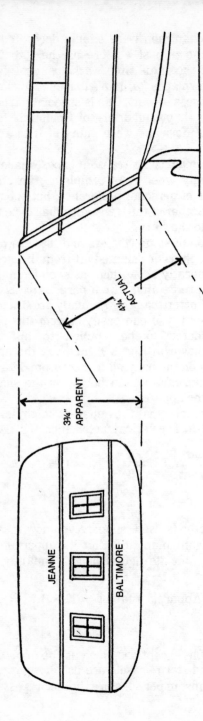

Fig. 8-9. Stern view parallax.

a continuous curve. At its simplest, such a stern bears only the vessel's name and home port. Fancier vessels, such as clippers, often carry a decorative wreath around the name. (See Fig. 8-10.)

The wreath is best made on a piece of card stock. Cut the card to the size and shape of the wreath and paint it to match the hull. Mount the decorations around the edges. The decorations may be gilt curlicues scavenged from cigar bands and labels, thread soaked in glue or shellac, contrasting paper cutouts, or whatever else is indicated. If the card must bend to adhere to the hull, make the decorations of flexible materials. If not, you can augment your material selection with powdered papier mache and Plaster of Paris sculpted with wet knife blades. See Fig. 8-11.

One very good source of gilded decorative swirls and curlicues is picture framing and art supply shops. I've also purchased them at Sherwin-Williams paint stores, where they are sold as decorative gilt-paper corners and borders for picture frames. They come in a vast assortment of sizes and patterns, either with a peel-off backing or an adhesive that must be wet. You can slice off little pieces, fashion them to your needs, and administer them with very good results.

The lettering for ships' names and ports of registry can also be obtained fairly easily. Model Shipways, for one, sells decals of common ship names and ports. If they don't have yours, you can buy several decals that have all the necessary letters and cut them up to construct the name. From art shops you can buy peel-off adhesive lettering in many sizes, and also lettering stencils and templates.

Sometimes a little ingenuity is called for. On the *Bear* model, for instance, I had to provide block letters four scale feet high to emblazon the transom. To do this, I used a one-inch stencil (the scale was $1/4'' = 1'$) to mark out the letters on black construction paper. I marked the letters backwards, on the back of the black paper so the pencil marks wouldn't show. Stencils always leave gaps, so I had to join the parts of the letters together. Finally, I cut out the letters with a sharp knife and cemented them to the white transom at marks indicating correct placement.

No matter what you have to do to your stern, it's best to do it off the hull and then cement the finished product in place.

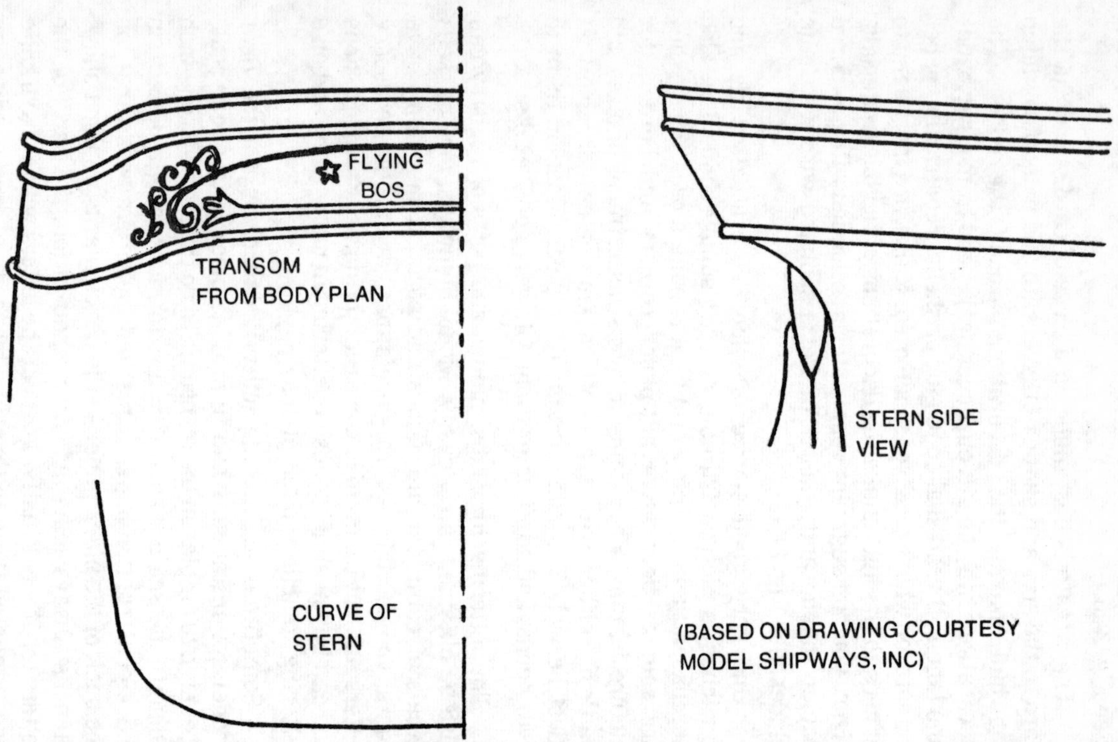

STERN SIDE VIEW

FLYING BOS

TRANSOM FROM BODY PLAN

CURVE OF STERN

(BASED ON DRAWING COURTESY MODEL SHIPWAYS, INC)

Fig. 8-10. Round stern decorations.

Squared Transoms

In its most elementary form, a squared transom is very simple. You cut a sheet to size and glue it on. For ships such as the *Charles W. Morgan,* the *Volante,* and the *Swordfish,* there really isn't much more to it than that, since all of these vessels have flush, unadorned sterns.

The task takes on a different magnitude when the transom carries windows, brightwork, and sculpture. To make *Old Ironsides* transom, which has all these things, will take several evenings.

There are two types of square transoms. The first is flush, which means that the sides of the ship and the edges of the transom form a corner. This type of transom should be made of balsa slightly oversized. When mounted you can sand down the transom edges to conform to the planking line.

The other type of transom is overhanging, usually found only on ships dating before the 1830s. In this configuration, the transom meets the counter but sticks out on the sides and above the taffrail. It usually covers the after sides of the quarter galleries as well. Thin hardwood sheets laminated to form a plywood are best for overhanging transoms.

You can obtain the shape of a flush transom by tracing through card stock held in place and rubbed around the end of the planking with the side of a pencil lead. For an overhanging transom, make a drawing of the outline on card stock based on the transom plan. Don't forget to use the height factor in finding vertical dimensions.

Cut out the transom outline and test it on the model to be sure it fits. This will now serve as a template for cutting out the sheet wood. Use thin sheet, preferably 1/32", laminated with

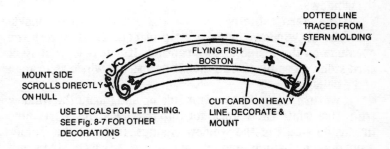

Fig. 8-11. Transom applique.

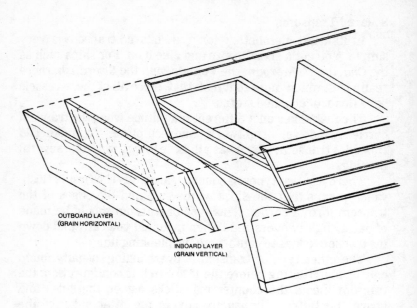

OUTBOARD LAYER
(GRAIN HORIZONTAL)

INBOARD LAYER
(GRAIN VERTICAL)

Fig. 8-12. Laminated transom.

two identical pieces. The interior piece should have the grain up and down, the exterior piece side to side. Join them with contact cement and bend them slightly to approximate the transom camber. Give the cement an hour to set, then seal and paint the transom. See Fig. 8-12.

Draw the window outlines and the wales on the template. Cut out the window openings (to the *insides* of the frames) and don't leave lattices. Lay the template in place on the transom, mark the openings, remove the template, and carefully cut out the windows.

If the stern cabin is finished and you want to see inside through the windows, glue a strip of cellophane across the openings on the inside of the transom. If not, paint a strip of card stock gloss black and glue it across the windows instead of the cellophane.

Now turn the transom right side up and mount the window trim. Use white card stock cut into narrow strips. First, line the inside edges of the window casings, then put the frames around each opening, and last, put in the lattices of strips half the width of the frames as described in the earlier section on quarter galleries. See Fig. 8-13.

196

Install the decorative moldings next. These should be made of 1/32″ thick plastic strips painted to match the hull wales. If this is a flush transom, it's best to make the moldings now, but defer installation until the transom has been mounted and the edges sanded and refinished.

From here on, it's all fancy work. Put on the lettering and then do all the details indicated by the transom plan. Some common transom sculpture—dolphins, mermaids, eagles, and the like—can be purchased from parts makers as white metal fittings. Other sources for brightwork have already been suggested in this chapter.

If sculpture is unavoidable, you'll find that the best results are obtained with boxwood stripping. Work out the form and refine it on the end of the stick so you've got something to hold onto. It may be necessary to rent or buy an electric hand drill with a variety of burrs for working in details. When the sculpture is completed, paint it while still on the stick, and cut it off only when all work is done.

If it's an animal or human form, however, don't overlook the possibility of using model railroad figures. You can usually find them made of plastic, and a sharp knife and a bit of ingenuity will modify them to suit your needs.

To mount the transom, apply liquid glue to the joint surfaces on the hull, then press the transom in place with one hand while wiping away the excess glue with the other. Because of the camber, the transom will probably tend to pull away from the joint along the sides.

Use either a fast-drying glue and hold the edges firmly in place with your thumbs, or else drive some pins through the transom into the frame. When the glue has set, withdraw the pins and apply a drop of water to each pinhole to swell it shut.

One additional step is needed with a flush transom. Fill the gaps along the joint, sand the edges to a smooth line with the hull planking, and paint the bare wood. If you have held the decorative moldings aside, install them now to complete the transom.

CHEEKS

Cheeks are heavy reinforcement carried outboard on either side of the bow. They seldom appear on clippers and small craft, but on most other medium-to-large vessels the

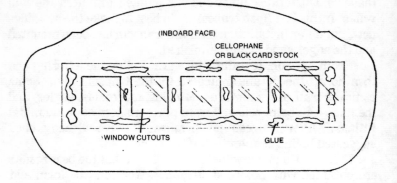

(INBOARD FACE)

CELLOPHANE
OR BLACK CARD STOCK

WINDOW CUTOUTS

GLUE

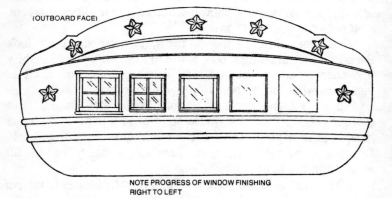

(OUTBOARD FACE)

NOTE PROGRESS OF WINDOW FINISHING
RIGHT TO LEFT

Fig. 8-13. Transom windows.

cheeks are pierced by the hawse holes, which are oval lipped openings for passing the anchor cables. See Fig. 8-14.

The cheeks take the great weight and friction off the anchor cables, thus protecting the hull planking. On some vessels, their function was enlarged to become decorative as well, with some builders carrying trailboards (extensions of the cheeks) forward onto the beakhead and embellishing them with all manner of swirls and curlicues.

Make the cheeks from 1/32″ balsa sheet. The grain should run vertically with respect to the hull to enable the cheeks to bend around the bow. If thicker cheeks are indicated on the drafts, build them up with additional 1/32″ sheets. Cut separate 1/32″ pieces to carry forward on the beakhead, and round the intersections with the cheeks by filling them with wood filler and sanding with sandpaper wrapped around a dowel. See Fig. 8-15.

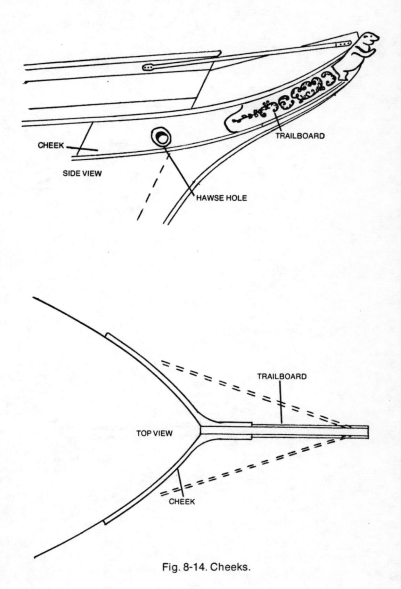

Fig. 8-14. Cheeks.

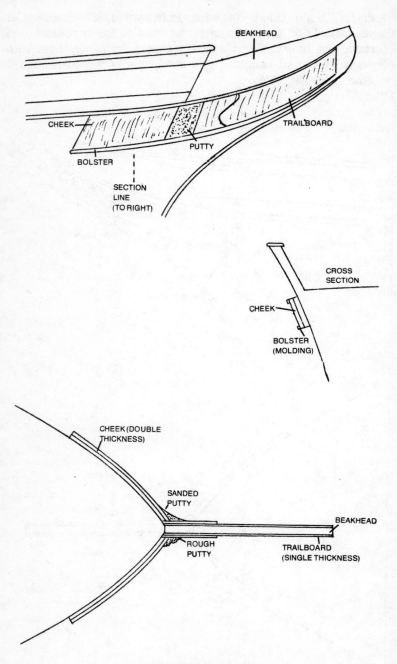

Fig. 8-15. Making cheeks.

Carefully sand or file the edges of built-up cheeks to make them smooth, as though of one piece. Install upper and lower edge moldings made of 1/32″ plastic strip, then paint everything to match the hull.

Hawse pipe lips can be purchased as white metal fittings. Prime them before painting them a dull black. If your ship is not black, paint the areas enclosed by the lips black after you have glued them in place.

To decorate the trailboards, buy decals or use some of the tricks you learned doing the quarter galleries and transom.

HEADRAILS

The headrails comprise a basket of curved railings carried under the bowsprit between the beakhead and the bow planking. They are found on large ships dating up to around 1840. Frequently there is a grate nestled within the headrails to provide a small deck. This assembly, commonly called the head, served not only decorative purposes, but as the crew's privy as well: hence the term "head" to describe a bathroom.

Headrails can be very tricky to make. It is difficult to get the rails on both sides to come out the same, so that the ship doesn't look lopsided if viewed from ahead. Don't be discouraged if you have to throw away a few bad tries. Trial and error seems to be the only way to achieve good headrails.

First, make the headrail support brackets. (See Fig. 8-16.) These are seen on the sheer plan (side view) as vertical timbers appearing in the spaces between the rails. They rest atop the beakhead. Using the three projection drawings, and applying techniques discussed elsewhere in this book, you can determine the width of each bracket and its height relative to the point of mounting on the beakhead. Carefully fashion the brackets from hardwood sheet. Paint them whatever color the headrails will be. For ease of fitting them, you may want to cut small notches into the top curve of the beakhead. (See Fig. 8-17.)

A number of materials can be used to make the actual rails. The least satisfactory is wood. The rails are flat if viewed from above; that is, they curve only up and down, not side to side, relative to the vessel's centerline. Thus, they can be cut from sheet wood, but there is no way to make the grain follow the curve, so the rails will be fragile and probably will break even before you have finished cutting them out.

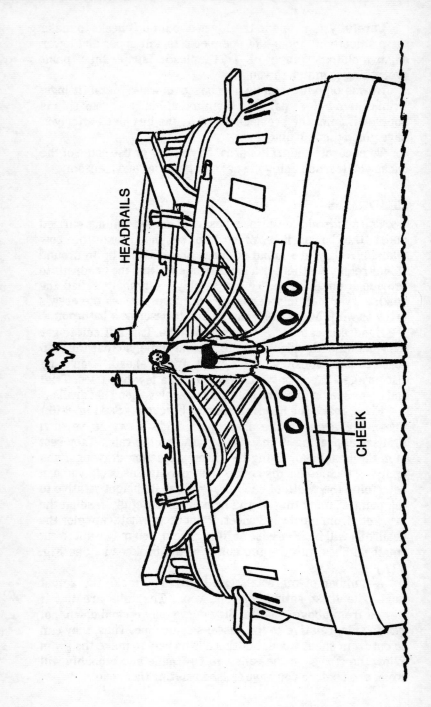

HEADRAILS

CHEEK

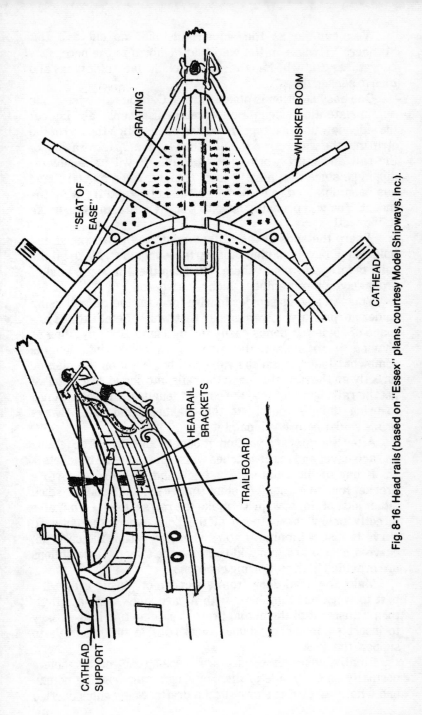

Fig. 8-16. Head rails (based on "Essex" plans, courtesy Model Shipways, Inc.).

GRATING

WHISKER BOOM

"SEAT OF EASE"

CATHEAD

HEADRAIL BRACKETS

TRAILBOARD

CATHEAD SUPPORT

You can do as the shipwrights did; go out and find "timbers" (twigs) in the wild that conform to the necessary curvatures. But who has time to search the forest for twigs and then to season them?

One easy solution is plastic strips. Get square strips of the appropriate dimensions. Boil water in a saucepan and lay out the side view under a sheet of waxed paper. Stick the end of the strip into the water for a minute, then lay it atop the drawing of the rail and start working it to shape. It will take several dippings, since thin plastic cools rapidly. When a good shape has been obtained, cut the rail off the strip and try it on the model. You will probably have to work it a little more to make it fit exactly.

Where the ends of the railing mount to the beakhead and hull, shave bevels to blend the surfaces together. Make all the rails before you mount them, but keep them in some kind of order so you'll remember which goes where.

You can also use solder in wire form for the rails. If using solder surprises you, remember that white metal fittings are made of solder. It bends easily to any shape. Start by filing or shaving it to square the sides, then cut it into lengths somewhat longer than the rails will be. Work on the plan or directly on the model to bend the rails into shape. Once you've got the rail right, cut it to the correct length and bevel the ends to bring them smoothly to the beakhead and hull. Always prime solder before you paint it.

After the rails are painted, mount them with a drop of glue on each bevel and in the notches where they join the brackets.

If one of the rails sweeps back and outboard to form a bracket for the cathead (a stout timber extending outboard on either side of the bowsprit), make the rail so that it terminates directly below the cathead at the point where the outward curve is just beginning. Later, when you mount the cathead, carve a bracket to join and continue the sweep. (Instructions are provided in the following chapter.)

Make the head deck from a wooden or plastic grate. It's best to work out the shape with a card stock template first, then transfer it to the actual grate. You may find it necessary to insert some inconspicuous blocks inside the headrails to support the deck.

Finally, install the "seats of ease" (one- or two-holers normally on each side of the bow), handrails, rigging points, and whatever else is shown in the drafts. Many ships carried

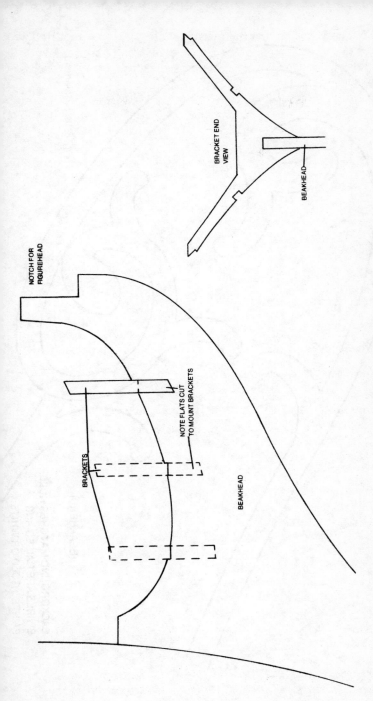

NOTCH FOR FIGUREHEAD

BRACKETS

NOTE FLATS CUT TO MOUNT BRACKETS

BEAKHEAD

BRACKET END VIEW

BEAKHEAD

Fig. 8-17. Headrail brackets.

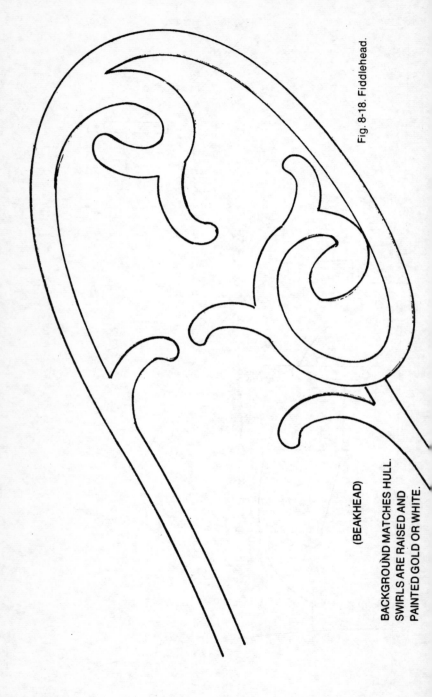

(BEAKHEAD)

BACKGROUND MATCHES HULL.
SWIRLS ARE RAISED AND
PAINTED GOLD OR WHITE.

Fig. 8-18. Fiddlehead.

long slender whisker booms—timbers angling horizontally forward—anchored in the headrails. Make them of strip hardwood and paint them black, then mount them as indicated.

FIGUREHEADS

Figureheads were carried on almost every vessel larger than auxiliary harbor craft. By long tradition, the figurehead is mounted to the very tip of the beakhead, the foremost part of the hull. The figurehead was unique to each ship, a piece of wooden sculpture gaudily painted, often even gilded.

The survival of the figurehead over many centuries on vessels of all nationalities attests to the universal appeal of this rather strange bauble. Yet there is ample evidence that to the sailor, forced to repaint it almost continuously while dangling in a dangerous and inconvenient place, the figurehead was an object to be despised. On the frigate *Constellation*, for example, the entire crew openly rejoiced when they found that the figurehead had been shot off in an engagement.

Figureheads fall into three general categories: humans, animals, and fiddleheads. The latter is not truly a figurehead, but rather a decorative scrolled carving that resembles the end of the neck of a violin. (See Fig. 8-18). Human forms often represent gods such as Neptune and Jupiter or stylized warrior figures on warships. Frequently merchantmen thrust forward buxom females. Animal forms included fish and birds.

You can buy white metal figureheads for some of the favorite vessels of modelers, occasionally in more than one scale. You can't buy fiddleheads, but they're easy to make and can often be carved right into the beakhead. If you can't find your figurehead, though, and it's not a fiddlehead, you have to start scrounging.

Check model railroad figures for human forms, and check hobby shops for military figurines. Toy stores, too, sell both human and animal forms in many different sizes.

Chances are you won't find exactly what the plans call for, but keep an eye out for the proper size and general characteristics. You can always repaint, cut off the legs, reposition the arms, so long as the basic figure is right. You can also make shields, spears, and such, and glue them onto the emerging figurehead. If all else fails, then, and only then, sculpt.

Plate 2. Fancy trailboard and fiddlehead on Constellation beakhead. Headrails are removed in this picture and catwalks mounted for restoration.

Chapter 9

Decks and Furniture

~~~~~~

With the exterior of the hull now completed, it's time to turn your attention to the areas between the bulwarks, where the people lived and worked.

FINISHING THE BULWARKS

Depending on the type of ship you are building, this step can range from a mere paint job to a real construction project. Study your plans, both the side view and the cutaway, looking for breaks in the bulwarks. These breaks might be anything from hawse holes to gunports. Ignore small openings such as scuppers (deck drains) and sheaves (built-in pulleys), which can be drilled. Almost every ship has a few openings in the bulwarks.

Hawse holes are oval-shaped openings ordinarily found at either end of the main deck in the vicinity of bitts (large posts for securing mooring lines). They are used to pass the hawsers through the bulwarks for mooring the ship.

The easiest way to make hawse holes is to buy a pair of hawse pipe lips for each hole and install them. These are oval donut-like fittings sold by partsmakers. Trim away any casting flash with a sharp knife and paint them with metal primer.

Glue a lip to the outside of the bulwark and cut away the planking inside its donut hole, then glue the other lip on the

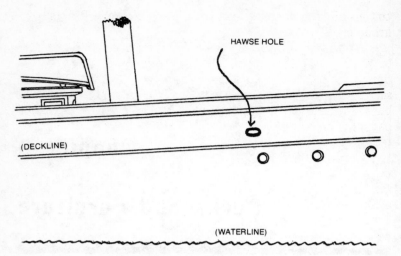

Fig. 9-1. Hawse hole in the bulwark.

inboard face of the bulwark. Use a small round file to smooth out the hawse hole, then paint the outer lip and the hole itself to match the hull exterior. See Fig. 9-1.

Boarding gates and gunports are basically the same, except that the gates go all the way to the deck and the ports usually have a sill a foot or so above deck level. Using the fore sides of the deck beams as section reference lines, find and mark these openings on the inside of the bulwark planking, making sure they are vertical.

Make timberheads to serve as side frames from the same stock as the original timberheads. These are not needed if you have laminated the bulwarks. These frames, like the timberheads, must be glued to the inside of both the hull and bulwark planking. Use glue, not contact cement.

Roll the hull on its side, deck facing you, and place a balsa block under the opening to be cut. Use a new X-acto #11 or equivalent blade to cut away the planking between the side frames. For a boarding gate, cut all the way to the top of the hull planking. For a gunport, cut down to the top of the lowest or second-lowest bulwark plank. (See Fig. 9-2.) Pay careful attention to where you are cutting; if the gunports are close together, it's easy to cut away the intervening planking rather than the ports themselves.

When the openings are all cut, use a small file to smooth the edges and bring them flush with the frames. Across the bottom of each opening, cement a piece of timberhead stock inside the planking to form a sill.

If yours is a warship, you will probably have to plank the bulwark interiors. Check the cutaway deck view. If no timberheads appear on the bulwark, it is planked. Most merchant ships did not go to the expense of fully planked bulwarks, but it is best to check anyway. Many ships carried partial planking called the *ceiling* on the upper half of the bulwark interiors. Do *not* install the ceiling at this time.

Plank the bulwark interior just as you did the exterior, using 1/32″ hardwood strips applied to the timberheads. Make the large openings as you go, and complete the hawse holes after the cement has set hard.

Smooth out any irregularities on the bulwark interiors with fine sandpaper wrapped around a stick or your fingertip. Be careful not to take the sharpness off the corners of exposed timberheads. The bulwarks are now ready for a paint job.

Color schemes can vary. Most modelers' plans have a paint schedule, so if you're working from such plans check to

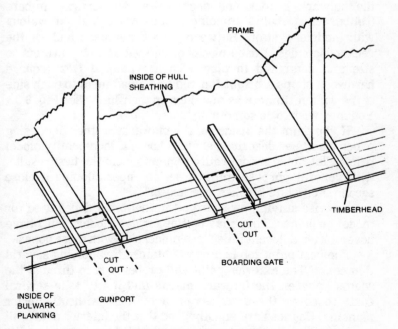

Fig. 9-2. Bulwark openings.

see what color to paint here. Otherwise, a little research may be necessary. Chappelle's books all have passages on painting schemes, but they're not indexed and you have to hunt through the text. Other resources like *Greyhounds of the Sea* refer to colors, and you can often find paintings of your ship's general type in books such as *Men, Ships, and the Sea.*

In general, warships followed a pretty standard pattern. Until around 1815, the bulwark interiors were dark red. After that time, they were usually white above the spar deck, and in frigates either red or white on the gun deck. The same holds true for revenue cutters.

Merchant vessels were much more fanciful, and often the colors both inside and out changed with captains. McKay's clippers tended to have white bulwark interiors, Webb's were natural, but again the captain's preference ruled, and some were downright garish. After all, at sea the only color you see is blue, which gets awfully monotonous. Thus, especially in small ships like brigs, you are pretty much at liberty to do as you please with interior decoration.

On the *Flying Fish*, I used a very striking color scheme for the bulwark insides and deckhouses. All vertical timbers (timberheads, cabin moldings, etc.) were stained walnut with modelers' stain. Between each timberhead and for the deckhouse sides, I used pieces of unlined 3″ × 5″ card cut to size and cemented in place. Then I painted 1/32″ square hardwood strips a bright flat red and glued them to each side of the walnut timbers as moldings on the white. (See Fig. 9-3.) You may wish to do something like this, too.

If you paint the insides of the bulwarks, rather than using paper inserts as described above, choose a good-quality model paint. Flat-finish model railroad paints yield the best results, with general purpose military-series dopes running a close second. For white finishes, use gesso.

I advise staying away from the fuel-proof dopes used for model airplanes. They may be fine for gas models, but I have never gotten a decent finish on a model ship with these dopes.

The best paint job is always obtained by applying several thin coats. The exterior paint will probably seep through the seams between the bulwark planks and it will take several coats to cover these stripes on a bulwark without interior planking. Chances are equally good that the interior paint will seep outside too. Your best bet is to let it seep, and when the

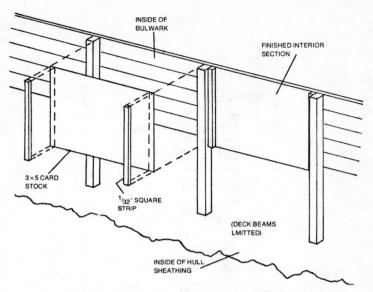

FINISHED INTERIOR
SECTION

3 × 5 CARD
STOCK

¹/₃₂" SQUARE
STRIP

(DECK BEAMS
LMITTED)

INSIDE OF HULL
SHEATHING

Fig. 9-3. One way to finish the insides of the bulwark.

last coat is dry on the inside, use a small brush to touch up the outside.

If the interior is not planked, install the ceiling after the paint is dry. Usually a 1/16″ thick hardwood strip of the appropriate width will suffice for the ceiling. If possible, make it a single strip for the entire length of the ship, or at least wherever it is visible. Paint the exposed side of the plank, then mount it to the upper part of the timberheads using contact cement.

Vertical alignment is important here. Lay a beam athwartships atop the bulwarks and use it as a gauge. Bring the ceiling up until it just touches the beam at any point. This will give the bulwark tops a level surface suitable for mounting the railing. See Figs. 9-4 and 9-5.

If you have planked the bulwarks inside, use the gauge beam to find out where you need to trim the top of the interior planking to bring it level. You may also find it necessary to cut down the tops of timberheads.

GUNWALE

The *gunwale* is the railing covering the top of the planking. In most 19th Century sailing vessels, this railing runs

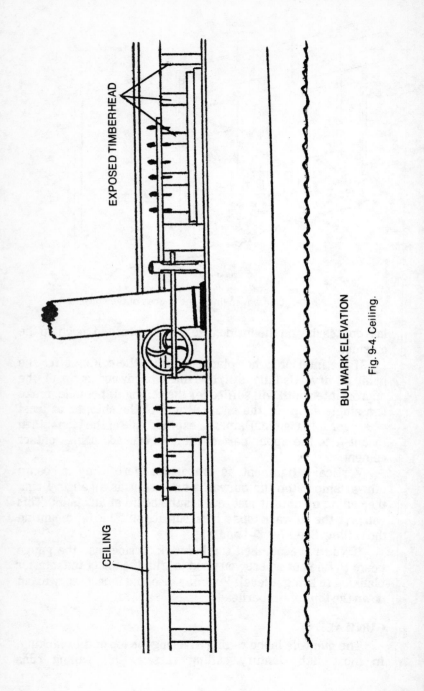

EXPOSED TIMBERHEAD

CEILING

BULWARK ELEVATION

Fig. 9-4. Ceiling.

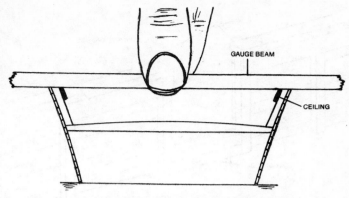

Fig. 9-5. Placing gauge beam across ceilings.

continuously all the way around the ship, almost flush with raised decks fore and aft and about five feet above the main deck.

The best material for the gunwale railing is balsa because it easily bends to conform to curves in the planksheer. Use strip balsa six scale inches thick and as wide as necessary to lay flush with the ceiling and the exterior planking (see cross section in Fig. 9-6). If this width is not a standard balsa dimension use the next wider size (for example, if the width is 7/32″ use 1/4″ balsa), install it flush with the inside planking, and carefully shave it flush with the exterior planking using a sharp knife.

On sharply curved bows and round sterns, it may not be possible to bend the balsa to fit. For this you will need to make a pattern and cut the railings from sheet balsa. Lay a sheet of paper atop the bulwarks and run the side of the lead of a soft pencil around the curve to trace it. (See Fig. 9-7.) Cut along the lines and use the pattern as a template. The grain of the piece should generally follow the curve (be straight at the center of the curve). If necessary, piece the railing in several sections, making the seams as tight and unobtrusive as possible.

Generally, gunwales were either white or natural. They can be painted or stained in place, but this, like any paint job, is better done before mounting.

DECKS

The *decks* of sailing ships are ordinarily made of tightly-seamed and caulked planks four to six inches thick and

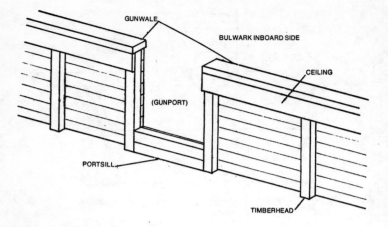

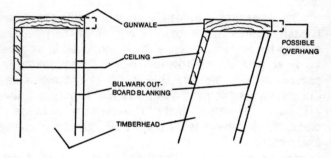

Fig. 9-6. Gunwale.

six to twelve inches wide. For a model, use hardwood strips 1/16″ thick and one scale foot wide.

You can buy hardwood sheet in 3″ widths that is scored to simulate decking, but this material has a lot of problems. If the main deck, for example, is wider than 3″, the material makes an unsightly seam. Also, it doesn't crown very well, and getting the exact shape of the deck is difficult. The positioning of hatch openings is yet another problem. In short, though a deck of strips takes a little longer, it yields much better results and is easier to lay.

Lay the lowest decks first, and always be sure the inboard works are completed before decking over them. This includes painting, installation of grates, guns, coamings, cargo, and all the other things that finish the work. It is almost impossible to do this sort of work through a hatch.

Start the deck by finding and marking the ship's centerline on every deck beam. If the frame is solid, you can simply carry the centerline mark from the face onto the deck beam. If it is a pieced frame or an unframed hull, measure the beam from bulwark to bulwark and mark the midpoint.

Sight down the length to make sure the centerline is straight. If it is not straight, your hull is bent or twisted. To

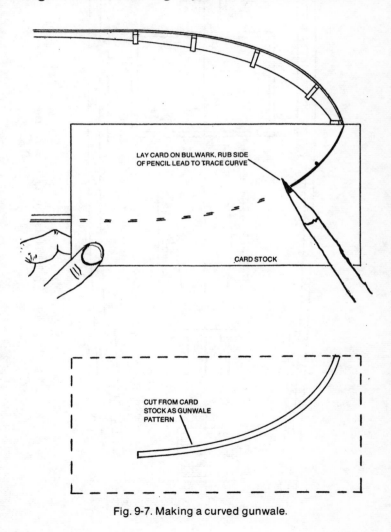

LAY CARD ON BULWARK, RUB SIDE OF PENCIL LEAD TO TRACE CURVE

CARD STOCK

CUT FROM CARD STOCK AS GUNWALE PATTERN

Fig. 9-7. Making a curved gunwale.

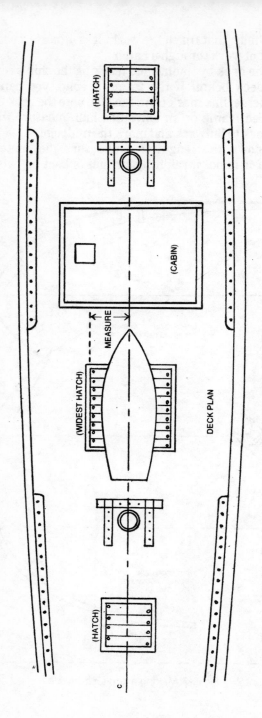

Fig. 9-8. Measuring for first deck planks.

correct the centerline, lay a straightedge on the centerline marks of the second or third deck beam from each end. Mark every beam with a red pencil to indicate the effective centerline, which will serve as your reference in laying the deck.

Refer to the deck plan to find the distance from the centerline to the edge of the widest opening on the deck. If there are to be no openings in your model's deck, skip this step, instead lay the first plank with its edge on the centerline. Measuring port and starboard from the centerline, mark this measurement on every deck beam that will support the deck being built. (See Fig. 9-8.)

Lay the first two planks with their inboard edges on these marks. Deck planks should be straight, clear, smooth strips. These first two planks ought to be continuous, but if the deck is too long, butt them on a deck beam. Just be very sure they are perfectly straight and accurately placed, because all the other deck planks will be lined up with them.

Use contact cement to fasten down the deck. Lay a strip on the beams and mark each beam's location on the strip with a soft pencil. Use this strip as a guide for applying the cement. Lay it on the table, marks up, and lay several deck planks beside it. Paint these planks with contact cement adjacent to each mark. Then paint contact cement on each beam from the first-plank marks outboard to the bulwarks, as shown in Fig. 9-9.

Lay succeeding planks outboard from the first strips. The work goes very fast at this stage, but don't get carried away; make sure each plank makes a tight seam with its neighbor.

If you must butt deck planks because of length, scatter the butts around among beams. The butt must never occur on the same beam in any group of three planks. (See Fig. 7-7 in Chapter 7.)

Sooner or later the easy technique will end as you near the bulwarks. The deck planking does not have to make a neat joint with the bulwarks. This will be done later with a timber called the *waterway*. For now, it will suffice to sliver the ends of the planks so that they will come within 1/8″ or so of the bulwarks. See Fig. 9-10.

When you have planked all the way to the bulwarks on both sides, it is time to deal with the deck openings along the centerline. (Again, if you have no openings in your model's deck, skip this step, for your deck is completed.)

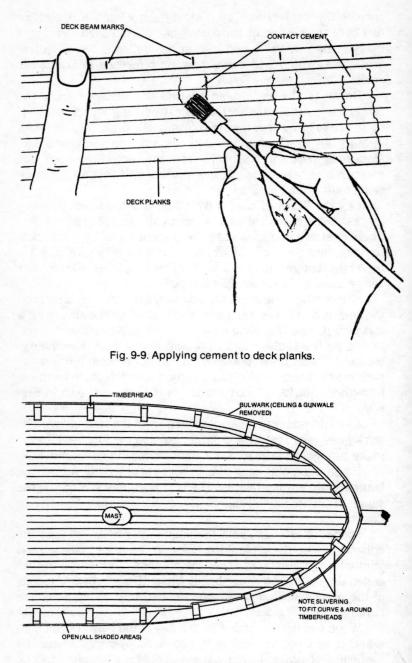

Fig. 9-9. Applying cement to deck planks.

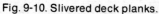

Fig. 9-10. Slivered deck planks.

First, install the false masts if they are not already in place. (See Chapter 5 or 6, depending on your hull construction.) Now refer to the deck plan to find the ends of the openings relative to the nearest section line (the deck beam). Except where the end of an opening falls directly on a deck beam, you will have to make false deck beams to support the new planking.

False deck beams are supports glued to the underside of the deck planking already in place. Their location should correspond to the ends of the openings. Make the beams from 1/4″ × 1/8″ hardwood, and shave them to achieve the same crown as the true deck beams. The beams should be an inch longer than the distance between the two first deck planks, so that each end will have a 1/2″ bonding surface with the underside of the existing decking. See Fig. 9-11.

Measure fore or aft to the inside of each deck opening from a nearby section line. Measuring from the corresponding deck beam, find and mark these distances by making a little tic on the inside edge of the decking with a soft pencil. Mark both sides of the central gap in the deck.

Install the false beams with a fast-drying acetone-base glue such as Duco. Put a drop on the top of the beam about a quarter inch from each end. Put the beam into gap at an angle, then straighten it athwartships and bring it up under the planking, aligned with the marks. Hold it snugly in place for about one minute until the glue has set enough to keep it there. Use this time to clean away any glue that has oozed out on the edge of the planking.

Let the glue set for half an hour or so, then resume laying the deck. Cut each plank to fit, then mount it with contact cement. Lay corresponding pieces on either side of the centerline, so that you approach the center of the deck from both sides at the same rate.

After laying each pair of planks, check the deck plan to see if you need to begin making the narrower openings. If necessary, notch the planks to make the opening the right width, as in Fig. 9-12.

As the planking closes in on the mast, check the location of the beams and false beams. If a deck plank terminating at the mast will lay on only one beam, you will again have to employ a false beam. Use a piece of scrap hardwood about an inch long glued to the undersides of the planks nearest the mast. Don't worry about the crown. See Fig. 9-13.

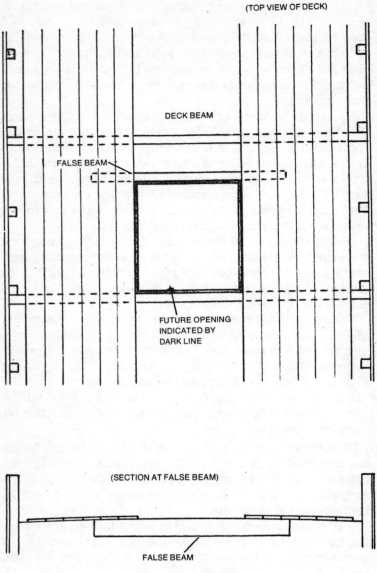

Fig. 9-11. False deck beam.

Shape the planking around the mast carefully. These planks should almost, but not quite, touch this false mast, which will have to come out to be replaced by the real mast later.

222

Almost invariably it happens that you end up with a small gap in the planking at the centerline. If you have done the job right, though, this gap will be of a uniform width the whole length of the deck, so all you have to do is to split a wider plank to fill it in.

Use a fingernail file to smooth down the plank ends at the openings. With dividers, find the fore-and-aft length of each

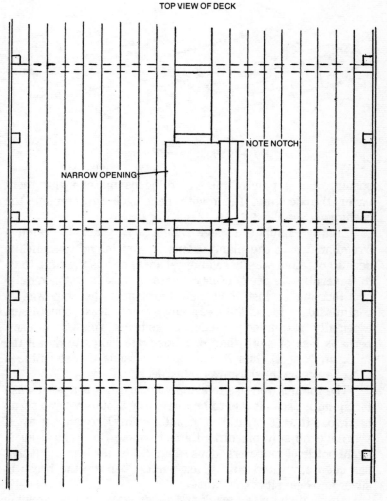

TOP VIEW OF DECK

NOTE NOTCH

NARROW OPENING

(NOTE USE OF FALSE DECK BEAMS)

Fig. 9-12. Starting a narrow opening.

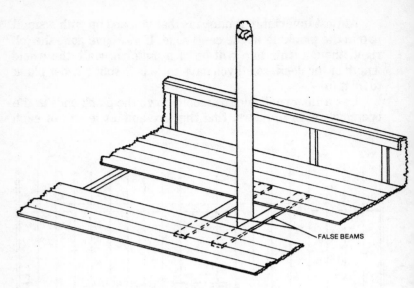

Fig. 9-13. False beams for mast.

opening, cut a pair of false framing beams and glue them under the decking, flush with each side to complete the openings. (See Fig. 9-14.)

Lightly sand the deck along the grain to remove irregularities in the plank seams. If you intend to stain the deck to obtain a weathered appearance, now is the time to do it. Generally the decks of naval vessels were holystoned daily and thus never lost their new look while the ship was in commission. Merchant captains were less punctilious, especially in smaller vessels such as brigs. This was a result perhaps less of sloth than of inadequate hands to do all the work on board. Thus it was often possible to determine a vessel's age by the darkness of her decks.

The thinner you use to clean your brushes is a good wash for aging a deck. It has to be dirty. Try it out on some scrap hardwood first. It should come out a grimy, irregular gray. If you have no suitable dirty thinner, make the wash using a small bottle of modelers' dope thinner. Clean a brush in it that has been saturated with black paint. Then dip the brush in silver and clean it in the thinner.

Alternate between black and silver, occasionally throwing in a little green, yellow, blue, and red, and testing it on scraps until the proper weathered look is achieved. It sounds awful,

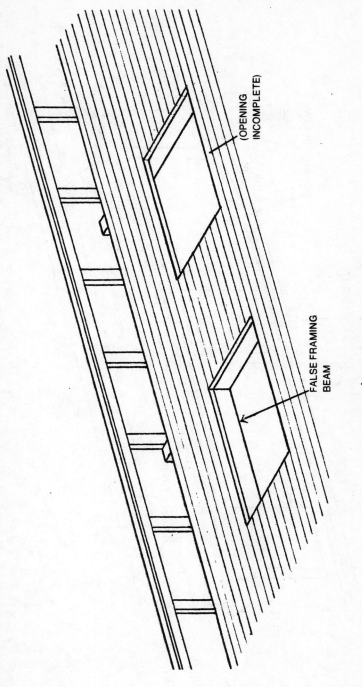

(OPENING INCOMPLETE)

FALSE FRAMING BEAM

Fig. 9-14. Finishing deck openings.

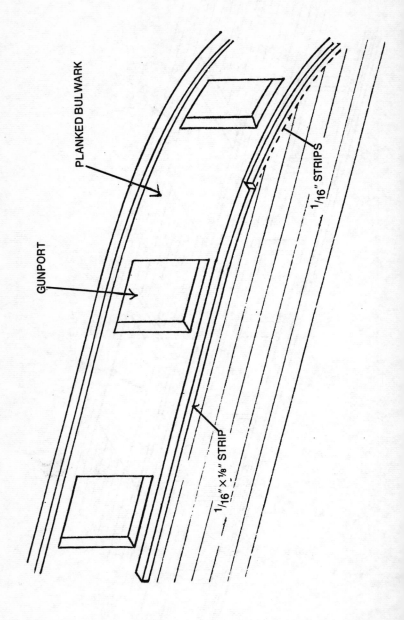

PLANKED BULWARK

GUNPORT

1/16" STRIPS

1/16" × 1/8" STRIP

226

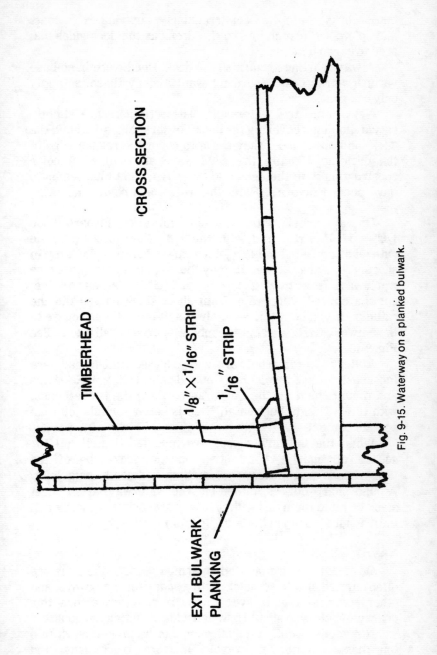

TIMBERHEAD

CROSS SECTION

1/8" × 1/16" STRIP

1/16" STRIP

EXT. BULWARK
PLANKING

Fig. 9-15. Waterway on a planked bulwark.

but it works. Stain the deck irregularly, applying extra coats and splotches in such low traffic areas as the deck sides and around cargo hatches.

Always shellac or varnish the deck. Plastic urethane-base varnish works best. You don't want a shiny finish, so apply only one coat.

Next come the waterways. These timbers are slightly raised moldings covering the deck-bulwark joint all around the deck, and on a model they serve to cover the ragged edge of the decking. Usually the waterways are painted a color constrasting with the deck and bulwarks; light blue seems to have been a favorite. Paint the waterways before mounting them.

On a model with planked bulwarks inboard, use 1/8″ × 1/16″ strip, laid with the 1/8″ side horizontal. The outboard edge must make a joint with the bulwark planking. In sharply curving areas, it may be necessary to piece the waterways from two strips 1/16″ × 1/16″. As an alternative, cut the curved waterways from sheet stock as you did the railings. If you do it this way, always fit the outboard curve to the bulwark first, then cut the inboard curve parallel to it. See Fig. 9-15.

Waterways for a bulwark with exposed timberheads are most easily made by piecing. Cut and paint 1/8″ × 1/16″ strips and mount them on the bulwarks between the timberheads, with the 1/8″ side horizontal. Glue is better for this job than contact cement.

When the bulwark pieces are mounted, install a 1/16″ square or quarter-round strip on the deck side of the timberheads and waterways, making a smooth snug joint. Around sharp curves, either cut the waterways from sheet stock or build them out with 1/16″ square strip as described in the previous paragraph. (See Fig. 9-16.)

NAVAL GUNS

On frigates and many other armed vessels, the guns are often carried on a lower deck, with a spar deck, gangways, and other structures built over them. If your vessel has this characteristic, you should now consider mounting the guns.

Nineteenth Century naval guns can be broken down into four basic categories: swivels, mortars, truck guns, and carronades. The first two are quite rare. Swivels are very

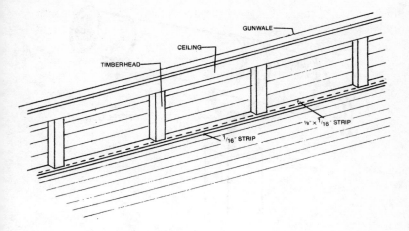

Fig. 9-16. Waterway around exposed timberheads.

small pistol-grip cannon mounted on the railings. They were ordinarily brought out only during action, and they gradually disappeared early in the century. Mortars were huge stubby guns nested in a cockpit on a special type of ship called a bomb ketch. Those ships were readily recognizable because they lacked a foremast. Plans for bomb ketches always include detailed drawings of the mortar mounting, a fact which makes a detailed description of this unusual weapon unnecessary here. See Fig. 9-17.

Truck Guns

Truck guns are by far the most familiar type of naval cannon. They are mounted on a four-wheeled gun carriage and the elevation can be raised and lowered by a wedge under the breech. Sizes are measured in terms of the weight of the shot thrown by the gun, ranging from four pounds up to around 24. Truck guns were the basic weapon of the 19th Century sailing navy. Able to hurl a shot about a mile, they were eminently suited to long-range gunnery. See Fig. 9-18.

A truck gun tends to recoil when fired. Thus they are lashed to stout eyebolts on either side of the gunport by a heavy slack hawser called the breeching, which passes through a ring on the backside of the gun's breech. This hawser checks the recoil of the gun at a point where it can be reloaded through the muzzle. Before firing again, the gun has

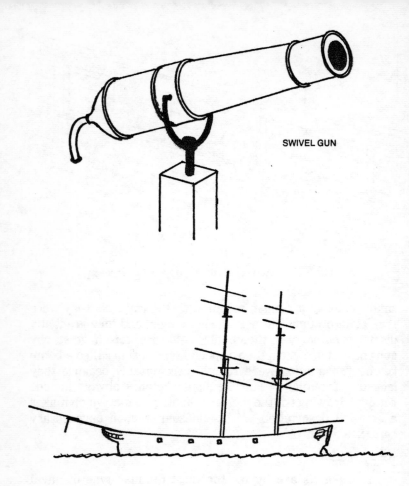

SWIVEL GUN

BOMB KETCH

Fig. 9-17. Unusual armaments.

to be run out, which is accomplished by blocks and tackles linking the carriage with eyebolts on each side of the gunport.

A means also must be provided for hauling the gun inboard and holding it there against the rolling of the ship. For this, another tackle is run from the carriage backside to a ring in the deck near the ship's centerline. A typical arrangement of gun lashings is shown in Fig. 9-19.

The loading and servicing of a cannon requires special tools with long handles. Called by such strange names as

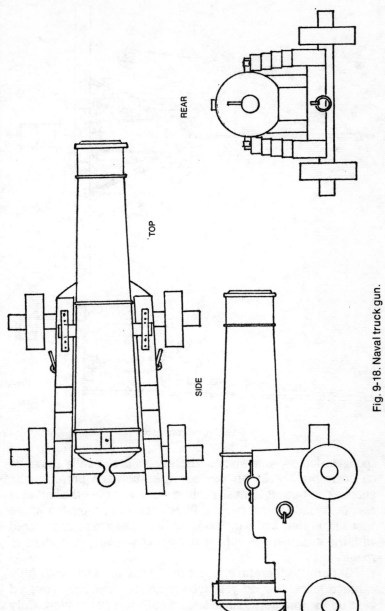

REAR

TOP

SIDE

Fig. 9-18. Naval truck gun.

231

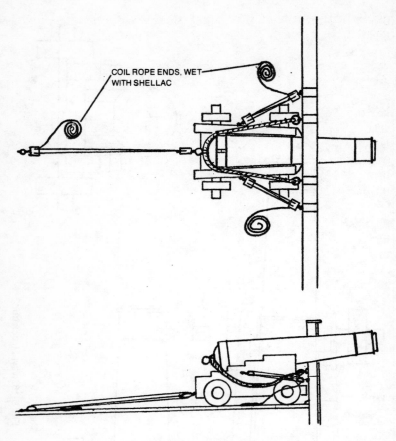

Fig. 9-19. Truck gun lashings.

sponges, ladles, and worms, these tools are usually mounted on horizontal racks on the bulwarks between ports on the gundeck. A bucket to dash cooling sea water over the barrel is also provided for every gun. Where guns are mounted in the open air on spar and quarter decks, the tools are seldom stored with the guns because of the danger of washing overboard in rough seas.

Generally, therefore, you won't need gun tools with fully exposed guns. Nor do you need them for most fully covered guns on the gun deck, since such details are lost to view. Only in the vicinity of an open waist or a large hatch providing visibility below deck will you need them. Unless the scale is large (3/16″ or larger) or you are a stickler for detail, you can get by with pieces of 1/32″ strip cut five scale feet long and glued to the bulwark. Otherwise, partsmakers sell gun tools.

You can likewise eliminate the lashings on concealed guns, except the breechings, which are often visible through open gunports.

Buy the guns from a hobby shop or parts catalog. Both the barrels and carriages are available, and often come in sets with a price break. Prime them before painting. If the bulwarks are red, so are the carriages; if not, paint the carriages brown or a dull yellowish tan. Barrels are black or tarnished-brass green. Glue the barrel into its carriage after painting, and glue the gun in place on deck.

Buy at least fifteen dozen brass jackstay eyebolts. These are tiny pieces of brass wire in the shape of a question mark, available at hobby shops, and you will find them indispensable in ship modeling. (See Fig. 9-20.)

Use jackstay eyebolts to anchor the gun lashings to the ship's sides. Wherever an eyebolt is needed, drill a hole at an

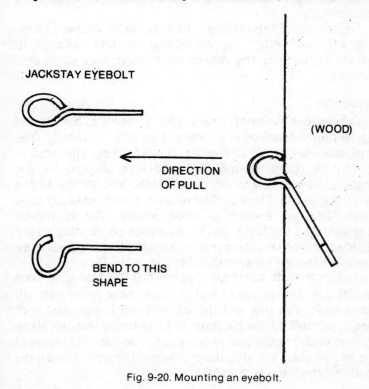

Fig. 9-20. Mounting an eyebolt.

angle to the direction of pull using a #72 bit. Hold the head of the eyebolt flat with needlenose pliers and bend the shank away from the hook. Put a drop of fast-drying glue on the tip of the shank and insert it into the hole, then give the glue a few minutes to set before tying anything to it.

Make the breechings from heavy natural cuttyhunk. Seize it (there is a section on seizing in Chapter 11) at each eyebolt, draping it loosely over the ball at the backside of the gun breech. Wet the breeching with shellac to stiffen it into a natural draped shape.

For the tackles, use fine natural cuttyhunk or tan sewing thread run through beeswax. It may be necessary to drill the carriages and mount eyebolts in them for anchoring the tackles. If you do, you'll probably break a few bits. It helps to wet the bit with a drop of oil before drilling each hole. For the blocks, use the smallest boxwood single blocks you can buy. It's okay to substitute small tan hobby beads, which are much easier to work with, where the gun is somewhat away from close scrutiny.

Before doing the lashings, find out about becket blocks, tying off, and other rigging-related matters detailed in Chapter 11. Lashing the guns is the most tedious job in ship modeling.

Carronades

Carronades resemble truck guns somewhat, but beyond their common function of gunnery, they differ radically. The carronade, developed in Carron, Scotland, first appeared in the British Navy around 1800 and was adopted by the Americans soon thereafter. Lightweight and stubby in the barrel, it was capable of hurling massive rounds as heavy as 64 pounds into an enemy in close action. The carronade complemented the truck gun's long-range penetrating power with short-range smashing power, and thus the two types were often mixed on the same vessel. See Fig. 9-21.

The carronade carriage does not roll like that of a truck gun. Rather, the outboard end is fixed to the lower port sill with a stout iron peg and the inboard end is equipped with wheels, permitting the carriage to be swiveled through about 90°, thus enabling the gun to be aimed. The barrel is mounted on a sliding platform atop the carriage, in order to absorb the recoil and run the gun in and out.

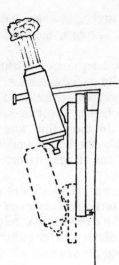

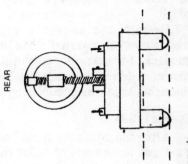

REAR

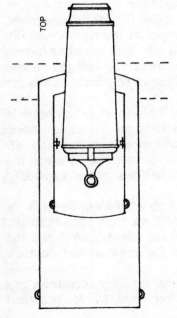

TOP

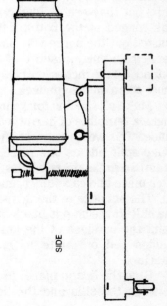

SIDE

Fig. 9-21. Carronade.

Carronades in many sizes can be purchased wherever you buy your fittings. Their paint schedule, lashings, and gun tools are the same as for truck guns.

On American and British frigates, long guns are usually carried on the gun deck and occasionally on the foredeck, and carronades on the quarter deck. One notable exception to this general rule is the frigate *Essex*, a modelers' favorite, which carried almost entirely carronades. In fact, this was the reason for her loss in the War of 1812; she was pounded to surrender by long-range British guns out of her carronades' reach.

Despite the evidence of numerous battle paintings, frigates never carried guns in the foremost ports on the gundeck. Likewise, large ships, like the *Constitution*, seldom showed a gun at the ports just forward of the quarter galleries, since this area was occupied by the captain's day cabin.

Gunport Lids

After mounting the guns, install the gunport lids. This is a good use for scraps of 1/32″ thick hardwood. There are two types of lids, solid and split. Solid lids are made of one piece that covers the entire port, hinged at the top and hoisted out by a purchase as shown in Fig. 9-22. Split lids also cover the entire port, but they are divided horizontally at midpoint, the lower half hinged at the bottom, the upper at the top and usually hoisted out the same way as solid lids. Split lids often have a semicircle cut in each half to let the tip of the gun muzzle extend a few inches outboard. This arrangement makes for more room on the gundeck.

Make all the lids for your model at once. The best bet is to make a template of hardwood or stiff paper to use as a cutting guide. The wood grain of the ports should run fore and aft. Make split lids as one piece, then cut them in two along the grain. To make muzzle holes, cut a half-hexagon in one edge of each piece and carefully round it.

The outsides of the lids should match the paint on most of the hull. If the ship is black but carries a white gunport stripe, paint the outsides of the lids and the edges black. Paint the insides red or white to match the color of the bulwark interiors.

Glue the lids in place. In reality, the hinges created a gap between the sills and the lids when open, but for practical

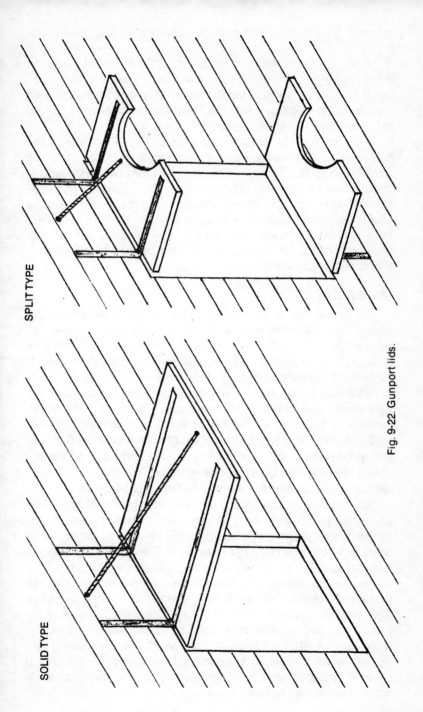

SPLIT TYPE

SOLID TYPE

Fig. 9-22. Gunport lids.

237

reasons, on a model you can glue the lids slightly inside tne ports.

Once the glue sets, cement very thin strips of paper in place as hinges. On black lids, use black construction paper; on other colors, use card stock painted to match the hull. These represent strap hinges running from the lower edge of the lid to the top, then up on the bulwark at least 18″.

Finally, add the hoisting purchases. Drill a pinhole in the hull a scale foot above the port and another in the upper or solid lid near the bottom edge. Use fine natural cuttyhunk or sewing thread run through beeswax. Tie a knot in one end, draw it through the bulwark hole from the inside using a needle threader, then draw it down through the hole in the lid. Secure it on the underside with a drop of glue. Cut off any waste after the glue is hard. If the inside of the lid looks messy, touch it up with paint.

UPPER DECKS

Upper decks of various sorts are often found on sailing ships. The most common are the forecastle (pronounced "fo′ csle") and quarterdecks. The forecastle is located in the bow forward of the foremast and usually flush with the gunwales. It contains the crew quarters on most vessels.

The quarterdeck is on the other end, beginning abaft the mainmast and running to the stern. Ordinarily the quarterdeck is pierced by the mizzenmast and contains cabins, skylights, and hatches. Officers' country begins at the break of the quarterdeck, off limits to seamen except for necessary duties. Below the quarterdeck are the wardroom, officers' cabins, and passenger accommodations. See Fig. 9-23.

On warships, the forecastle and quarterdecks are often joined by gangways along the bulwarks. As the man of war evolved, the gangways widened until finally the upper decks merged into one, called the *spar deck*. The open waist became a large hatch beamed over and carrying the ship's boats.

In the late 1800s, the introduction of steam auxiliary power on sailing ships led to the development of the hurricane deck. This is a deck joined to but slightly above the after edge of the forecastle, and running at a height of about eight feet off the main deck to the vicinity of the mainmast. Beneath it are usually a deckhouse and the engine room cover, and atop it several skylights and a wheelhouse, plus the smokestack. It functioned somewhat like the bridge on a modern vessel.

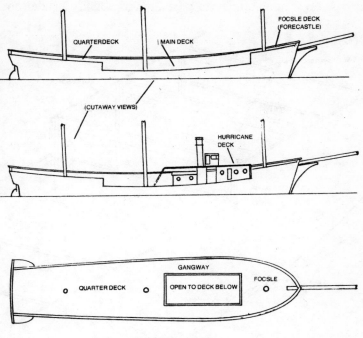

QUARTERDECK | MAIN DECK

FOCSLE DECK (FORECASTLE)

(CUTAWAY VIEWS)

HURRICANE DECK

GANGWAY

QUARTER DECK   OPEN TO DECK BELOW   FOCSLE

SPAR DECK SEEN FROM ABOVE

Fig. 9-23. Raised deck types.

The construction of an upper deck does not differ much from that of the main deck. Every inch or so along the bulwarks starting at the break of the deck, cement a $1/8'' \times 1/4''$ stanchion with the $1/8''$ edge forming the joint. Rest the bottom of the stanchion on the main deck, and bring the top up to $1/4''$ short of the upper deck height. See Fig. 9-24.

Cut deck beams from the same stock, at a length to cross from bulwark to bulwark. Carve in the crown along the $1/8''$ edge and glue them in place atop the stanchions.

Now lay the deck as you did the main deck. The waterways here will be narrower, so try to bring the planks right up to the bulwarks. Also, make the break of the deck perfectly flush with the beam. This will require a bit of shaving and fitting, but it yields satisfying results and saves later aggravation. Don't forget to make openings for cabins and hatches on the quarterdeck if you intend to leave them open.

Ordinarily a bulkhead is found at the break of the quarterdeck, forming a wall on the main deck. Some ships also

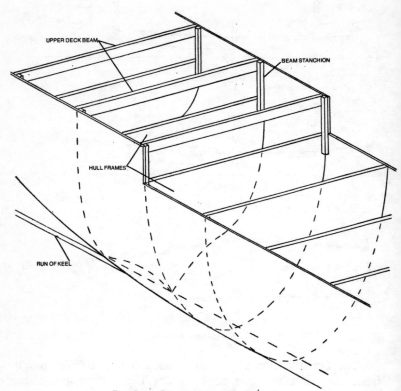

UPPER DECK BEAM

BEAM STANCHION

HULL FRAMES

RUN OF KEEL

Fig. 9-24. Framing an upper deck.

carry a similar bulkhead at the break of the forecastle. Work out the exact shape of this bulkhead by making and fitting a template of card stock. Cut 1/32" wood sheet according to the template.

Bulkheads are usually plain and unadorned, being finished the same as the inboard face of the bulwarks. Sometimes, however, they are decorated in the manner of deckhouse exteriors. You will have to study your plans carefully. Always do as much of the decorations and detailing as you can before mounting pieces. The deckhouse instructions later in the chapter also provide hints applicable to bulkhead adornments.

When the bulkhead is finished, mount it on the vertical face of the upper deck beam with contact cement, and glue a waterway molding in the joint with the main deck.

HATCH COAMINGS

Hatch coamings are enclosures built around unhoused deck openings to prevent water from entering the ship. They are ordinarily 12″ square timbers covered with sheet metal.

To make them, use strip wood a scale foot square. Cut the four sides each two scale feet longer than the hatch dimensions, then mitre the ends at a 45° angle so that when assembled, the coaming resembles a picture frame. Fit it in place around the hatch without glue and make adjustments until the inside edges of the coaming are flush with the deck opening all the way around. Paint the pieces and glue them together at the mitres, as shown in Fig. 9-25.

The coamings of cargo hatches require a few finishing touches. Two small moldings, which can be made from 1/32″ square strip painted to match the coaming, run around the outside of the coaming. They are parallel and about 1/16″ apart, the upper one flush with the coaming top. Their purpose is to provide a batten slot for tying down the canvas cover.

Inside the cargo hatch, cement another strip of the same size along each fore-and-aft edge and 1/16″ below the coaming top. These are hatch cover rests, and should be installed even if the hatch is closed. If the hatch is open, paint the rests to match the coaming. Finally, cement the coaming to the hatch opening.

Hatch covers are boards with handles at each end. They run athwartships, nesting inside the coaming on the hatch cover rests. A closed hatch should be completely covered by them; on an open hatch they may be eliminated, but it adds to the realism of the model to stack them in disorder next to the hatch.

Make cargo hatch covers from hardwood strip 1/16″ thick and of the width indicated by the deck plan. At each end, on diagonally opposite corners, drill a pinhole and cement in a jackstay eyebolt, then paint the hatch covers a light gray.

GRATES

Grates sometimes appear in hatches, especially on warships. They are also found around the helm, where they provide drainage to give secure footing. See Fig. 9-26.

You can make grates, but the process is very time-consuming and maddeningly tedious. The partsmakers sell them in a variety of sizes, made of white metal, stamped

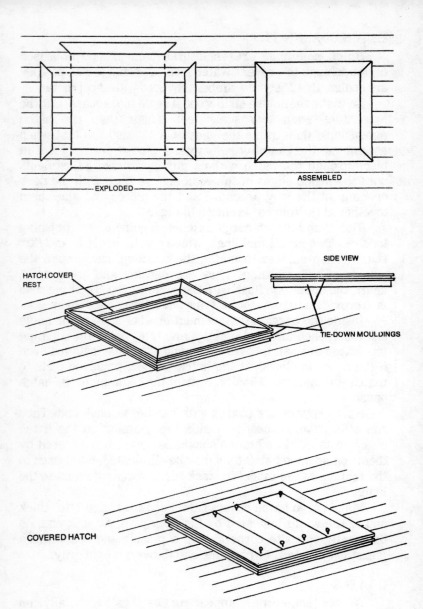

Fig. 9-25. Cargo hatch coamings.

brass, wood-tone plastic, or hardwood strips. It is worth the money to buy the grates and cut them to fit. Install them in hatches as you would install hatch covers.

LADDERS

Ladders, too, appear in hatches and at changes in deck level. Like grates, they can be purchased as metal fittings in a variety of scales and widths, which is the easiest way to go.

Simply cut the ladder to the required length, prime and paint it, and glue it in place. Note that the term ladder is somewhat misleading; landsmen would call them steep stairways. Ordinarily a ship's ladder inclines at about 60°.

DECKHOUSES

Deckhouses are seldom found on warships, but often on merchantmen. From the middle of the 19th Century onward, most ocean-going trading vessels carried two main deck-

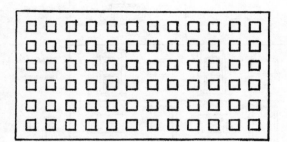

GRATE
TOP VIEW

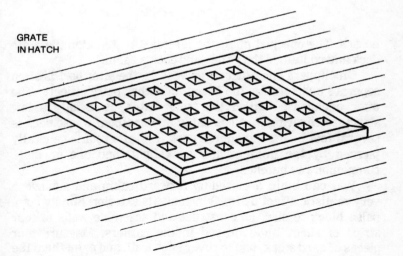

GRATE
IN HATCH

Fig. 9-26. Grates.

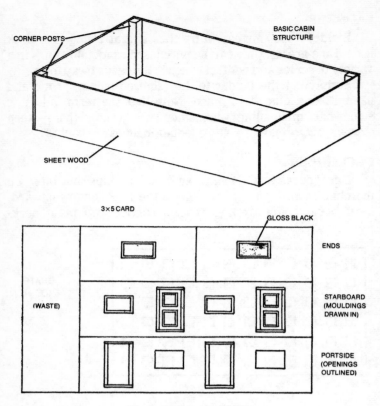

Fig. 9-27. Forward cabin.

houses. The one just abaft the foremast rested atop the main deck and contained the galley and cook's cabin.

On clippers and other large vessels, the after part is often separate quarters for the bosun and other petty officers. The after deckhouse, called the trunk cabin, is usually a low structure covering a saloon cabin or wardroom whose deck is several feet below the quarterdeck level. Its roof is generally pierced by the mizzenmast, a skylight, and one or more companionway hatches.

You can build a closed-up forward cabin and achieve a very realistic effect by finishing only its exterior. Simply cut a balsa block to size, or construct and assemble walls of four strips of sheet wood braced in the corners. Measure four pieces of card stock, one to cover each wall, and paint them the basic color of the cabin. See Fig. 9-27.

Using a sharp, hard-lead pencil and straightedge, mark the outlines of the doors and windows on the stock, but not of the moldings around them. If the doors have wainscotting or panels, mark these outlines as well. Paint the windows gloss black.

Next, paint a card the color of the moldings. With a sharp knife or scissors, slice off thin strips as you need them. Piece the strips around the doors and windows, as vertical moldings, and wherever else the plans indicate, except at the bottom and the corners. To apply the strips, use Elmer's glue, or an equivalent, very sparingly. Be sure your fingertips are clean and dry before you begin the gluing.

Cut around the outlines of the sides. With contact cement, mount them to the cabin walls. Now you can put the corner moldings on. Eliminate the white edges at the very corners with a 000 brush and the same paint as the moldings.

Deckhouse roofs are often painted a color similar to battleship gray. Unless you have evidence otherwise, it's safe to use that color for your cabin roofs. Cut the roof from 1/32" wood sheet with the grain oriented fore and aft. Note that the roof must overhang the cabin sides by at least the thickness of the moldings you will soon be mounting around the tops of the walls. Paint the roof with at least two coats, sanding lightly with fine sandpaper between coats. Don't forget the edges and the underside of the overhang.

While the roof is drying, paint a 1/16" × 1/32" hardwood strip the same color as the cabin moldings. Cut two pieces of this strip and glue them flush with the tops of the fore and aft cabin walls, 1/16" sides vertical. Next, measure and cut the sidewall strips so that their ends will cover the ends of the moldings you just mounted. After gluing them on, paint the bare ends.

Run a sparing bead of glue around the tops of the cabin walls and place the roof so it overhangs uniformly on all sides. Rest the cabin assembly on a level place and put a small weight such as a paperback book atop it while it dries.

BOATS

On many ships, the forward cabin roof is used as a place to store boats. The boats are rested and tied down skids across the width of the cabin roof. Now is the time to install or make them.

If at all possible, you should purchase your ship's boats. They come as fittings in either white metal or rough-shaped pine, in many sizes and types. The metal boats are better, because all you have to do is file down the flashing and prime them before painting. With paper strips and wood scraps you can finish them inside with ribs and seats, or glue ballooner scraps tightly over the gunwales for a covered boat. Wooden boats need final shaping and sanding. If you rout them carefully you can produce a thin shell suitable for interior finishing, but it's a difficult job. They are fine, however, for covered launches, after you've mounted the keel and posts.

Sometimes you just can't find a boat that fills the bill, though, and when that happens you have three choices: substitute with the nearest thing you can get, omit the boat altogether, or make the boat. This situation is particularly prevalent with whalers, since whaling boats are a very important part of the ship but difficult to find in a variety of sizes. Longboats for other vessels types are less critical, but even here you may run up against a void in the product line.

Construction

To carve a boat, select a piece of stock with clear straight grain, all of the dimensions of which exceed those of the boat. The grain must run fore and aft. Make a template of the boat's top view and cut the piece to this shape. Along the centerline on one side, cement a narrow hardwood strip to act as a false keel, then carefully carve the contours of the bow, the run, and the stern. When you are satisfied with the rough shape, sand it into final form. Remove the false keel, or else modify if to serve as the real keel.

If the boat is to be finished inside, rout the interior with woodcarving tools. This operation is a miniature version of the hollow-hull technique discussed in Chapter 5. You probably should not try it on a balsa boat, as the thin shell will become so fragile it may break simply by holding it. Leave as much material in the bow and stern as you can. Cut down to a flat floor at the grate level. See Fig. 9-28.

The last shaping step, hollow or solid, is to cut in the sheer. Pay careful attention in addressing the grain as you shave in the sweep downward from the bow and stern.

All wooden boats, whether you purchase or carve them, have to have the keel and end posts mounted. Make these of

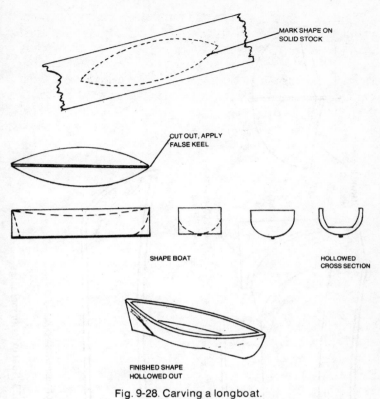

Fig. 9-28. Carving a longboat.

1/32″ strip stock. On a square-stern boat install the sternpost first, its heel even with the bottom, then set in the keel and cut it off at the trailing edge of the sternpost. On double-ended launches such as whaling boats install the keel first, bringing it up to the start of the rise at both ends, and treat both posts as stems.

To make the stem, cut a piece of strip 1/32″ thick and maybe 1/4″ wide. Shape the 1/32″ edge to fit the curve of the cutwater and glue the piece to the boat. When the glue is hard, carve down the excess to parallel curve 1/32″ out from the joint. See Fig. 9-29.

Upon examining your boat drawings you may find that they are of clinker (or lapstrake) construction, in which the top edge of each hull strake is overlapped by the lower edge of the next in a way similar to house siding. If this is the case, plank the boat hull with narrow strips of card stock. You will

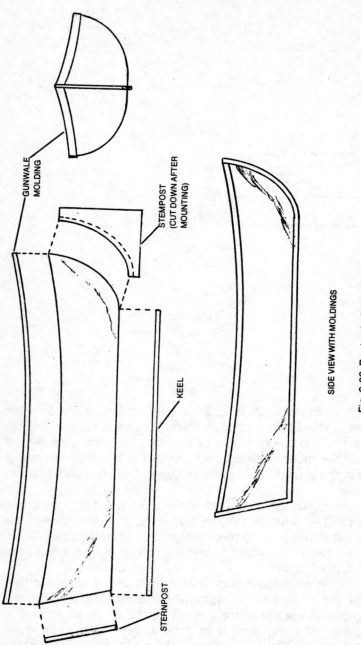

GUNWALE MOLDING

STEMPOST
(CUT DOWN AFTER
MOUNTING)

KEEL

STERNPOST

SIDE VIEW WITH MOLDINGS

Fig. 9-29. Boat exterior moldings.

have to reverse the order of planking from that used on the ship hull, working instead from the keel toward the waterline, and this will require careful piecing to make the planksheer come out right.

Some boats have a thin external gunwale molding. If your boat is to be covered by a tarp, omit it. On an open boat, use two or three thicknesses of card stock to build it out.

To cover a boat, cut a scrap of ballooner to the boat's top shape, leaving at least 1/2" of excess all around. Run a bead of glue, bow to stern, along one gunwale and glue the cover to that side. When it is dry and secure, run another bead on the other gunwale, pull the ballooner taut without wrinkles and hold it in place until the bond is set. You will want to use fast-drying glue for this.

Trim away the excess ballooner to about 1/16" from the gunwales and glue this extra cloth to the sides, so it comes over the edges of the gunwales. You may want to trim the ballooner instead to a scalloped pattern, and glue lines under the boat from point to opposite point on the scallops to simulate lashings.

Finish the inside with odds and ends. For a floor grate, lay crisscross strips of wood tone paper across a bottom painted black. Use card stock cut into tiny strips for ribs. Seats can be 1/32" thick scraps or even card stock, set on moldings that act as seat rests. Buy white metal oars, paint them a wood tone, and glue them to the seats. Make the detachable rudder and tiller from wood scraps and glue it to the seats in the stern. Coil a length of light rigging line to lay in the bow. See Fig. 9-30.

Whaling boats have a great many other pieces of gear—sails, harpoons, rope buckets, boat hooks, etc.—most of which can be purchased or made quite easily from scraps. Before finishing the interior of a whaling boat, consult one of the numerous pictorial works on whaling.

Davits are required to suspend boats capable of being hoisted outboard. For details, see Chapter 12. Here, we are concerned with boats lashed atop the fore cabin.

Lashing

There are several ways to lash down a boat. In every case, a line should be run from the skid over the boat and back to the skid. (See Fig. 9-31.) For a fancier effect you can also run

249

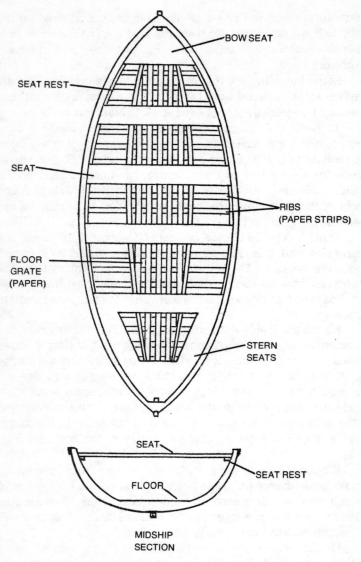

BOW SEAT

SEAT REST

SEAT

RIBS
(PAPER STRIPS)

FLOOR
GRATE
(PAPER)

STERN
SEATS

SEAT

SEAT REST

FLOOR

MIDSHIP
SECTION

Fig. 9-30. Boat interior.

crisscross lines from one tiedown point to the opposite tiedown point of the other skid. Use lightweight tan rigging line run through beeswax.

If more than one boat is carried on the roof, make the tiedowns between the boats first, since they're hard to reach with the boats in place. Fasten the boats to the skids with strong glue, and set up the lashings after the glue has hardened.

On the deck, measure and mark the locations of the cabin corners. Turn the deckhouse upside down and run a bead of

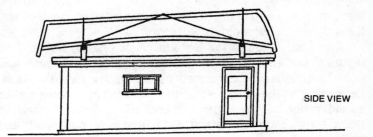

SIDE VIEW

SKID

EYEBOLT

END VIEW

CROSSED LASHINGS

TOP VIEW

"NORMAL" LASHINGS

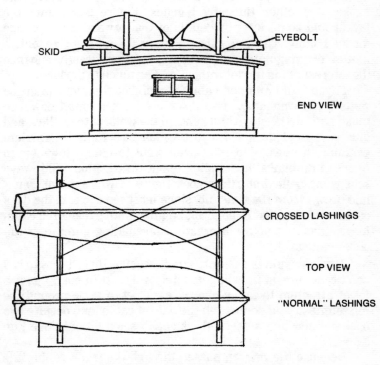

Fig. 9-31. Boats placed atop fore cabin.

glue all around the cabin wall bottoms, then place the cabin right side up on the marks. The sides should exactly parallel the deck planking. Use a weight to hold it firmly in place until the glue sets.

Make and mount moldings for the wall-deck joint, just as you did for the wall-roof line. Because of the crown of the deck, there may be a gap along the cabin sides between the deck and the wall, which the molding will cover.

The final touch is the installation of Charlie Noble. This mythical seafarer dwells, in this case, atop the deckhouse, and is more mundanely described as the galley exhaust stack. Depending on the period, Charlie differs in appearance rather considerably, but the fittings makers sell all types of stacks in many sizes. Paint the stack dirty bronze or dull black and mount it with a drop of strong glue.

I like to have the fore deckhouse open, with cellophane windows (wrappers from cigarettes and packaged food items do nicely) and open doors giving a glimpse of the stove, the bunks, and other finishing touches. Figure 9-32 shows the layout and some interior details of the forward cabin on one model I built. These arrangements were, to some extent, a matter of imagination on my part, but they greatly enhance the interest of the model without adding much to the labor.

If you build an open cabin, remember to paint the inside walls and furnishings. Use discs cut from a small dowel to make pots on the stove and hung on the walls of the galley, and glue scraps of dark cloth to the quarters walls to simulate clothing on pegs. You may even want to glue a few human figures into bunks or standing about inside. Model Shipways sells a big-bellied shirtless cook figure of white metal; paint him brown from the waist up, since most sea cooks in the days of sail were blacks. In general, be imaginative about the cabin furnishings and you will create a fascinating glimpse of life under canvas.

A trunk cabin is easier to build, because there's less to it. I don't recommend finishing its interior. On one model, I gave a lot of attention to fancy chairs, a carpet, a table around the mizzenmast, and so forth in the saloon cabin, and despite two open hatches and a skylight, you can't see a bit of it. See Fig. 9-33.

Because the mizzen passed through the trunk cabin, it is best to erect four walls of strip wood braced at the corners.

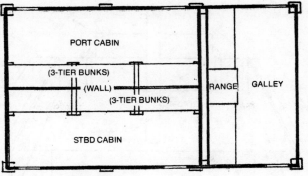

PORT CABIN

(3-TIER BUNKS)

(WALL)

(3-TIER BUNKS)

RANGE

GALLEY

STBD CABIN

FLOOR PLAN

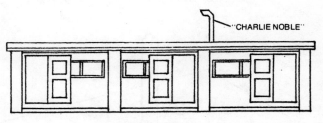

"CHARLIE NOBLE"

SIDE ELEVATION

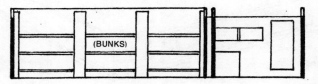

(BUNKS)

SIDE CUTAWAY

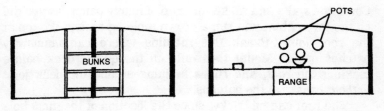

BUNKS

POTS

RANGE

CABIN CUTAWAY

GALLEY CUTAWAY

Fig. 9-32. Open fore cabin details.

253

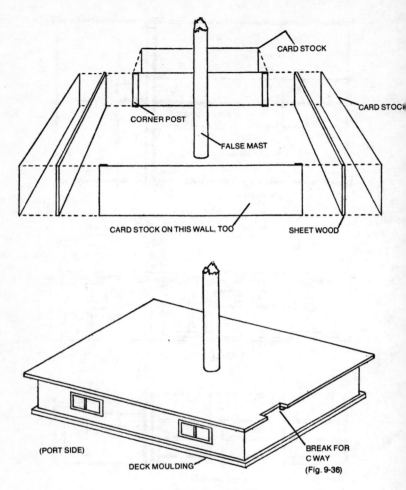

Fig. 9-33. Trunk cabin.

Cover the walls and make the trim of heavy paper, as you did on the fore cabin, and run a crown molding around the top at the roof joint. Break this molding where campanionway hatches occur. Mount the walls on the quarterdeck before tackling the roof, and run a molding around the deck joint *without* breaks at the hatches.

The roof can be tricky, since the location of the mast hole is critical. It is best to make a template from card stock and test it out on the cabin with the false mast in place. Adjust the location of the hole if necessary (this is best done by making a new template incorporating the corrections), and when the template fits just right, use it as a pattern for cutting the wood sheet.

Paint the roof top and sides and gently impale it on the mast. Run a bead of glue around the cabin wall tops and snug the roof in place, making sure the mast can be withdrawn without damaging the roof.

Trunk cabins often carry a skylight to provide light and ventilation below, and a view of the sails so the officers can

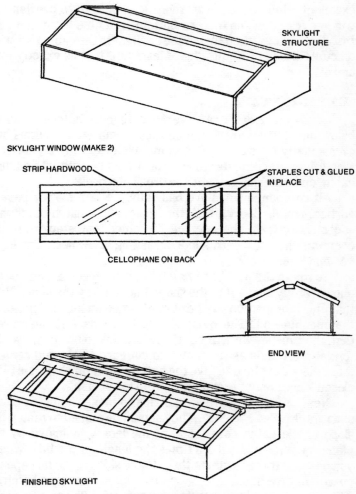

Fig. 9-34. Skylight.

check their trim without going on deck. Typically the windows are barred on the outside to protect them from falling rope and other objects, and each side of the skylight's slanted roof is hinged at the center peak, permitting it to be lifted for ventilation. See Fig. 9-34.

Skylights are most easily made by cutting solid balsa to the proper size and shape and covering all visible surfaces with card stock. Paint the slanted top surfaces with several coats of gloss black, then mount moldings of card strips or 1/32" hardwood to frame the windows. Paper staples make excellent window bars. Cut them long enough to overlap the window frame edges top and bottom, and glue them in place. Install moldings, then fasten the skylight to the cabin roof with a couple drops of liquid glue. Make sure it runs exactly fore and aft.

COMPANIONWAYS

Companionways are covered personnel hatches leading below deck. They are found on most commercial vessels and occasionally on warships. A companionway may be either a small, free-standing deckhouse, or it may be built into a trunk cabin, and occasionally into the break of a deck.

All companionways are basically the same. They have a vertical double door, a high threshold, and a hatch cover that slides away from the opening. To enter, one steps over the coaming, then descends a ladder leading below deck. See Figs. 9-35 and 9-36.

To make the overhead hatch lid, cut a piece of solid balsa and carefully shave it to the shape indicated by the plans. Note that most companionway lids are crowned on top and higher at the opening end. The balsa should be made 1/16" narrower than the finished lid will be. If the hatch is to be open, use the fore and aft ends as templates to cut card stock, and cement these pieces in place to give the hatch ends a finish. If it is to be closed, cover only the end away from the opening.

Next, cut 1/32" hardwood strips to make the hatch cover slide tracks. See Fig. 9-37. They should be angled to match the slope of the hatch cover, and of the length indicated by the plans (generally about 2.5 times the length of the lid). Where you position them in gluing them to the sides of the lid depends on whether the hatch is to be open or closed; usually a hatch lid will slide almost its own length on the tracks. To make sure the

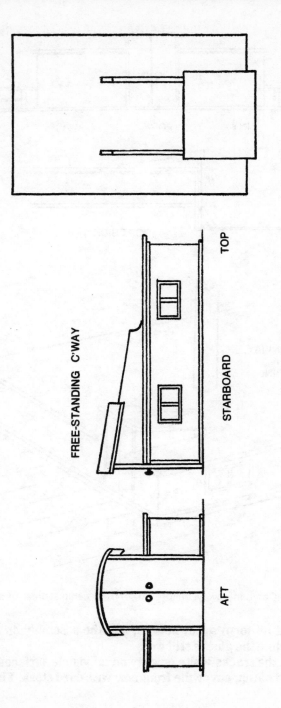

FREE-STANDING C'WAY

STARBOARD

TOP

AFT

Fig. 9-35. Companionway types.

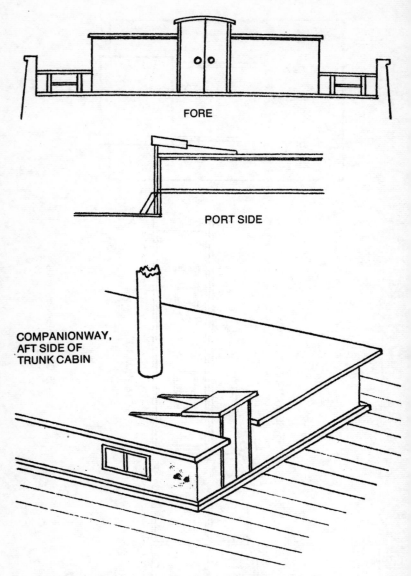

FORE

PORT SIDE

COMPANIONWAY,
AFT SIDE OF
TRUNK CABIN

Fig. 9-36. Companionway, on fore side of trunk cabin at break of deck.

slides and lid form a flat bottom, test the assembly on a flat surface while the glue is still wet.

Paint the tracks white or gray on all visible surfaces. If it is a closed hatch, cover the front now with card stock. Finally, cut a piece of card stock or 1/32" balsa sheet to form a roof that overhangs all four sides, and after it is cemented on, paint it to match the other deckhouse roofs.

To mount a companionway on the truck cabin or deck break, first find and mark the hatch location. You may have to notch the roof overhang, making it flush with the side wall and the width of the hatch doorway. Next, make doors of card stock or 1/32" wood sheet, from the top of the deck-joint molding to the top of the roof line. Use the same technique to wainscot the doors as you did other cabin doors. Mount the

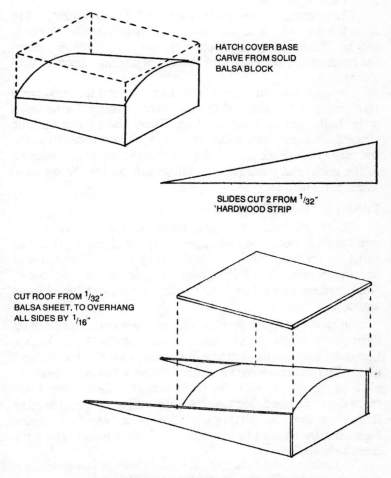

HATCH COVER BASE
CARVE FROM SOLID
BALSA BLOCK

SLIDES CUT 2 FROM ¹/₃₂"
'HARDWOOD STRIP

CUT ROOF FROM ¹/₃₂"
BALSA SHEET, TO OVERHANG
ALL SIDES BY ¹/₁₆"

Fig. 9-37. Making a companionway hatch cover.

doors, then glue on the hatch lid, front edge flush with the doors.

Make a closed free-standing hatch housing from solid balsa cut to shape and size, and finished like the other deckhouses. Mount it on the deck and install lower moldings at the deck joint before you cement the doors and hatch lid in place.

An open companionway is a nice touch, and lends a sense of reality to a model by suggesting it has an inside. The space below should be finished at least to the extent of being painted black, or having a deck that extends out of view. Install a ladder leading below.

The housing is most easily made of 1/8" wood sheet, cut to form the two sides and the closed end. Ideally, the inside walls will be flush with the deck opening, but if they are not, place the housing so that a uniform amount of decking shows at both sides.

Install a coaming across the doorway, and if necessary a roof beam at the edge of the overhead opening. Using wood strip, build up the doorway sides. Finish the outside like the other deckhouses and paint the inside white before mounting the roof. Glue on the hatch lid, then glue the completed housing to the deck. Put deck-joint moldings around the three closed sides. See Fig. 9-38.

FANCY RAILINGS

Fancy railings are often found in the vicinity of the quarterdeck, especially on clipper ships, and around the open waist on frigates. They serve the very practical purpose of keeping people from falling over deck breaks or overboard; what makes them fancy are the often elaborately turned stanchions.

Unless you have a precision lathe, these stanchions can be difficult to make. I suggest you buy them. A. J. Fisher Company has a great variety of turned brass stanchions, and all the partsmakers carry some. Choose a size and shape as close as possible to what the plans indicate. Always buy a few more than you need, because they are easy to drop and hard to find when they do. Prime the stanchions before you paint them, but be careful to leave the ends bare metal. The ends must be filed flat.

To make straight railings at deck breaks or to segregate a flush quarterdeck, the stanchions usually rest on a raised

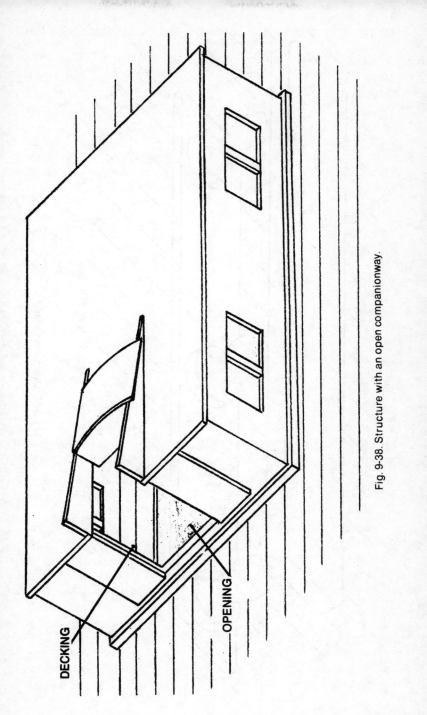

DECKING

OPENING

Fig. 9-38. Structure with an open companionway.

261

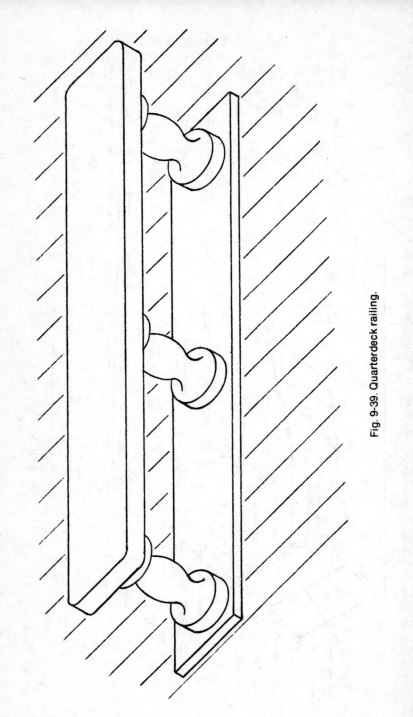

Fig. 9-39. Quarterdeck railing.

plank bolted to the deck. Cut these base planks to the same length and width as the railing above from 1/32" hardwood strip. Paint them to match the railing, or, if you prefer, the waterways. Mark the exact center of each stanshion on the base with a lead pencil, then cement the base planks to the deck.

Put a drop of glue on the bottom of a stanchion and, using the center mark on the base as a guide, carefully set it in place on the base plank. Install the hardest to reach first, working toward the most accessible. Sight along the stanchion line frequently to be sure they line up.

When all the stanchions are installed, make the railing from hardwood at least 1/16" thick. Apply several sparing coats of paint (or varnish on a stained rail), sanding between coats to achieve a fine finish. Be sure to finish both top and bottom. To mount it, put a drop of glue on each stanchion top and set the railing in place. Use a lightweight to clamp it until the glue sets.

Curved railings around the stern are made in a similar fashion, except you have to add a step before the stanchions are mounted. Lay a piece of card stock on the curved part of the stern and rub it with the side of a pencil lead to obtain a tracing of the curve. Cut this tracing out with a sharp knife to be used as a pattern for the taffrail. See Fig. 9-40.

Such railings are best made by creating a sort of plywood lamination. For the lower layer of the railing, cut the shape of the pattern from 1/32" sheet wood, with the grain running fore and aft. Cut an identical upper layer from the same stock, but with the grain running athwartships.

Cement them together with contact cement, and lay the railing atop the gunwales to make sure it fits the curve exactly. Be careful in evening up the edges that the inboard-outboard breadth of the railing remains constant and the curve smooth.

Finish the railing and proceed with installation as described previously. Butt the curved and straight parts of the railing on a stanchion, and fill the seam and refinish it after the other work is done.

PINRAILS

Pinrails mount on the bulwarks to serve as tying-off points for running rigging. They are generally symmetrical in

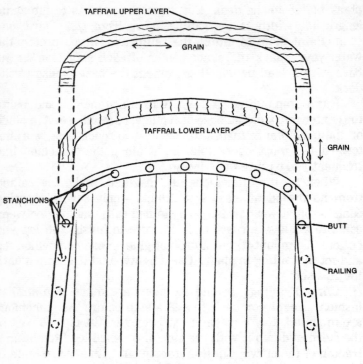

Fig. 9-40. A laminated curved taffrail.

distribution; that is, the port and starboard pinrails for each mast are identical and directly opposite one another just abaft each mast. See Fig. 9-41.

Like most other small parts, belaying pins are best purchased. They should be two scale feet long and made of turned brass. Count the number you need and buy at least a dozen more.

Make the pinrails one at a time. Cut the rail from a good piece of hardwood at least 1/16″ thick. Shave it to make a solid joint with the bulwark or ceiling where it will be mounted. Mark and drill the holes for the pins using a #70 bit. It is easiest to insert the belaying pins with needlenose pliers; generally no glue is necessary. Once the pins are all inserted, prime them, then paint the whole works the same color. If you want contrasting pins, touch them up later.

When you rig your model, you're going to be tying off a lot of lines at the pins, which will exert a strong upward pull on the pinrails. For this reason, a very strong joint is required in mounting the pinrails to the bulwark.

An easy way to brace the pinrail is to glue a small bracket at each end of the rail in the angle formed by the bulwark. The problem with this method is that it usually violates accuracy.

Another way to brace the pinrail is to drill two holes through the rail from the inboard edge to the bulwark joint. After the rail is glued in place, roll the model on its side and drive lill pins through the holes into the bulwark. See Fig. 9-42.

CATHEADS

Catheads are stout timbers extending outboard on either side of the bowsprit, used as booms in handling the anchors and also frequently as supports for the bowsprit rigging.

Make the catheads from square stock cut to the indicated length. Hardwood is best, but balsa will do. If the cathead passes through the bulwark, you will have to cut a square hole flush with the deck and the cathead sides.

In most cases, the cathead passes over the gunwale. It takes a bit of carving and fitting, but you can cut out a chunk

Fig. 9-41. Pinrails on board the Constellation. Note the way the lines are coiled and fixed to the belaying pins. Note also the bosun's chair lashed to the bitts. It is rigged to the mizzen top for restoration work on the frigate.

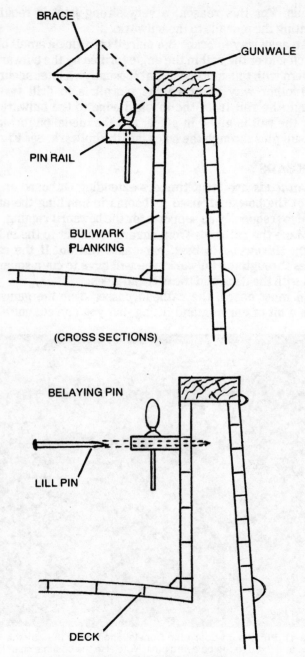

BRACE

GUNWALE

PIN RAIL

BULWARK
PLANKING

(CROSS SECTIONS)

BELAYING PIN

LILL PIN

DECK

Fig. 9-42. Bracing pinrails: Two alternative ways.

from the cathead to fit over the gunwale neatly. The slope of the deck at the sides will tend to make the cathead droop outboard, so shave the underside of the cathead's deck end to make it slant slightly upward. See Fig. 9-43.

Sand the outboard end flat and smooth, then paint the cathead, except where it joins the deck and gunwale. Note that the outboard ends have some grooves in the top and bottom. These are *sheaves*—built-in pulley wheels—that accommodate the line passing down to a block on the anchor as it is being

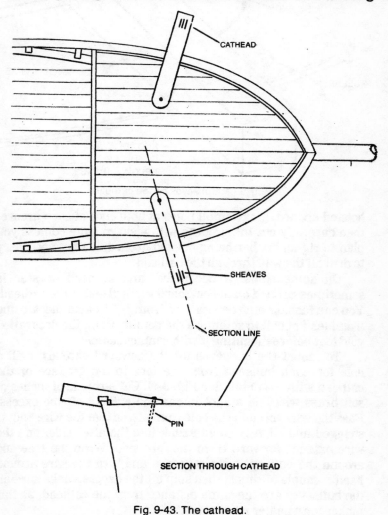

Fig. 9-43. The cathead.

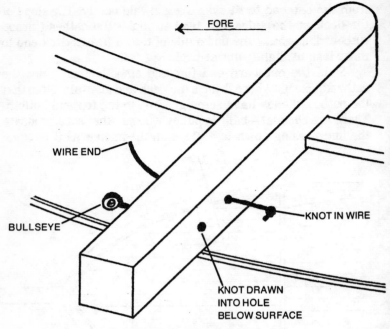

FORE

WIRE END

BULLSEYE

KNOT IN WIRE

KNOT DRAWN
INTO HOLE
BELOW SURFACE

Fig. 9-44. Bullseyes on the cathead.

hoisted aboard. Make small holes at both ends of each groove, then carefully cut the grooves with a sharp knife. Unless you plan to rig an anchor being hoisted aboard, it's not necessary to drill all the way through the cathead.

On some ships, a decorative animal head or star is sometimes carried on the outboard vertical end of the cathead. You can fashion such decorations from 1/32" balsa sheet, using a dull lead pencil to sculpture the details. Paint the decoration gold leaf before mounting it with contact cement.

To mount the bullseyes for the bowsprit shrouds, drill a hole for each bullseye from the fore to the aft face of the cathead with a #70 bit. See Fig. 9-44. Cut a couple of inches of soft brass wire, tie a knot in one end and cut off the excess. Pass the wire through the hole from aft, so that the wire knot is snugged and slightly countersunk into the after side, and the wire extends forward from the fore side. Wrap the free end around the bullseye's strop groove and turn the wire around itself a couple of times, then snip off the excess. Make sure all the bullseyes are the same distance from the cathead, as this makes for a neater rigging job.

Paint the brass wire around the bullseye dull black. On the after side, using an awl or some such pointed instrument, shove the wire knot below the wood surface, fill in the hole, sand it, and refinish the area.

Use glue to mount the cathead. Put a drop in the mortise that fits over the gunwale and another near the inboard end. Push a lill pin down into the deck to anchor the cathead. Paint the pinhead to match.

BILLBOARDS

Billboards are metal plates on the ship's sides a few feet abaft the catheads. Their purpose is to protect the wooden planking from damage by the points (*bills*) of the anchor as it is being hoisted on deck for storage. (See Fig. 9-45.)

Make the billboards from balsa sheet cemented between the moldings and flush with them on the surface. Paint the edges to match the hull. Then, over the balsa and moldings, cement card stock cut to size and shape. Bring it up over the gunwale and cement it to the inside atop the waterway. Paint the card stock to match the hull, even on the gunwale. Don't carry contrasting molding colors across it as a stripe.

FIFE RAILS

Fife rails are the free-standing pinrails at the feet of the fore and main masts. Usually they have three straight sides and can easily be made from wood scraps, but if you prefer, or if the fife rail curves, you can buy white metal units from partsmakers. Either way, you will have to drill them and mount belaying pins as you did on the pinrails.

Secure mounting of the fife rail to the deck is crucial. Like the pinrails, the fiferails are subject to a powerful upward pull. Make sure the feet of the stanchions are clean, smooth, and suitable for a good bonding surface. Use a casein glue, or else jury-rig a tiedown scheme.

To do this, drill two #70 holes in the deck directly under the fiferail, one on either side, and insert eyebolts with their shanks bent at a right angle. Then pass a piece of tan thread through the eye and tie it taut atop the rail.

This is definitely not done on real ships, and purists may shudder, but it works, it saves a real disaster from happening later, and the resulting eyesore vanishes when the rigging is done. See Fig. 9-46.

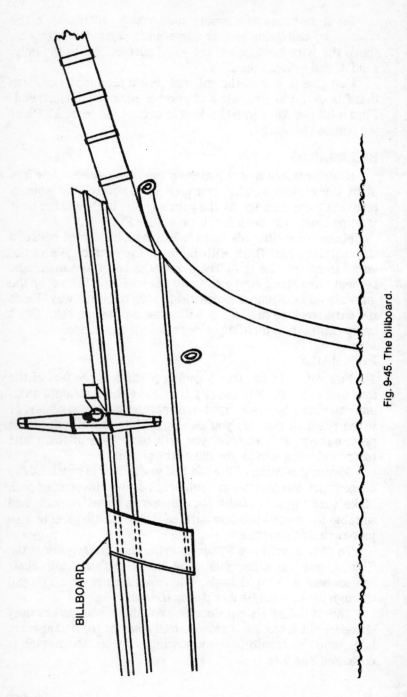

Fig. 9-45. The billboard.

BILLBOARD

BILGE PUMPS

Bilge pumps of many different sorts appear on ships, depending upon the ship's size and period. Don't look for a pump on a frigate, since it is carried well aft on the gun deck where it cannot be seen. On pre-1840 ships, the pumps are usually found abaft the mainmast and resemble long-handled pumps that used to be found on farms. After about 1840, an arrangement of wheels on a crankshaft mounted on an extension of the main fife rail came into use. Whatever the case on your ship, you should buy these parts.

Incidentally, deck furniture of this sort is usually painted white to increase its visibility to those moving about in the dark. Such is the case with the long handled bilge pump. With the wheel pump, however, an exception is almost universally

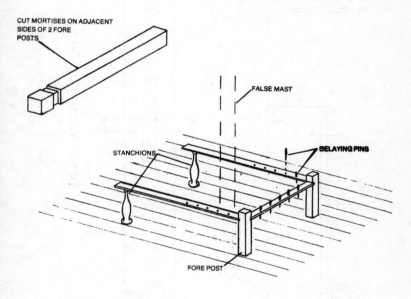

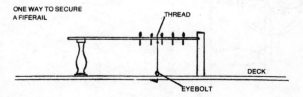

Fig. 9-46. The fife rail.

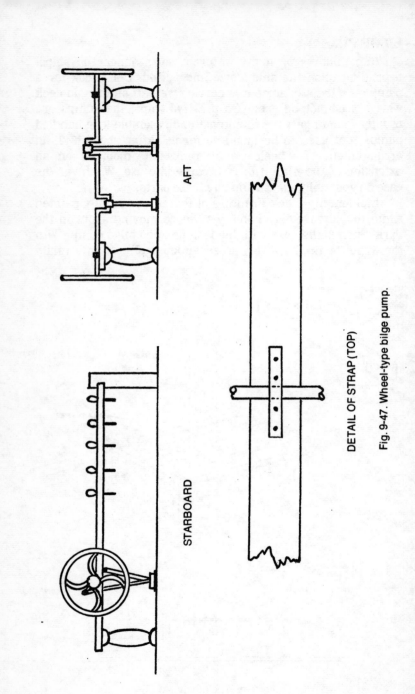

AFT

STARBOARD

DETAIL OF STRAP (TOP)

Fig. 9-47. Wheel-type bilge pump.

made. Paint the wheels gloss red, and the shaft, rods, and deck boots a flat black. Where the crankshaft rests on the fife rail, glue on a small strip of black construction paper to simulate a metal strap. See Fig. 9-47.

THE HELM

The *helm* is composed of several pieces. Usually a small steering gear enclosure stands directly above the rudder, where the rudder shaft pierces the deck if long enough. This is really a miniature chest-high deckhouse with the wheel mounted on its fore side. Make this enclosure from a piece of balsa, finished to match the other quarterdeck structures, including corner moldings and a roof. Buy the wheel itself. All the partsmakers sell wheels in a variety of sizes and spoke counts. Drill a hole in the housing to accommodate the wheel shaft, and glue it in there. See Figs. 9-48 and 9-49.

On warships and some merchant vessels, the wheel may be free standing in either a single, double, or sometimes even a triple wheel design. These assemblies, too, can be purchased. In this arrangement, a line comes up through the deck, makes several passes around a barrel on the wheel shaft, then goes back down through the deck on the other side. This can be easily simulated by drilling a couple of holes and winding a piece of tan thread around the barrel. Glue the ends in the holes, then wet the line with shellac.

The deck plan will indicate grates before or beside the helm. Use purchased grating for this, glued directly to the deck. Make sure you frame or otherwise finish the grates' edges.

The *binnacle* is a case containing the compass, charts, and other navigational necessities, located directly forward of the helm. This can be purchased as a white metal fitting, or made fairly easy from scraps. It is almost always painted white.

ANCHORS

Anchors come in all sorts of shapes and sizes. The most common one, which you will always find on a ship, is the stock anchor. It has long hooked arms with barbed bills at one end, and a stout timber perpendicular to the arms at the other. The shaft terminates in a shackle to which the cable is seized. Ordinarily, this type of anchor is stored next to the cathead with one arm around the cathead inboard end and the stock

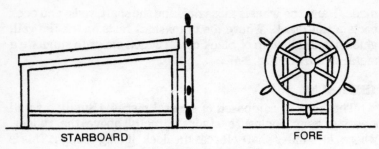

STARBOARD

FORE

STEERING GEAR HOUSING

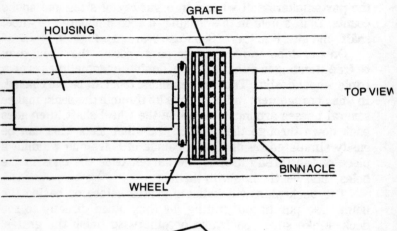

HOUSING

GRATE

TOP VIEW

WHEEL

BINNACLE

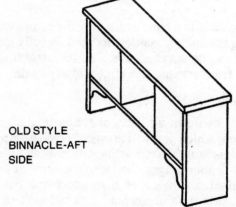

OLD STYLE
BINNACLE-AFT
SIDE

Fig. 9-48. Helm details.

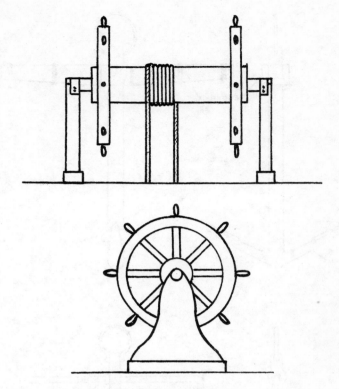

Fig. 9-49. Double wheel.

outboard of the gunwale and vertical. If only one stock anchor is carried, it usually goes on the starboard side.

Another common anchor is the iron stock anchor, also called the *kedge*. This is primarily an auxilliary anchor, so it's usually a bit smaller than the stock anchor. The two are similar in basic shape, except that on the kedge the stock is missing. In its place is a metal rod, hooked on one end, that slips through a sleeve in the shaft. When the anchor is in use, the rod locks at its center to give the same effect as a stock, but when stored, the rod is pulled out to the hook and lashed to the shaft or an arm. In this way, the anchor takes up less room and is easier to handle. It is usually stored the same way as a stock anchor. (See Fig. 9-50.)

Modelers' plans will tell you what size and types of anchors to buy, usually by depicting them at the catheads. If you are working from builders' plans or historic drawings, you

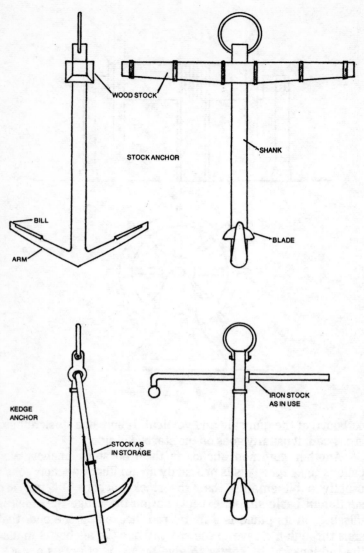

WOOD STOCK

STOCK ANCHOR

SHANK

BILL

ARM

BLADE

KEDGE
ANCHOR

STOCK AS
IN STORAGE

IRON STOCK
AS IN USE

Fig. 9-50. Anchor types.

should consult an authority such as the *Young Sea Officer's Sheet Anchor* for anchor formulas.

DECK DETAILS

Deck details such as bitts, bollards, capstans, eyebolts, scuttles, and shot racks appear on the deck drawings. Most of

Plate 3. Above, planked bulwark on Constellation. Note the finish of the gunports, the pinrail, the waterway, and the way the gunwale crosses the ports. Below is the helm area of the Constellation. The reconstructed frigate does not have gratings at the helm. Note the two skylights and the becket blocks seized to eyebolts in the quarterdeck.

these parts can be bought in whatever shapes and sizes the plans call for. Refer to your catalogs and work with the drawings to make up a list of what you need. Check the items on the drawings with a black-lead pencil as you list them. Check them with a blue pencil when you have acquired them, and in red when they're been installed.

You can make shot racks by gluing beebees or ball bearings to wood strips. To make capstan bar racks, use 1/32" hardwood strips glued to larger strips at right angles. Many other details can be added to enhance your model and give it a highly realistic appearance by using a few scraps and a little imagination.

Chapter 10

Mounting The Hull

▲▲▲▲▲▲▲▲▲▲▲▲▲▲▲▲▲▲▲▲▲▲▲▲▲▲▲▲▲▲

Mounting the hull is the most important single step in the building of a ship model. It is not truly a part of the ship building process, but if you fail to do it properly, you will regret it later.

There are many ways to mount a model, some of which are covered here and most of which you'll probably work out on your own. No matter how you choose to mount the model, two criteria are essential: the model must be stable, and it must be secure.

You are by now well aware that the hull of a ship model has amazing strength. To this tough hull, however, you have attached a great deal of exceedingly fragile detail. The rigging, soon to follow, is the most delicate of all. Should your model, through careless mounting, tip over or fall to the floor, you'll spend more time in bitter repairs than you spent in enjoyable construction—if you can salvage it at all.

CRADLE

A cradle is the most stable and secure mounting for any type of ship model. In its simplest form, the cradle is little more than a nicely finished hardwood version of the temporary construction cradle. How elaborate it can become is up to you.

An excellent material for the cradle is the thin hardwood used in drawers. If you can get an old dresser drawer from an

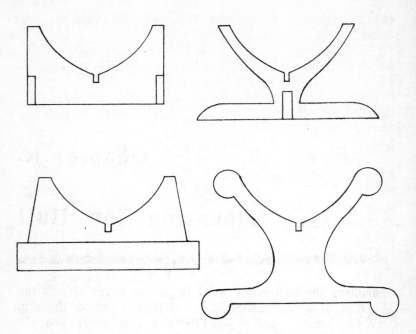

Fig. 10-1. Examples of cradle ends.

antique dealer or out of someone's attic it's especially nice, since old wood has an inimitable mellowness that survives staining and adds a touch of grandeur.

If a simple box-type cradle doesn't appeal to you, get out the jigsaw and make something fancier. You'll do well to work from a pattern to make both ends the same (except, of course, for the hull cutout). Scrolls, cutwork, modified urn forms are all possible. Let your imagination be your guide. Do keep in mind, though, that the ship is the important thing, not the cradle, and the cradle should never distract the eye or overwhelm the model it holds. See Fig. 10-1 for examples of cradle ends.

If your vessel is a warship with headrails, quarter galleries, an elaborate stern, and other embellishments, a scrolled cradle is fine. But it just won't do with a sharp, sleek clipper. In general, the simpler the ship's lines and decorations, the plainer the cradle ought to be.

After the cradles are cut, test them on the model. They should fit the hull exactly, with no gaps and irregularities, yet they should not squeeze the hull. You may have to trim and sand the cuts to get them right. It's a good idea, by the way, to mark the keel so you know where the cradle belongs.

Cradles have the inherent disadvantage of interfering with the view of hull lines. You can minimize this problem by doing away with the box sides and using, instead, a central longitudinal member to link the end cradles. Make the longitudinal piece of good quality 1" × 1", and cut interlocking mortises near its ends and in the cradles, as shown in Fig. 10-2. Use a liquid glue, preferably casein, in the joints.

Before assembling the cradle you should finish it. Sand all surfaces to a satin smoothness. To avoid distracting the eye, stain it a fairly dark wood tone such as cherry or walnut, using a wiping stain. Apply several coats of semigloss polyurethane varnish, sanding lightly between coats to bring out a good smooth finish.

Once the cradle is assembled, place the ship in it for a final pre-mounting test. The waterline should be level. So should the deck from the end view. Lay a long stick across the gunwales and measure the height of the ends from the table. They will be the same height if the hull is level. Try wiggling the hull to make sure it is secure.

Mark the keel where it rests in the cradle and remove the hull. Drill a small hole from side to side through the keel, at

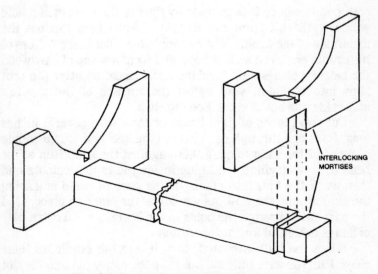

INTERLOCKING MORTISES

Fig. 10-2. Assembling a cradle without box sides.

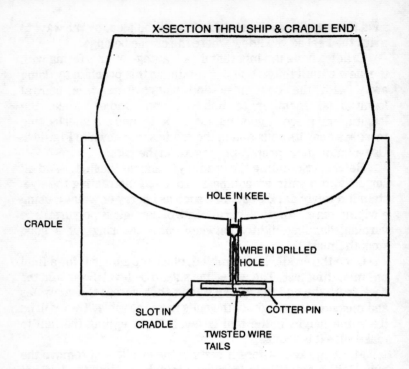

X-SECTION THRU SHIP & CRADLE END

HOLE IN KEEL

CRADLE

WIRE IN DRILLED HOLE

SLOT IN CRADLE

COTTER PIN

TWISTED WIRE TAILS

Fig. 10-3. Wiring the ship to the cradle.

both points where it is gripped by the cradle. Next drill a hole with a 1/16″ bit from the bottom of each keel slot out the underside of the cradle. Cut an "invisible" slot in the bottom of the cradle centered on this hole, and from a scrap of hardwood (or better yet a small finishing nail) make a cotter pin that slips into the slot, well below the surface of the cradle's underside and out of sight. See Fig. 10-3.

Cut two pieces of light brass or steel wire several inches long. Pass one through each hole in the keel and take a couple of turns of the tails to snug them against the keel. Run a fine bead of slow-drying liquid glue inside the cradle cutouts and then work the hull into place, taking care to avoid smearing the glue around the hull. As you lower the hull into place, feed the wire tails through the holes in the keel slots. An extra pair of hands is helpful for this operation.

When the hull is seated, turn it and the cradle on their sides. Pull the wire tails out, and slip the cotter pin into the slot with the tails on opposite sides. Twist the tails securely against the pin, taking half a dozen turns, and nip off the excess. Bend the twisted end into the slot so it won't mar the surface beneath the cradle.

The model is now firmly mounted. Once you set it upright, you'll probably never have to tip it again.

BASEBOARDS

Baseboards also make very stable, secure bases. The hull can be secured by a cradle built on the baseboard, or by other means such as mounting pedestals.

A baseboard may be a simple piece of shelving stock, but modelers generally prefer a nice piece of maple or fruitwood cut to an oval, or with scalloped corners and molded edges. The board may be large enough to accommodate not only the model, but a case too.

Some of the partsmakers sell baseboards through their catalogs. Baseboards are fairly expensive, especially when you add shipping charges. An excellent alternative is to check decoupage boards in craft shops. These come in a vast assortment of sizes and styles, usually in solid unfinished maple, and they make very fine baseboards. They're hard to find in larger sizes, however.

Always sand the baseboard to a satiny surface (unless you buy it already finished), and don't neglect the molded edges, even though they are inconvenient to work on. Like the cradle, the board requires a good wiping stain and several coats of semigloss polyurethane varnish. Be sure to varnish all surfaces including the underside, and especially the grain ends, because unless it is imperviously sealed, a solid board will soak up humidity and warp.

If you make a cradle for the hull, you can mount it directly on the board before or after the hull is placed in the cradle. Situate the cradle and trace its outline on the board with a soft pencil. Then, apply contact cement within the outline and on the cradle's underside and press them together to form a permanent bond.

Mounting Pedestals

Any hull but a plank-on-frame can also use mounting pedestals with the board. Usually these have the external appearance of a brass ball or a column base. Some have a large cylindrical tenon below to fit a hole in the board and a

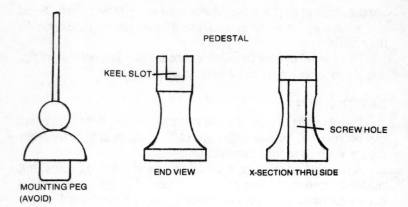

KEEL SLOT

PEDESTAL

SCREW HOLE

MOUNTING PEG
(AVOID)

END VIEW

X-SECTION THRU SIDE

Fig. 10-4. Mounting pedestals.

long peg above which enters the hull via the keel. I suggest you avoid such pedestals, because they offer little security. Other pedestals grip the keel and are drilled to accommodate a screw that passes from the underside of the board into the hull. These are excellent, but they don't work with a plank-on-frame model because the screw has nothing to grip. See Fig. 10-4.

Mark the pedestal locations on the board's top surface and drill a hole the same diameter as the screw. On the underside, enlarge the screw hole to permit countersinking the head. Pass the screws up through the holes and impale the pedestals. Hold the hull so the tips of the screws touch the points of entry and mark the keel to indicate those points.

Carefully cut pieces out of the keel so that the screws will meet the hull, but only remove as much as is absolutely necessary. The keel slot in the top of the pedestal will hide these cuts if it's properly done. Drill a hole for each screw into the hull, making sure it's perfectly vertical. Use a bit 1/16" smaller in diameter than the screw. See Fig. 10-5.

Slip the pedestals over the keel and again impale them on the screws. Have someone hold the hull while you drive the screws. The best way is to sit on the floor and place the end of the board over the table's edge so you can get at the screw from beneath. Don't drive it tightly, just snugly.

It's a nice finishing touch to put a flocked surface on the underside of the board. This keeps the board from marring furniture, and at the same time it has less tendency to slip around. You can buy adhesive flocked sheets such as contact paper in hardware stores and kitchenware departments.

Crossed Baseboards

Crossed baseboards can be made as a lower-cost variation on the solid baseboard. In this case, two narrow boards are joined in the form of a cross, with the shorter arms centered.

Make the cross as shown in the exploded view in Fig. 10-6, joining the pieces with contact cement. If you want to simulate a routed edge, mitre and mount a decorative or coping molding on the edges of the crossed members. Sand and finish the assembly after it is put together.

You can mount the hull with screw pedestals just as you would on a board. Ordinarily they are placed an inch or two

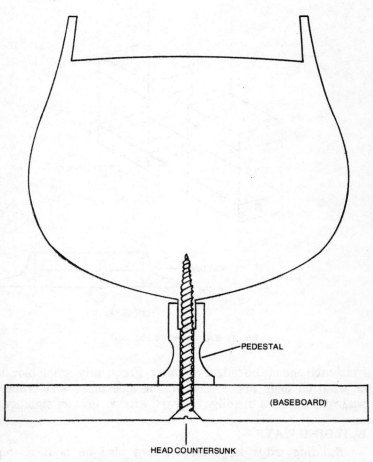

PEDESTAL

(BASEBOARD)

HEAD COUNTERSUNK

Fig. 10-5. A section of the pedestal mounting.

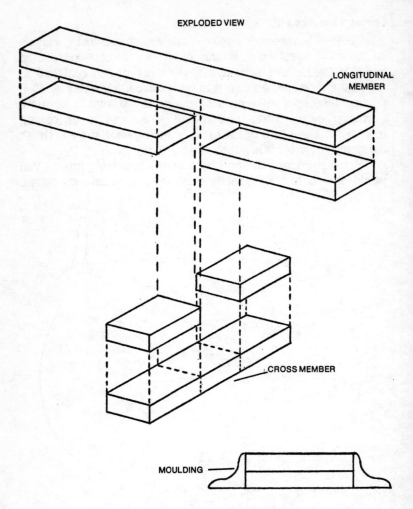

EXPLODED VIEW

LONGITUDINAL MEMBER

CROSS MEMBER

MOULDING

CROSS SECTION

Fig. 10-6. Crossed baseboard.

from each end of the longer member. Frequently, small blocks or whittled pegs are placed on the side arms and braced against the turn of the bilge to give the model greater stability.

BUILDING WAYS

Building ways in miniature can also be built as an interesting mounting for a small vessel, particularly one with a

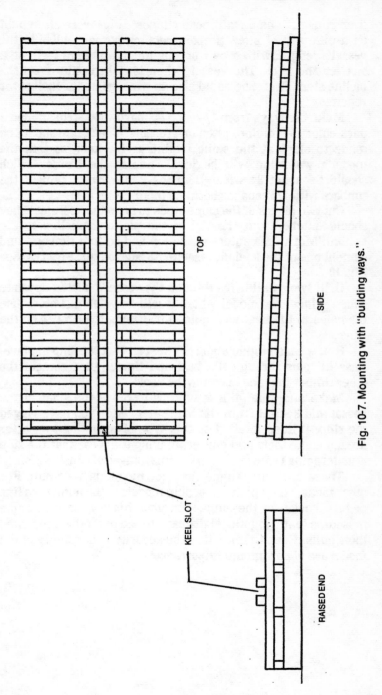

KEEL SLOT

RAISED END

TOP

SIDE

Fig. 10-7. Mounting with "building ways."

287

deep run, such as a Baltimore clipper. Ships were often built on a platform of stout timbers running perpendicular to the vessel's length, with a pair of longitudinal timbers forming a slot for the keel. The vessel, when launched, slid down the incline stern first. She could also be winched up the incline for repairs.

Make the ways from 1/4″ × 1/4″ hardwood strip stained a dark color to simulate pitch or creosote. The frame should be made to slant at the same incline as the keel, so that the model's waterline will be level. Across the frame, which should be about 3″ wider than the hull's beam, cement the timbers with 1/8″ spaces between them.

Cut two pieces of the same stock to form the keel slot. They should extend from the top of the platform incline to the bottom. Mark the centers of the top and bottom timbers, and cement one of the keel pieces with its edge on these marks. See Fig. 10-7.

Drill two small holes through the vessel's keel at opposite ends. Place the model where it will be when mounted, use the holes in the keel as a guide for drilling the timber on the ways.

Run a bead of glue along the keel and set the ship in place. Pass lill pins through the keel and timber then cement the other timber in place to clamp the keel.

Make and glue on a few props to brace the sides of the vessel and keep it from tipping. Later, after you have rigged the ship, it adds interest to this type of mounting to scatter around some tools and clutter, making it appear that the ship is undergoing repairs or is in the final stages of construction.

These are some suggestions for mounting your hull. For other ideas, study pictures of ship models in the numerous fine picture books on the subject in your library, or visit some museums featuring model displays to see how others mounted their hulls. Keep in mind that the security and stability of the model are of paramount importance.

Chapter 11

Rigging The Ship

Volumes have been written on the topic of rigging, and the subject still isn't exhausted. This chapter provides a general guide to rigging. For a comprehensive treatment, see *Steele's Elements of Mastmaking, Sailmaking, and Rigging*. This book, first published in 1794, has gone through innumerable reprints and is still the ultimate authority on the subject. Copies are sold in hobby shops and through magazines and catalogs. Many public libraries have the book, too.

The rigging of a ship, especially on a ship that is square-rigged, looks terribly complex and difficult, but it is really a marvel of functional simplicity. What gives it such an awesome aspect is the sheer number of lines. There are only about half a dozen basic line configurations which merely repeat on each yard of each mast. Once you have done one or two of each type, you'll know how to do all the rest. When you see a finished model with seeming miles of cordage aloft, and it appears to you all at once, it looks as though someone with hundreds of hands did the whole thing instantly. But when you are the rigger, you put in one line at a time, and it's a lot easier than it looks.

ANATOMY

All the masts, spars, lines, blocks, hoops, and poles above the vessel's decks are collectively called the *top hamper*.

289

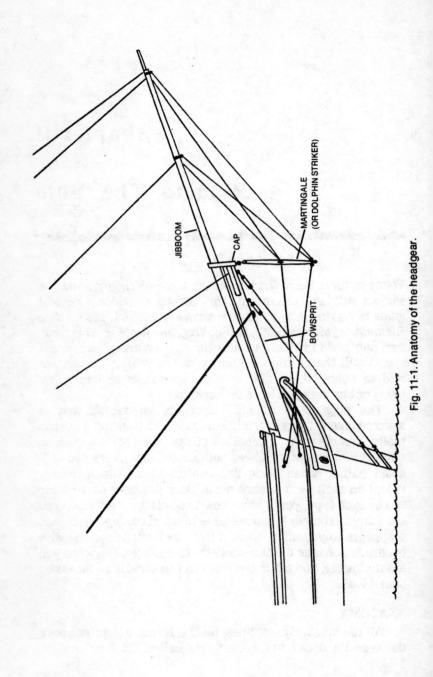

Fig. 11-1. Anatomy of the headgear.

MARTINGALE
(OR DOLPHIN STRIKER)

JIBBOOM

CAP

BOWSPRIT

Aside from the sails, which will be discussed later, the top hamper is divided into two main categories: the spars and the rigging.

Spars are poles. On nearly all sailing vessels, the spars were made of fir trunks selected for their straightness and turned on a large lathe to smooth and taper them. The spars fall into several categories depending on their placement and use:

> The *bowsprit* is a short stout mast thrusting forward from the bows of the vessel. To it is generally attached a much longer, slender spar called the *jibbom*. See Fig. 11-1.

> The *masts* are vertical spars set in the decks and braced against the keelson to hold the sails aloft. The order of masts from bow to stern is fore, main, and mizzen. On vessels of more than three masts, the continuing order is jigger, spanker, and driver.

> Unless the vessel is quite small, each mast is usually made of several spars. The lowest is called simply the mast, the next higher the topmast, the third the topgallant mast. The latter is further subdivided into the topgallant mast, royal mast, and pole, though it is all of one piece.

The lower end of a mast is its *heel*, the top is its *head*. Where masts join is the *doubling*.

> The heel of the upper mast rests in a frame known as the *crosstrees*, at the head of the lower mast the doubling ends in another brace called the *cap*. On the lower crosstrees, one usually finds the *top*, a platform of crescent shape on a merchantman, square on a man-of-war. See Fig. 11-2.

> The *yards* are horizontal spars for spreading the sails. Most vessels carry the same number of yards on each mast, which may vary from three to six. In ascending order, these are the main (fore on the foremast, cross jack on the mizzen), topsail, topgallant, royal, and skysail yards. Late clippers also carried an even higher yard called the moonsail yard. Large vessels of the late 1800s occasionally had a split topsail on the fore and main, thus carrying an upper and lower yard on the topmasts. In this rig the upper topsail yard,

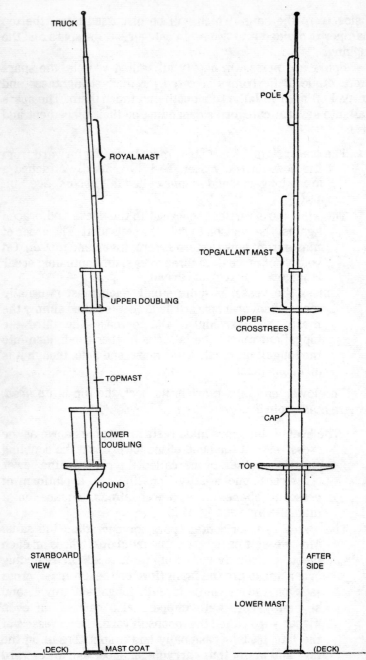

Fig. 11-2. Anatomy of a mast.

with sails furled, is lowered to rest on the lower yard. See Fig. 11-3.

Booms and *gaffs* are spars carried on the after sides of masts. The boom secures the lower edge of a fore-and-aft-rigged sail, and generally remains horizontal and fixed to the mast at one place. The gaff secures the upper edge of the sail. It is raised and lowered with the sail, and when raised it angles upwards from the mast. In older vessels, both the gaff and boom had jaws that surrounded the mast on three sides and were lashed in place on the open side. Later, a universal joint called the gooseneck was developed for the boom, and gaffs either retained jaws or had heel fittings that slid in a track on the mast. See Fig. 11-4.

RIGGING TYPES

The rigging of a ship is divided into two main types: *standing* and *running*. Standing rigging is ordinarily tarred for preservation against the elements. It is a structural part of the top hamper which provides support and does not move. Both ends of a standing line are securely fixed to the hull or a spar, often with one end seized about a deadeye so that lanyards may be used to adjust tension.

Running Lines

Running rigging, on the other hand, is natural hemp, usually of a lighter weight than standing cordage. Its purpose is to move spars and sails aloft. Running lines are always rigged with one end secured and the other tied off at a belaying pin. To do their job, running lines, almost without exception, pass through a pulley of some sort. Pulleys built into a spar or bulwark are called *sheaves*; free pulleys tied to the end of another line or to an eyebolt are *blocks*. The assembly of lines and blocks to do a job is called a *tackle*.

All rigging is symmetrical. Every line on one side of the mast has a twin on the other side. Fore-and-aft standing lines, called the *stays*, counterbalance each other to hold the mast rigid. Though it may not appear so at first glance, all the top hamper components of a vessel are interrelated to the extent that a change in the tension of one line will change the tension of all the others.

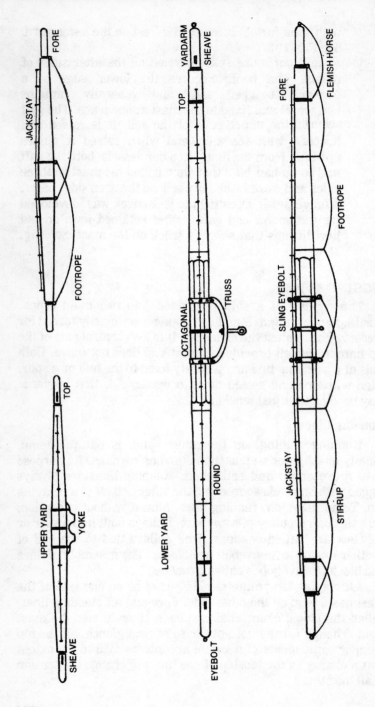

Fig. 11-3. Anatomy of a yard.

294

Standing Lines

There are two basic types of standing lines. The *shrouds* support the masts on the sides. Usually, the shrouds carry light footropes called *ratlines* to make them rope ladders for going aloft. The *stays* support the masts fore-and-aft. Stays secured to the fore side of a mast may run to the deck or down to the aft side of the next mast forward. Backstays run down to

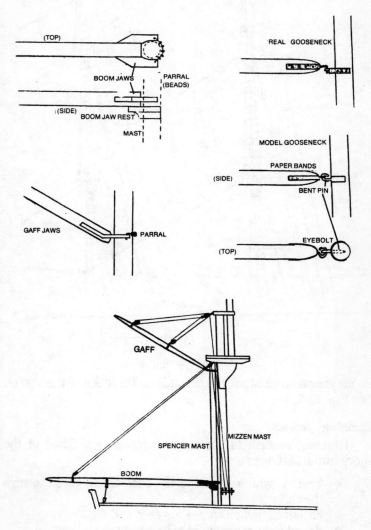

Fig. 11-4. Booms and gaffs.

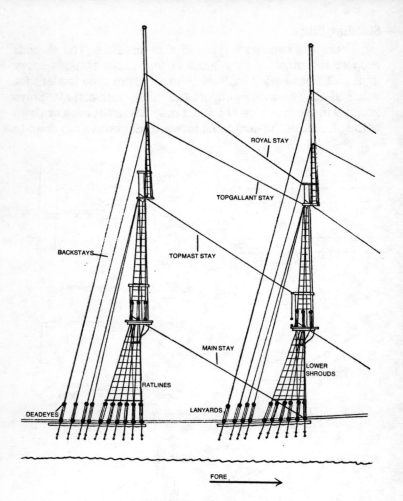

ROYAL STAY

TOPGALLANT STAY

BACKSTAYS

TOPMAST STAY

MAIN STAY

LOWER
SHROUDS

RATLINES

DEADEYES

LANYARDS

FORE

Fig. 11-5. Standing rigging.

deadeyes secured abaft the shrouds on the sides of the vessel.
See Fig. 11-5.

Running Tackles

Running tackles fall into many categories. Some of the
more important ones are:

- **braces**, which fasten to the ends of the yards to turn
  the sails
- **halliards**, which raise the yards and sails
- **downhauls**, which help to lower yards and sails

- **lifts,** which hold yards horizontal
- **sheets,** which draw the lower corners of a sail down to the yard below
- **clews,** which hoist a sail to its yard

With very few exceptions, running lines are rigged with the belayiing end on deck to minimize the hazards of going aloft. This made it necessary to send men aloft only when making and shortening sail. Donald McKay developed but never perfected rigging techniques that would have made it possible to do all sail handling from the deck; the clipper era ended just as his ideas were catching on.

In general, everything about the top hamper grows smaller, the higher one goes on the mast. The spars become more slender, the yards shorter, the sails smaller. This is true, too, of the rigging.

A realistic effect can be achieved by using three different sizes of cordage, heaviest at the bottom, decreasing the diameter on the topmast, and using the lightest cord above the upper crosstrees. Standing rigging should be 25 percent to 50 percent heavier than running.

RIGGING ORDER

The order of rigging is a matter of personal preference. You can erect all the masts, then install all the standing rigging, then mount all the spars and running lines. Or you can do one mast at a time, or do similar jobs on each mast sequentially. The only fixed rule of order is to do the standing rigging before the running, lest you mess up the tension and have to readjust all the running lines.

I enjoy rigging more than any other part of ship modeling, but I've found that too much of any one thing gets boring after a while. For this reason, I suggest you do one mast at a time, building and rigging as much as you can, and after all the masts are built and rigged, go back and set up the running lines between masts. It's easiest to work from bow to stern, rigging the head gear, then the fore, main, and finally the mizzen masts.

It's also easiest to work your way up the mast. First, erect the lower mast in the deck, then the upper masts. Set up all the standing lines from heel to head, including those going to masts you've already done. Then, again from bottom to top, build, mount, and rig each yard. When the uppermost yard is completed, go on to the next mast.

After all masts are rigged individually, return foreward. Complete the bowsprit and headsail running rigging. If the foremast carries a trysail gaff (clippers and schooner-type rigs have them on the after side of the lower mast), mount and completely rig it first, then rig the fore braces.

The braces run from yard to adjacent mast to deck. Fore braces run aft to the mainmast. Main braces, too, run aft to the mizzen, but mizzen braces run forward to the mainmast, which creates a dense web of lines between the main and mizzen.

Since the braces soon fill your working space between masts, they can interfere with feeding the lines down the mast to the deck. For this stage of rigging, then, it's best to reverse the order and work from the highest yard down.

Before you rig the main and mizzen braces, be sure you've done all the detail work on deck. Once the braces are set up, you'll have trouble getting your hands to unfinished details. Also, rig the main trysail gaff if your ship has one.

Rig corresponding yards on the main and mizzen together; that is, rig both royal yards first, then both topgallant yards, and so on.

The final step is to rig the lower yard braces, which run to the gunwales or boomkins set in the ship's sides.

MATERIALS

Spars are generally round, having been turned from fir trunks. You can use dowels in an assortment of sizes for spars and achieve satisfactory results. If you're willing to work a little harder, you can make spars by rounding hardwood strips. Done well, this produces more accurate results than dowels, since the spars can be sized exactly to scale. Don't use balsa for masts or yards, because they'll break.

All spars taper, since that is in the nature of trees. Steele's book gives complex formulas for determining the degree of taper in various spars, and Chapelle provides similar data more simply stated.

For best results, your spars should taper. Dowels, of course, do not taper, and to make them taper is difficult without a hobbyist's lathe. It's easier if you round square stock. Or you can buy spars already tapered from the Marine

Models catalog, which sells them tapered from heel too head for masts and booms, and tapered both ways from the center for yards. These spars need sanding to take out the roughness, but the price is reasonable.

Cord

Cord for rigging is available in many places. The best cord is cuttyhunk, a linen twine made in the form of a miniature rope. You can obtain it from some hobby shops and most parts catalogs. Buy plenty. You will need three sizes each of black and natural cord, for the three basic levels of the masts. The black at each level should be 50 percent larger in diameter than the natural cord. It comes both on spools and cards.

On your rigging plan, write each size cord you bought so that you'll know what to buy if you need more. You will also need spools of ordinary black and tan sewing thread to be used for seizing ratlines and miscellaneous lashings that would ordinarily take light rope.

Buy also a disc of beeswax. You can get it where sewing supplies are sold, for about 15 cents. All rigging line should be pulled through the edge of the wax disc twice in the same direction before use. This has the dual benefit of eliminating the unrealistic fuzz on the thread and of sealing the thread so it won't sag and tighten as humidity changes.

Blocks

Blocks, as we mentioned, are pulleys. They are made by placing a sheave between two slabs of wood and securing the whole works with an iron band. Double and triple blocks are made essentially the same way. The block itself is left natural in color. At its top, as part of the band, is a ring to which a line is seized. Some blocks also have a ring at the bottom for securing the standing end of a line that travels to another block and returns to pass through the first block. This is called a becket block. See Fig. 11-6.

The size of a block is dictated by the size of the line that passes through it: the larger the line, the larger the block. If you use three sizes of running line, buy three sizes of blocks in direct proportion to the diameters of the thread.

You can buy boxwood blocks from the partsmakers, or by the dozen from hobby shops. They come in single through triple configurations in many sizes measured in increments of

SIDE

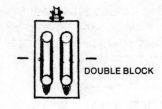

DOUBLE BLOCK

TRIPLE
BLOCK

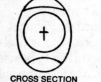

CROSS SECTION
OF BLOCK

SINGLE
BLOCK

SHEAVE

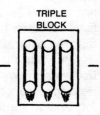

BECKET
BLOCK

HAULING
END

STANDING BLOCK

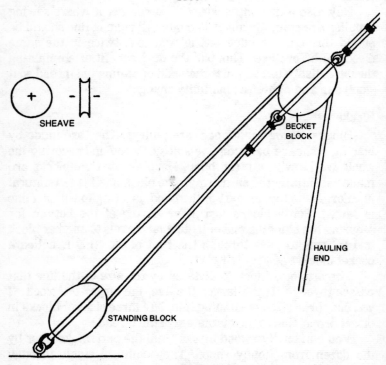

Fig. 11-6. Blocks.

1/32" along the length. These blocks are predrilled and have a stropping groove.

You'll probably find it necessary to redrill the holes, since most manufacturers use a bit too small to accommodate a needle threader and the thread. Grasp the block in needlenose pliers and bore into the existing hole with a #70 bit in your pin vise.

Wire

Wire comes in very handy when rigging, especially for lines such as footropes that need to have a catenary. Wire can also be used to strip blocks and fasten them to spars. Use a fine-gauge annealed wire.

Jackstay Eyebolts

Jackstay eyebolts are in absolute necessity in rigging. Buy many dozens. They will be used not only for their primary purpose of providing sail mountings atop the yards, but as mounting rings for blocks and seizing points for standing lines.

Canvas

If you plan to fit the ship with a full suit of billowing sails or to furl the sails on the yards, buy a type of fine cotton called ballooner. This is similar to percale in that it is closely woven. It approximates a scale canvas. You can buy it by the yard from some partsmakers in white, or try a fabric shop, where you may be able to buy it in a more realistic unbleached color. A yard will last a long, long time.

Tools

The tools you will need, in addition to those with which you are already familiar are:

> several needle threaders (see Chapter 2)
> good manicure or surgical scissors
> small wire nippers
> hooked dental forceps
> clamp-type clothespins
> small hobbyist's vise

KNOTS

Knots are the source of much nautical lore. Seamen, living in a spiderweb of hemp, developed an almost endless variety

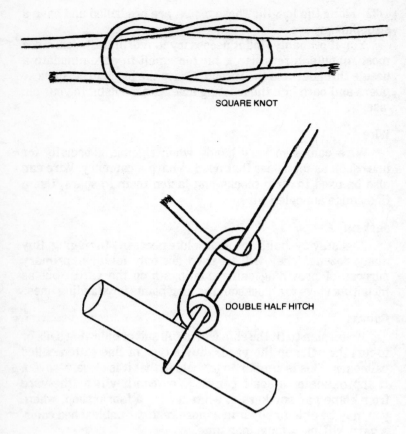

SQUARE KNOT

DOUBLE HALF HITCH

Fig. 11-7. Basic knots.

of special-purpose knots. They're very interesting, and there's no reason you couldn't incorporate many of them in a model. The effort, however, would be largely wasted, because the intricacies are lost in slender thread.

For modeling, you can get along just fine knowing only two basic knots, the square knot and the double half-hitch. These two are really the same knot in that if you pull on one of the tails of a square knot hard enough, it will become a double half hitch. This latter knot has infinite uses on a ship model. It can be used to secure the standing end of a line to a spar or an eyebolt, to belay the running end, and even as a slip knot. See Fig. 11-7.

Even in easily accessible places, you will find that knots are best tied with the foreceps. Always cut the line a few inches longer than it will be when tied off to give yourself a free end to work with. First, tie the end that's hardest to get to, then reeve it through its blocks and tie off the other end.

Set up tension by tying a single half hitch with the line slack, then gently pull on the free end until the slackness is gone. Don't put any more tension into the line than necessary, for fear of distorting the top hamper and slackening other lines. When the tension is okay, take another half hitch or two around the line, then snip off the free end at the knot.

SEIZING

Seizing is a means for securing the standing end of a line too bulky to tie, such as a stay or the anchor hawser. A line is always seized around something: an eyebolt, a spar, the anchor ring, or a block. See Fig. 11-8.

To seize up a line, pass the end around the securing point. Use lighter cord of the same color to bind the doubled line into a noose form. Take several turns around the hawser, then tie off with a square knot and clip the ends of the light cord. For best results, use contact cement to fix the free and standing parts of the hawser before seizing it, and make a second seizing about two scale feet farther from the noose. Clip the waste from the hawser just above this second seizing.

Eyebands

Eyebands are frequently found on spars where lines of blocks are attached. These are metal hoops wrapped around the spar with eyes cut or welded on. You can buy them as fittings, but they are simple to make.

Where an eyeband is needed, cement a band of black construction paper around the spar, then drill #70 holes and mount jackstay eyebolts. This yields a perfectly satisfactory result for most vessels after 1812. See Fig. 11-9.

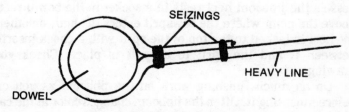

Fig. 11-8. Seizing around a dowel.

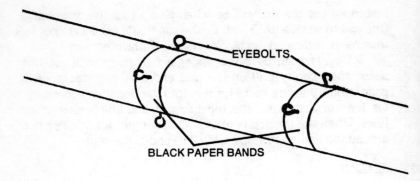

BLACK PAPER BANDS

Fig. 11-9. An eyeband.

Prior to 1812, wooldings were used instead of metal eyebands. To make a woolding, simply wrap black cord around the spar several times and apply a drop of glue. Snip off the ends, and tie your lines and blocks to the band with double half hitches.

HEADGEAR

The *headgear* should be rigged first. The size and period of the vessel will determine the complexity of the job; older warships have very elaborate headgear, whereas on clippers the rig of the bowsprit is clean and spare. See Figs. 11-10 and 11-11.

Start with the gammoning, which comprises a number of turns of heavy black line securing the bowsprit to the beakhead. On later vessels, this appears as a steel band. Next, rig the bobstay, which is a heavy double line or chain from the cutwater to the end of the bowsprit, seized to an eye at both ends.

From a dowel or tapering spar stock, cut the jibboom, the long spar thrusting forward from the bowsprit. On some vessels the jibboom heel rests in a socket in the bow directly above the point where the bowsprit enters the hull; on others, the heel is lashed to the top of the sprit with a chock inserted between it and the sprit to keep it in place. Check your drawings.

Do as much finishing work on the jibboom as you can before mounting it. Often the jibboom changes color at the cap, black or white inboard and natural inboard. Frequently, too, it

304

incorporates sheaves along its outboard portion for passing through running lines, which should be drilled, and the eyebands should be mounted.

If your jibboom is of the newer type, carefully cut a tenon in the inboard end and a corresponding mortise in the hull, taking care to make the tenon vertical in reference to the eyebands and sheaves. If it is lashed to the sprit, round the heel and fashion chocks to glue to the underside. When all is ready, glue the jibboom in place.

The bowsprit cap comes next. Again, this will vary with the period of the vessel. Newer vessels use a simple iron band secured around the tip of the sprit and the jibboom, which can be made of construction paper. On older vessels, a timber is used. Its thickness should be one-half its width. Make it from hardwood.

Drill a hole the diameter of the jibboom in the stock, then mark the outline and cut the cap out, with the grain oriented from side to side. After sanding the cap to final shape and finishing it, cut off the top at the sides of the hole. Glue the lower part to the forward end of the sprit and the top to the jibboom. If necessary, fill the seam and refinish it. Install eyebolts as necessary. See Fig. 11-12.

On newer type headgear, install saddle irons as indicated by your plans. These are bands that clamp the jibboom and bowsprit together at intervals along the doubling. Use black construction paper and contact cement.

The *bee seats* are flat timbers glued to the sides of the sprit just abaft the cap. Drill a single hole in each one. On older vessels the bees usually butt against the cap. Paint them to match the sprit.

The *martingale*, also called the dolphin striker, is a spar that hangs below the cap, used to bring the stays to the tip of the jibboom at a greater and, therefore, stronger angle than if they were run straight from the hull. Again, this spar varies with period. On older vessels, it is fixed to the cap by a couple of bolts, and the stays pass through holes in it. On newer ships, the martingale is more flexible in having two flanges that slip over a ring in the cap's underside with a bolt acting as a cotter pin. The stays pass through hook cleats bolted to either side of the martingale and are held there by tension.

In either case, a round toothpick makes a very fine martingale, or you can buy this spar as a metal fitting. A. J.

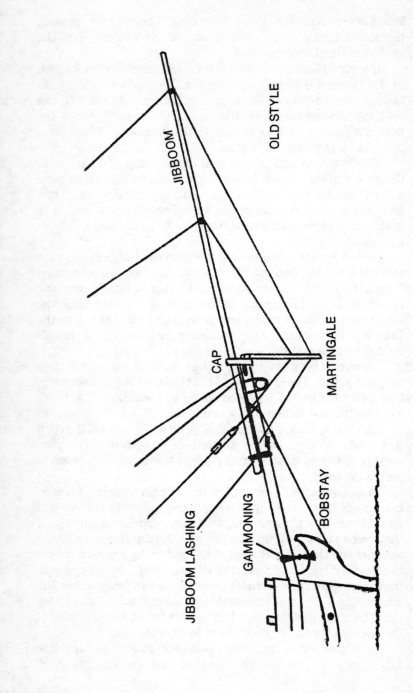

JIBBOOM

OLD STYLE

CAP

MARTINGALE

JIBBOOM LASHING

GAMMONING

BOBSTAY

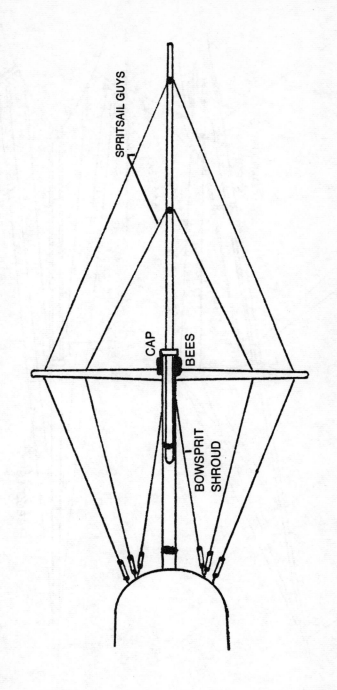

Fig. 11-10. Headgear: Old style.

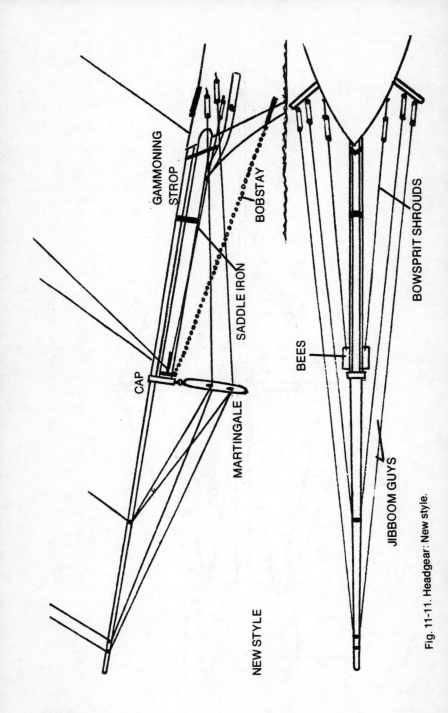

GAMMONING
STROP

BOBSTAY

SADDLE IRON

CAP

MARTINGALE

NEW STYLE

BEES

BOWSPRIT SHROUDS

JIBBOOM GUYS

Fig. 11-11. Headgear: New style.

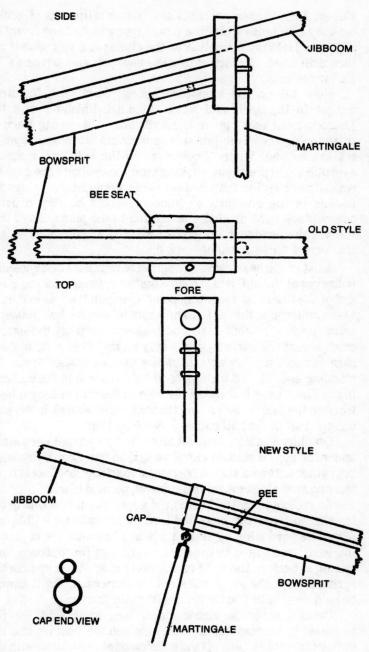

SIDE

JIBBOOM

MARTINGALE

BOWSPRIT

BEE SEAT

OLD STYLE

TOP

FORE

NEW STYLE

JIBBOOM

BEE

CAP

BOWSPRIT

CAP END VIEW

MARTINGALE

Fig. 11-12. Bowsprit caps.

Fisher, Inc., makes probably the best martingales of brass, but they cost quite a bit. The newer type can be hung from the cap by a jackstay eyebolt. For the older type, just glue it on, then drill a hole through it into the bowsprit and drive in a lill pin for security.

Now set up the standing rigging. Start with the lines closest to the sprit and work outboard, finishing with the jibboom guys that run to the catheads. Always rig lines in pairs, doing the same line on the port and starboard sides at the same time. Where lines come to the hull, use jackstay eyebolts to secure them, making sure the eyebolts are exactly opposite each other with respect to the stempost. Any stay that fastens to the bowsprit or jibboom should be rigged using heavy black cord or chain, according to the plans. Stays that run via the headgear up to the foremast are medium weight black cord. Guys are light black line.

Most of the head stays are seized to the spars and rigged to bullseyes at the hull end. To rig a bullseye, first, seize the other end of the line to its mounting point, then pull the free end back to the bullseye in the hull. About an inch from the hull bullseye, seize the line around a second bullseye. Snip off the excess cord. Mount the corresponding stay on the other side, making sure the bullseye is seized at the same distance from the standing end. Tie a 6 inch piece of light tan line to the bullseye in the line, reeve it through the hole in the hull bullseye, back through the line bullseye, and then take up the slack in the stay and tie it off at the hull bullseye. See Fig. 11-13.

On older vessels, you will often find a spritsail yard slung under the cap. It seldom carries a sail on 19th Century vessels, but rather acts as a sort of horizontal martingale. Make it from tapered spar stock or a slender dowel, painted black.

As indicated by the location of guys, mount eyebolts in the top side to reeve the guys and turn them toward the jibboom. Make the yard sling by seizing a heavy line near the center of the yard, passing it between the sprit and the jibboom, and seizing it back to the yard on the other side. When you rig the spritsail guys the yard will stabilize somewhat, but it cannot be held level until you rig braces from the foretop.

Certain other headgear lines, too, must wait for the foremast to be completed. These include the jibstays and the various forestays, plus all the running lines associated with the head sails.

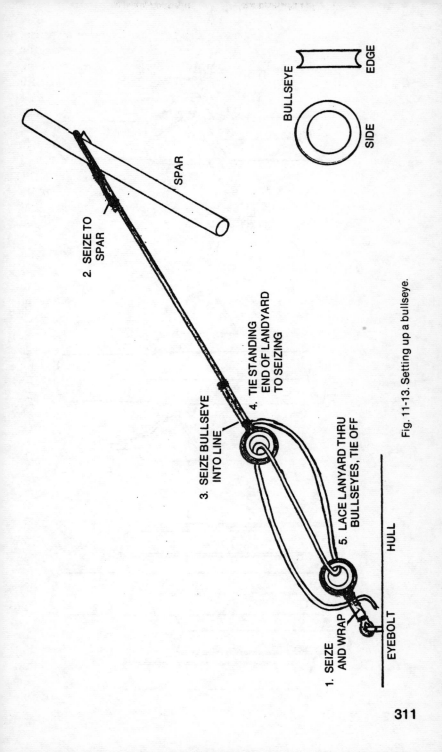

Fig. 11-13. Setting up a bullseye.

EDGE

BULLSEYE

SIDE

SPAR

2. SEIZE TO SPAR

3. SEIZE BULLSEYE INTO LINE

4. TIE STANDING END OF LANDYARD TO SEIZING

5. LACE LANYARD THRU BULLSEYES, TIE OFF

1. SEIZE AND WRAP

EYEBOLT

HULL

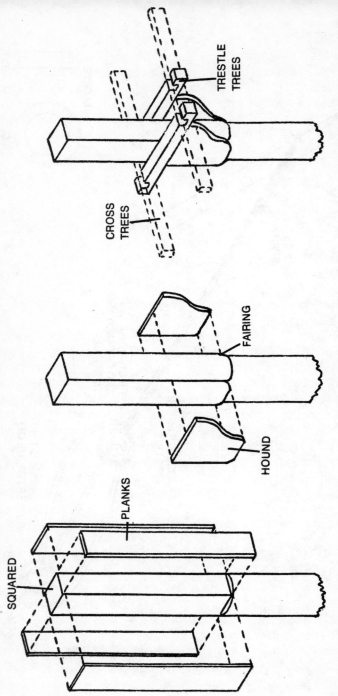

CROSS TREES

TRESTLE TREES

FAIRING

HOUND

PLANKS

SQUARED

Fig. 11-14. The masthead.

MASTING

The masting of the ship can now begin. All masts are similar regardless of period or position on the ship.

The first mast to be made is the lowest mast. The rigging plan of your ship will indicate the height of the mast above deck. To find the actual length you need to cut, mark the deck line on the false mast, withdraw the mast and add the distance below the mark to the indicated height above the deck. Cut a dowel of the appropriate diameter to this length.

Near the top of the lowest mast, supporting the doubling, are two curving timbers called the *hounds*. Measure the distance from the bottom of the hounds to the mast cap. Square this much of the dowel as shown in Fig. 5-22 of Chapter 5.

Use hardwood strips to build out the squared end to the same dimensions as the mast diameter, and fair the lower corners into the round. Cut a pair of hounds from hardwood sheet and cement them in place with their after edges flush with the square. Fair the lower ends of the hounds into the mast.

Paint the mast. If the doublings are of a different color, the color changes at the top of the hounds. On large vessels, lower masts are ordinarily made of several timbers banded together with metal hoops. Every two or three scale feet from deck to hounds, cement a narrow strip of black construction paper around the mast to simulate these bands. Step the mast to make sure it fits properly. The hounds must extend forward.

Where the mast enters the deck, a small circular platform is built around the mast. On real ships this platform, called the mast coat, is a group of wedges fitted into a watertight ring and covered with canvas. This part is best purchased in a diameter that fits the dowel. Slide it up over the heel of the lower mast and when the mast is stepped, press it down in contact with the deck. See Figs. 11-14 and 11-15.

It's easiest to build the top with the mast stepped. First, cut the trestle trees, a pair of timbers that rest atop the hounds. The trestle trees and crosstrees lock together with interlocking mortises. Cut these notches and cement the timbers to the hounds. Cut and mount chocks against the mast between the trestle trees. Next, cut the crosstrees from the same stock as the trestle trees. Outboard of the mortises, shave an upward taper into the crosstrees. Glue them in place with a drop of glue in each mortise.

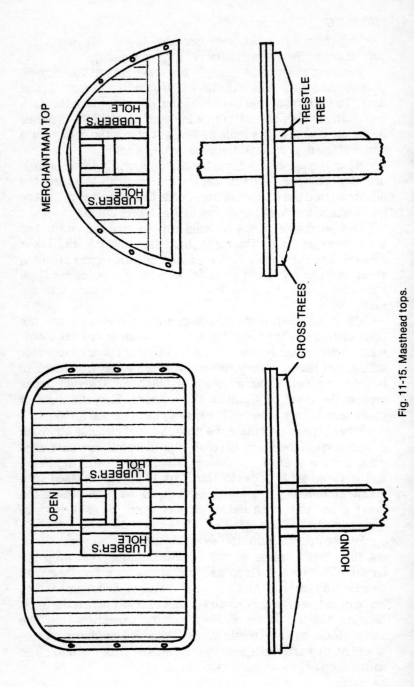

Fig. 11-15. Masthead tops.

MERCHANTMAN TOP

LUBBER'S HOLE

LUBBER'S HOLE

TRESTLE TREE

CROSS TREES

OPEN

LUBBER'S HOLE

LUBBER'S HOLE

HOUND

Plank them by laying 1/16″ × 1/32″ strips in whatever pattern the drafts indicate, leaving openings for the lubber's holes adjacent to the mast. All around the edge, shape and glue a raised rim atop the planking. Drill holes in the side rims to accommodate the futtock shrouds. Finally, paint the top and the trees white on all visible surfaces.

Next, make the topmast. The head of the mast is squared just like the lower masthead, but there are no hounds. There are likewise no mast bands, since this mast is slender enough to be made of one pole. The foot of the topmast should be squared for its last two or three scale feet, built out and faired into the round in imitation of the upper end. Set the mast in place, with the foot resting in the square opening forward of the chock and between the trestle trees. If the doubling is of a color contrasting with the mast, mark the lower mast cap location to serve as a color change line.

The foot of the topmast should extend no lower than the underside of the trestle trees. To keep the mast from falling through, glue a small wood chip on either side of the foot 1/8″ up from the end. See Fig. 11-16.

Withdraw the topmast and paint it. While the paint is drying, glue a small block from the same stock as the trestle trees to the fore side of the very top of the lower mast, extending from one edge to the other of the squared face. Now, very carefully and triple-checking alignment, cement the topmast in place with a drop of glue at the foot and on the block you just mounted.

When the glue is hard, wrap several thicknesses of black construction paper around the very top of the lower mast and on around the topmast to make a mast cap. Into the openings caused by the topmast's roundness, pack a little putty. Smooth it with a knife point and touch it up with black paint, and paint the exposed top surface of the mast.

Up at the topmast doubling, build another set of trestle trees and crosstrees of stock half the dimensions of the lower set. There is no platform on the upper crosstrees. See Fig. 11-17.

The topgallant and royal masts are all one spar, usually a very long, slender, tapering pole. It steps in the upper crosstrees, and so the foot should be made the same way as the topmast foot. The pole rising above the uppermost eyeband is usually painted to contrast with the lower part, and often

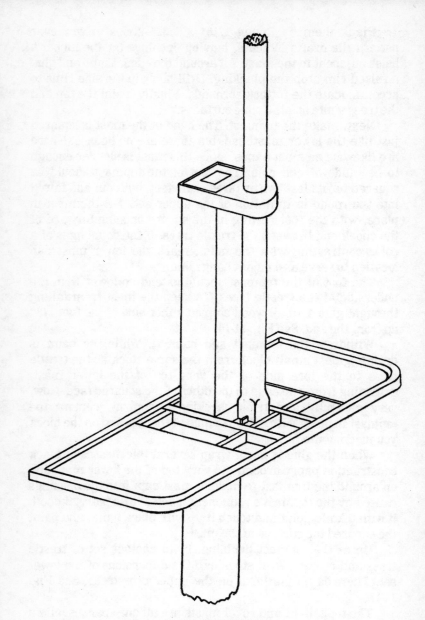

Fig. 11-16. Stepped topmast.

topped by a ball or disc called the truck. In such cases the mast tapers to a sharp point. Glue this mast on like the topmast, and make the cap the same way.

316

SHROUDS

The *shrouds* should now be rigged. Shrouds are rope supports on both sides of the mast which keep it from swaying as the ship rolls. By tying ratlines at 14 inch intervals up the shrouds they are also made to serve as ladders for going aloft.

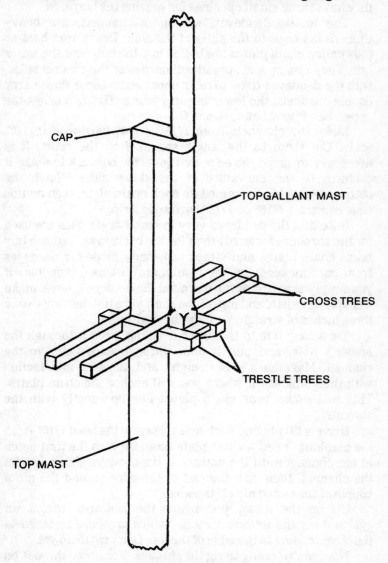

CAP

TOPGALLANT MAST

CROSS TREES

TRESTLE TREES

TOP MAST

Fig. 11-17. Upper doubling.

Because the masts continually strain against the shroud, it is necessary to adjust them frequently. For this purpose an arrangement of deadeyes and lanyards is incorporated into the lower end of each shroud. Deadeyes are similar to bullseyes, but instead of a single large "doughnut hole" in the center, they have three small openings for reeving the lanyards.

The lowest deadeyes, set up in channels, are heavy timbers fastened to the sides of the ship. Heavy iron bars or rods called *chain plates* are bolted into the hull near the water line. They rise up and spread outboard over the channel sides, with the deadeyes fixed to their upper ends. Some ships carry double channels, the lower channel four or five feet below the upper. See Figs. 11-18A, B, and C.

Make the channels from 1/16″ × 1/4″ hardwood in 1/8″ scale. Cut them to the length specified by the plans. It is necessary to shape the edge that joins the bulwark to make it conform to the curvature of the ship's sides. Notch the outboard edge to accommodate each chain plate, then on this edge cement a 1/16″ × 1/16″ hardwood strip.

Note that the deadeyes vary in size. Larger ones are used for the shrouds (forward) than for the backstays. You can buy brass chain plates and straps especially made for deadeyes from partsmakers, but the results are just as satisfactory if you simply use wire. Wrap it around the deadeye groove, make a couple of twists, and nip off the short wire tail, leaving two or three inches of straight wire for the chain plate.

Tie a long line to the lower doubling, drop it through the lubber's hole, and pull it down through each notch in the channel. Make sure it is straight, and mark its intersection with the plank seam where you will anchor the chain plates. This will make your chain plates line up exactly with the shrouds.

Drive a lill pin into each mark, leaving the head 1/16″ from the planking. Feed a chain plate down through the first notch in the channel until the bottom of the deadeye snugs against the channel, then turn the end of the wire around the pin a couple of times and nip off the waste.

Up on the mast, just below the platform, mount an eyeband for the futtock shrouds, which are lines fastened to the mast leading to the edge of the top. Don't rig them yet.

Now you're ready to rig the shrouds. For lower shrouds on the fore and main masts use heavy black line; on the mizzen use medium weight line. First to be rigged are the center shrouds, so if there are six shroud lines, start with the third and fourth. If there are five shrouds, start with the second and third. Cut a long piece and seize a deadeye at one end. Run the free end up through the lubber's hole, around the squared masthead, and back down to the channel. Seize the line at the masthead, making sure the deadeye is three to five diameters from the channel deadeye when pulled taut. In the free end, seize another deadeye the same distance from the channel.

Set up the lanyards in each pair of deadeyes. Rig all lanyards the same way. You can use either black or tan thread of small diameter. Cut about 6 inch of line, tie a double knot at one end, and clip off the excess. Thread it through the left hole from the back and pull it fairly taut, then lace it up and down through the deadeyes as shown in Fig. 11-18B. Tie it off around the bottom of the channel deadeye and clip the waste.

When both shrouds are rigged, turn the ship around and rig the corresponding shrouds on the opposite side. Now rig the shrouds on either side of those in place (second and fifth or first and fourth) the same way, except there is no seizing at the masthead for these shrouds. Make all the deadeyes come the same distance from the channels, so they make a level row. If there is an odd shroud (third, fifth, or seventh), rig it last. Set it up on the starboard side, take it up around the masthead and back down to the corresponding point on the port side.

To make ratlines, paint contact cement on the shrouds and on a piece of fine black line several inches long. As shown in Fig. 11-18C, wind the line to and fro up the shrouds at intervals of slightly over one scale foot. Press each ratline firmly against every shroud to form a good bond. When you've gone all the way to the top, trim the excess loops off each side of the shrouds.

After a couple of days, lightly paint the shrouds with flat black paint or else they'll collect dust and turn gray. To complete the lower shrouds, cut a 1/32″ square strip, paint it black, and cement it across the shrouds resting just above the deadeyes. This is called the sheer pole, and its purpose is to stiffen the shrouds.

To make the *futtock* shrouds, wire deadeyes as you did the channel deadeyes. Feed the wire tails down through the holes in the edges of the top and crimp them through eyebolts in the eyeband below the cheeks. Rig the topmast shrouds as you did

DEADEYE

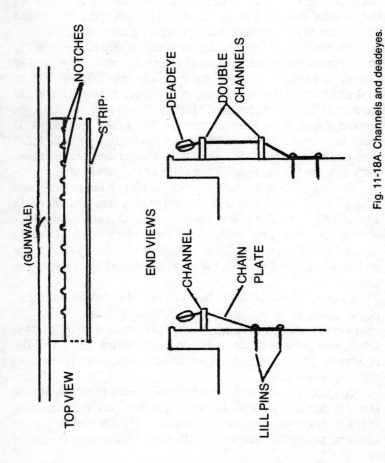

Fig. 11-18A. Channels and deadeyes.

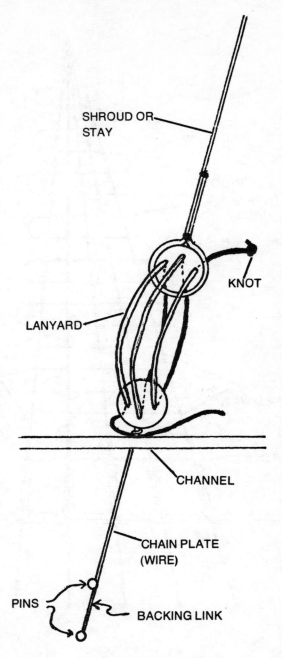

SHROUD OR
STAY

KNOT

LANYARD

CHANNEL

CHAIN PLATE
(WIRE)

PINS

BACKING LINK

Fig. 11-18B. Lanyards.

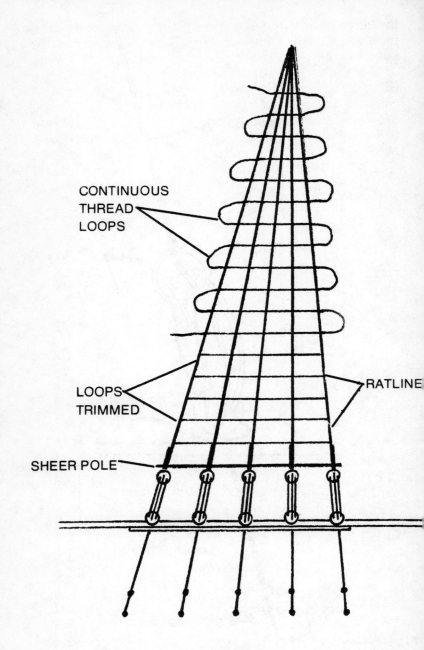

CONTINUOUS
THREAD
LOOPS

LOOPS
TRIMMED

RATLINE

SHEER POLE

Fig. 11-18C. Ratlines.

the lower shrouds, using medium black line on the fore and main and light line on the mizzen. Ratlines are applied the same way. See Fig. 11-19.

For the topgallant futtock shrouds, rig from an eyeband below the upper trestle trees to holes drilled at the ends of the crosstrees. You can use twine for these futtocks rather than wire. Instead of deadeyes, use small bullseyes with light cord for the shrouds, which terminate at the rigging point below the royal yard.

When all the masts are erected, set up the stays and backstays. Also, you can complete the rigging of the headgear now, including the running lines.

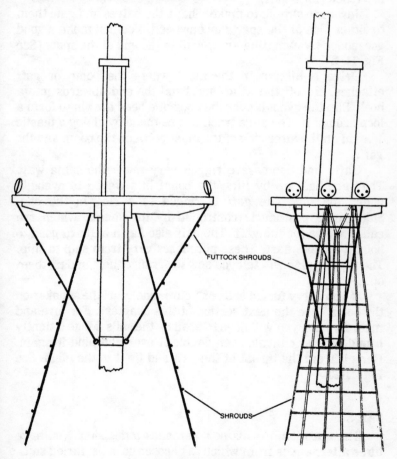

FUTTOCK SHROUDS

SHROUDS

Fig. 11-19. Futtock shrouds.

GAFFS AND BOOMS

Gaffs and booms should now be made and rigged. All ships carry a large fore-and-aft sail astern, called the spanker or mainsail depending on the rig. Some also carry trysail gaffs on the fore and main.

On older vessels, gaffs and booms join the mast by means of jaws, a y-shaped affair at the end of the spar. The jaws slip around the mast, with the open side secured by a lashing of lines with either rollers or a leather sleeve to permit the spar to move. In newer vessels, the jaws are replaced by a flexible gooseneck that either bolts to the mast (for a boom) or slides in a track (for a gaff).

Jaws are simple to make. Shape the halves and glue them to either side of the spar's inboard end. You can make a good gooseneck by mounting an eyebolt in the end of the spar. (See Fig. 11-4.)

Drive a lill pin in the mast where the boom or gaff attaches, cut off the head, and bend the end upwards into a hook. Slip the eyebolt over the hook and bend the pin to form a loop around it. The slide track can be made by gluing a plastic I-beam on the after side of the mast between the boom and the gaff.

Gaffs and booms are rigged very much the same way. They are held up by lifts, the boom lifts rigged to eyebolts under the top. The gaff is rigged to a ring in the cap. Side-to-side position is controlled by the sheets, which are called vangs for the gaff. The gaff also has a halliard used to hoist it up the mast. These purchases vary from ship to ship. The rigging plan will tell you how to arrange them and tie them off.

If you carry furled sails on your model, furl the spanker on the boom (see the next section of this chapter). For fore and main trysails, you will need to brail up the sails. Make a tightly bound tube of canvas, then double it over and bind it again. Hang it from the throat of the gaff and tie it to the mast. See Fig. 11-20.

SAILS

The question of sails now demands a decision. You have three alternatives from which to choose: no sails, furled sails, or a full suit of billowing canvas.

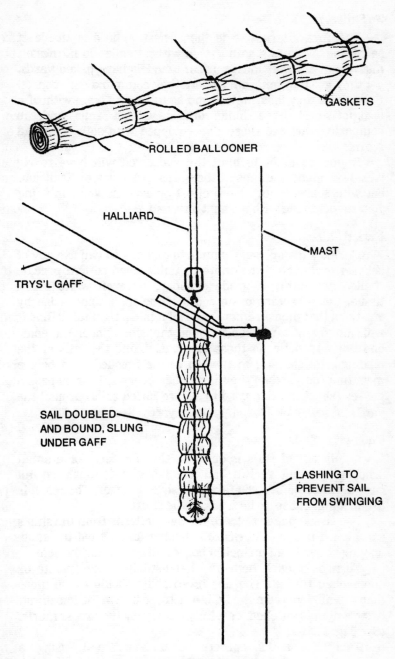

GASKETS

ROLLED BALLOONER

HALLIARD

MAST

TRYS'L GAFF

SAIL DOUBLED
AND BOUND, SLUNG
UNDER GAFF

LASHING TO
PREVENT SAIL
FROM SWINGING

Fig. 11-20. Brailed-up trysail.

No Sails

The first alternative is the easiest. It is also the least satisfying. What is a sailing ship without sails? In fairness, I must point out that most museum models have naked yards, yet they got into museums where they command our respect. But I think they look lifeless and as futile as a train without a locomotive. I have built models without sails and, in comparing them to those I've equipped with sails, I've had regrets.

If you do elect to omit the sails, you will have to rig jackstays along the tops of the yards. It's not a difficult job, but with scarcely any more effort or expense you can bring your model to life with the next alternative.

Furled Sails

Furled sails are very simple to make. You can use any of several materials: fine white or unbleached cottom percale (ballooner cloth), 00-grade silkspan, or even white facial tissue. Cut a rectangle the width of the sail's upper edge by one-third that measurement and roll it into a tight tube. Bind it with lengths of tan thread around the center, near the ends, and halfway between these lashings. Using the tails of the bindings, tie the sail to the top of the finished yard before mounting the yard on the mast. Then every 1/4" or so pass a gasket (short tan line used to secure furled sails) around the yard and sail to pull it snugly to the yard. (See Fig. 11-20.)

Full Suit of Sails

A full suit of sails is quite another matter. For a small schooner it's not such a bad job, but give it much careful consideration before you take on a square-rigger. The result is astonishing, but so, to be frank, is the effort.

Use tissue paper to trace the sail patterns from the ship's sail plan. Pin the patterns to ballooner and cut out the sails, leaving at least half an inch of border all around for the hem.

Turn over each hem and hand-stitch it using white or unbleached thread. The line of stitching should be no more than a scale foot from the fold. It helps to iron in the folds first. After a hem is stitched, carefully trim away the excess fabric. (See Fig. 11-21.)

Tack the sail's corners to a board and, using a straightedge and a sharp pencil, draw in the vertical stitch lines, reinforcements, and other features. See Steele's book and your sail plan for exact details.

In each lower corner of the sail use a needle to pull through a thread knotted on one end. Thumbtack the upper edge of the sail to the edge of a small piece of lumber, (for example, two feet of 1 inch × 6 inch shelving stock). Tack the corner threads to the board, so that when the board is held horizontal with the sail hanging down, the sail has the appearance of being bellied out on the wind. See Fig. 11-22.

Dunk the sail in a bowl containing a concentrated mixture of starch and water, at least ten times as much starch as the

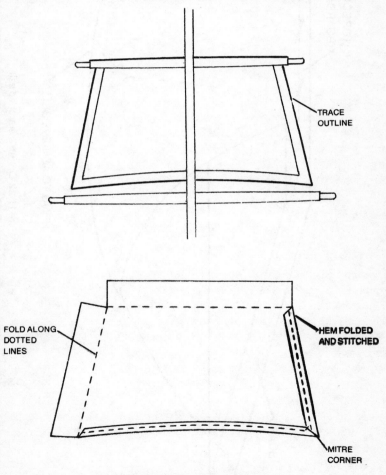

Fig. 11-21. Making a sail from a pattern.

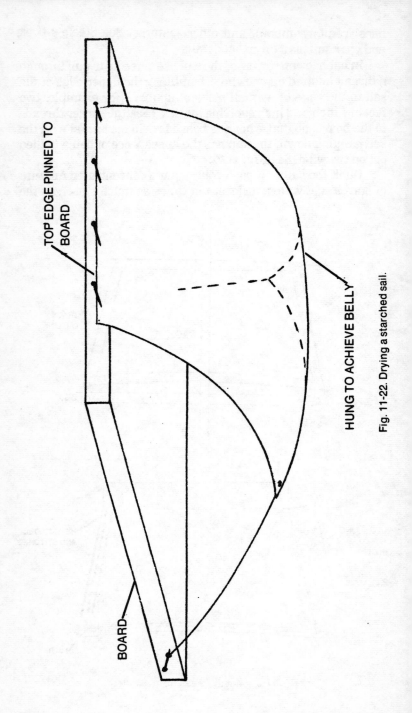

TOP EDGE PINNED TO BOARD

HUNG TO ACHIEVE BELLY

BOARD

Fig. 11-22. Drying a starched sail.

normal concentration. Hang the sail to dry bellied out under the board.

When it has dried, remove it from the board and carefully iron it with the iron on a low setting. Be especially careful to maintain the curl of the sail.

Finally, using Elmer's glue, cement on the reefing points (lengths of rope passing through the sail in rows). Attach blocks and lines as required, and glue the top of the sail to the completed yard.

As you can imagine, a suit of sails for a big square-rigger is a big job. A clipper takes about 25 sails. If you do it, you'll create something surpassing the magnificent, but the decision to do so should not be taken lightly.

Yards

Yards are more complex than the casual glance reveals, but not especially difficult to make. Study the rigging plan for your model, and note that the yards can be divided into the two categories of lower and upper. Lower yards include the course and topsail yards and the crossjack. These are heavy spars, octagonal at the center, then going to a round that tapers uniformly outward to the projecting tips, or yardarms, at the ends. The lowest yard attaches to the mast below the cheeks via an iron swivel truss. (See Fig. 11-3.)

On a single-topsail rig, the topsail yard, like the upper yards, slides up and down the mast but is secured to it by means of a parral passing from the yard around the mast and back to the yard. On the double-topsail rigs, popular during the clipper era, the lower topsail yard is usually a smaller copy of the course yard, including the truss. The upper yards—topgallant, royal, skysail—omit the octagonal section, being round from end to end. Otherwise, they are similar to the lower yards in their fittings and features. All upper yards have parrals. Their diameter decreases in direct proportion to length.

Because taper is important to the apperance of yards, it is easiest to make them from the tappered stock sold by Marine Models. If you want to make them yourself, use a square boxwood strip. Shave it to an octagonal shape and then cut in the tapers with a small plane, and finally round it as necessary by sanding the octagon edges. Note that the octagonal part of a lower yard does not taper, only the round. See Fig. 11-23.

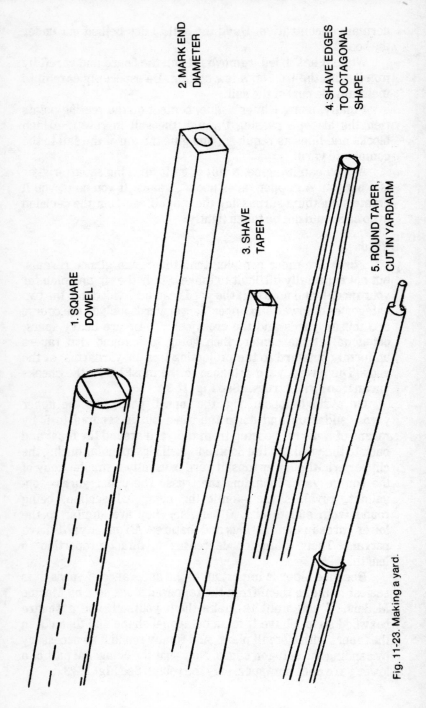

1. SQUARE DOWEL

2. MARK END DIAMETER

3. SHAVE TAPER

4. SHAVE EDGES TO OCTAGONAL SHAPE

5. ROUND TAPER, CUT IN YARDARM

Fig. 11-23. Making a yard.

Carve out the yardarms, making the ends round. According to the rigging plan, mount cleats and yokes made of small slivers of scrap wood. Drill holes for the sheaves using a #70 bit on the upper yards and a 1/32″ or even 1/16″ bit on the lower spars.

Shipwrights often got fanciful in painting the top hamper. Often, for instance, the lower yards are natural on the octagon and yardarms and black on the tapered round, with the upper spars reversing this scheme by being black between the center eyebands and at the arms and natural elsewhere. Use flat paints for colors and walnut modelers' stain for natural. No varnish is necessary.

Yard trusses are best purchased as brass or Britannia metal fittings. Where the swivel fitting occurs below the hounds, glue a black paper band around the mast and mount two jackstay eyebolts, one above the other. To mount the yard, slip the eye of the truss between the eyebolts and drop a lill pin through the three openings, then cut off the lower end of the pin.

Before you mount the yards, however, you have some work to do. First, use black paper strips to make the bands and mount jackstay eyebolts wherever lines tie to the yard. If your yards will be without sails, mount a row of eyebolts at intervals of 18 inches to 24 inches in scale along the top of the yard. Thread the jackstay—a piece of fine black line—through the eyebolts, tying it as the last eyebolt on each end to make it taut.

Sails or no, the next step is to mount footropes, upon which the seamen stand as they make the furl sail. On short yards, the footropes start at the yardarm eyeband and cross at the center. On long yards, they are periodically supported by stirrups. The Flemish horse, shown in Fig. 11-3, is added at the ends.

Make footropes from fine black annealed wire. Drill holes in the top of the yard for the stirrups, which are also wire. Cut a short length of wire, insert the tip in the hole and bring it down to hang under the yard. Straighten a long wire, turn it around the yardarm, and bring it to each stirrup. Crimp the end of the stirrup around the footrope and work the catenary into the footrope so that it appears to hang limp and natural. Use the same techniques to make the Flemish horse. A small vise is very handy during this stage of construction.

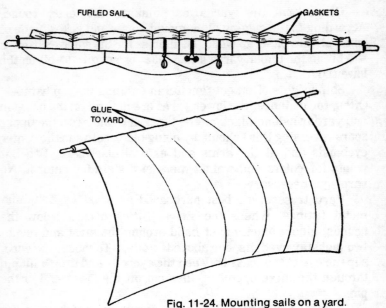

FURLED SAIL

GASKETS

GLUE TO YARD

Fig. 11-24. Mounting sails on a yard.

Now, if you have furled or unfurled sails to mount, attach them. Furled sails should be firmly tied down with a gasket every scale foot or so. Eliminate large bulges and lumps in the sail as you work outward from the center. Unfurled sails can be cemented to the yard using Elmers glue. Make sure it bellies out correctly with respect to the yokes or truss. (See Fig. 11-24.)

Mount the lowest yard first and work upward. You will find it necessary to rig temporary lifts to keep the yards from swinging around and possibly breaking their mountings. As you do, make each yard as nearly horizontal as possible.

The truss mounting was discussed a few paragraphs ago. Parral mountings are quite simple. Drill two small holes in each yoke and tie a 6 inch piece of black thread in one hole, leaving both tails. On each tail thread a few black hobby beads. Bring the yard to the mast and draw one of the tails through the other yoke hole. Tie the tails securely and tautly with a square knot, and clip off the excess. See Figs. 11-25A and B.

The course yard, lacking a halliard, is supported by a group of tackles known as the slings and jeers. On older vessels these tackles are seized up using heavy black hawsers.

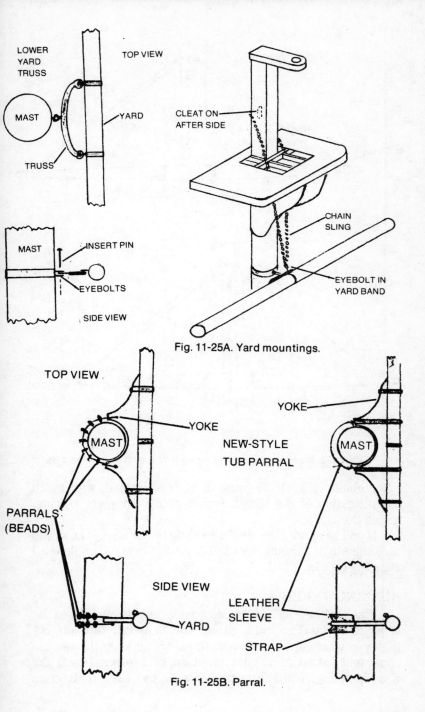

LOWER YARD TRUSS

MAST

YARD

TRUSS

TOP VIEW

MAST

INSERT PIN

EYEBOLTS

SIDE VIEW

CLEAT ON AFTER SIDE

CHAIN SLING

EYEBOLT IN YARD BAND

Fig. 11-25A. Yard mountings.

TOP VIEW

MAST

YOKE

YOKE

MAST

NEW-STYLE TUB PARRAL

PARRALS (BEADS)

SIDE VIEW

YARD

LEATHER SLEEVE

STRAP

Fig. 11-25B. Parral.

333

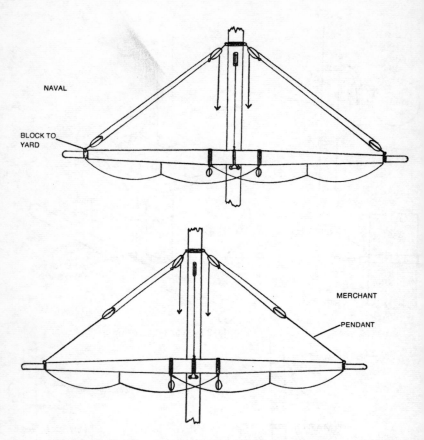

Fig. 11-26. Naval vs. merchant rigging (Lift shown as an example).

After about 1820, chain came to be used instead, with much simplification of the slings. Before doing any more rigging, install the tackles.

If you have not already done so, rig the backstays now, and also the stays running forward from the mast. Complete all standing rigging.

RUNNING RIGGING

The next several figures deal with running rigging, in the order in which it should be done. This is an intricate job, but highly rewarding. As you add lines, try to keep the tension consistent so that some lines do not sag while others twang like a violin string. While adjusting tension, pay careful attention

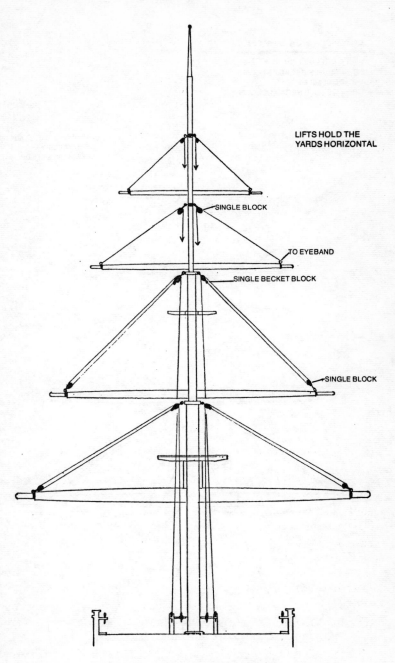

LIFTS HOLD THE
YARDS HORIZONTAL

SINGLE BLOCK

TO EYEBAND

SINGLE BECKET BLOCK

SINGLE BLOCK

Fig. 11-27. Lifts for a warship.

335

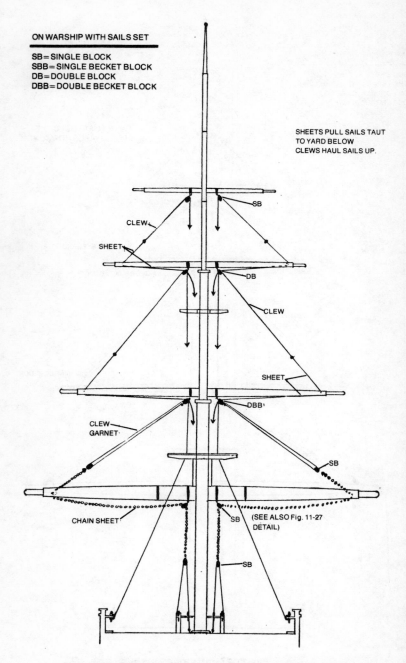

SHEETS PULL SAILS TAUT
TO YARD BELOW
CLEWS HAUL SAILS UP.

SB

CLEW

SHEET

DB

CLEW

SHEET

DBB

CLEW
GARNET

SB

CHAIN SHEET

SB

(SEE ALSO Fig. 11-27
DETAIL)

SB

Fig. 11-28. Sheets and clews with sails furled or omitted.

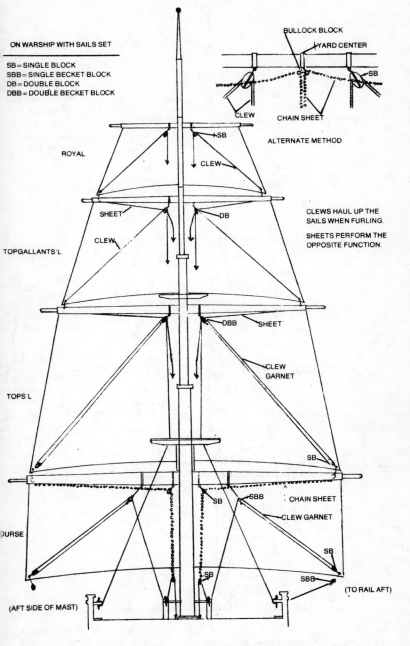

ON WARSHIP WITH SAILS SET

SB = SINGLE BLOCK
SBB = SINGLE BECKET BLOCK
DB = DOUBLE BLOCK
DBB = DOUBLE BECKET BLOCK

BULLOCK BLOCK
YARD CENTER
SB

CLEW   CHAIN SHEET

ALTERNATE METHOD

ROYAL

SB

CLEW

CLEWS HAUL UP THE
SAILS WHEN FURLING.

SHEETS PERFORM THE
OPPOSITE FUNCTION.

SHEET

DB

CLEW

TOPGALLANTS'L

DBB   SHEET

CLEW
GARNET

TOPS'L

SB

SB   SBB   CHAIN SHEET

CLEW GARNET

SB

OURSE

SB

SBB   (TO RAIL AFT)

(AFT SIDE OF MAST)

Fig. 11-29. Sheets and clews on warship with sails set.

337

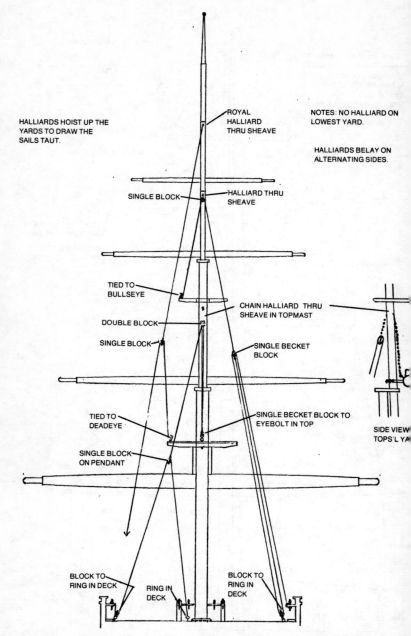

HALLIARDS HOIST UP THE
YARDS TO DRAW THE
SAILS TAUT.

ROYAL
HALLIARD
THRU SHEAVE

NOTES: NO HALLIARD ON
LOWEST YARD.

HALLIARDS BELAY ON
ALTERNATING SIDES.

SINGLE BLOCK

HALLIARD THRU
SHEAVE

TIED TO
BULLSEYE

CHAIN HALLIARD THRU
SHEAVE IN TOPMAST

DOUBLE BLOCK

SINGLE BLOCK

SINGLE BECKET
BLOCK

TIED TO
DEADEYE

SINGLE BECKET BLOCK TO
EYEBOLT IN TOP

SINGLE BLOCK
ON PENDANT

SIDE VIEW
TOPS'L YA

BLOCK TO
RING IN DECK

RING IN
DECK

BLOCK TO
RING IN
DECK

Fig. 11-30. Halliards hoist up the yards to draw the sails taut. Note there is no halliard on the lowest yard, and that halliards belay on alternating sides.

338

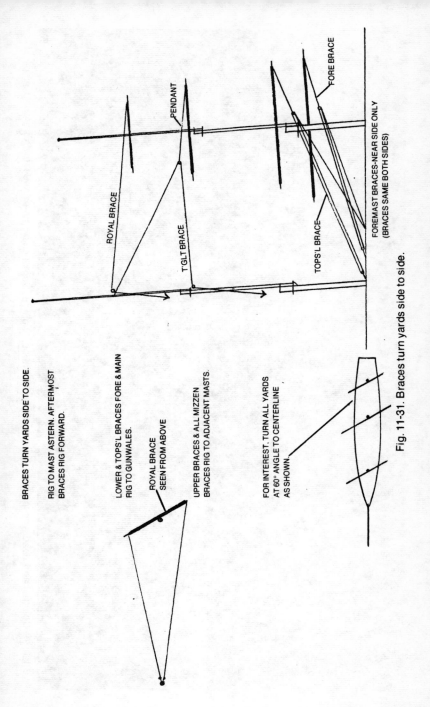

BRACES TURN YARDS SIDE TO SIDE.

RIG TO MAST ASTERN. AFTERMOST BRACES RIG FORWARD.

ROYAL BRACE

PENDANT

T'GLT BRACE

FORE BRACE

TOPS'L BRACE

FOREMAST BRACES–NEAR SIDE ONLY (BRACES SAME BOTH SIDES)

LOWER & TOPS'L BRACES FORE & MAIN RIG TO GUNWALES.

ROYAL BRACE SEEN FROM ABOVE

UPPER BRACES & ALL MIZZEN BRACES RIG TO ADJACENT MASTS.

FOR INTEREST, TURN ALL YARDS AT 60° ANGLE TO CENTERLINE AS SHOWN.

Fig. 11-31. Braces turn yards side to side.

339

Plate 4. Channel and deadeyes for main shrouds on "Constellation." Note spacing of chain plates and lanyards around gunports.

to what the other lines are doing. If some suddenly go slack, you are applying too much tension.

The drawings included here are for a warship. The only real difference between warship and merchant rigging has to do with economies of rope. Merchants favored the use of pendants to bring a block closer to its partner and thus save on hemp costs. This is demonstrated by the example of the lift shown in Fig. 11-26.

Figures 11-27 through 11-31 show the most common running lines. They are, of course, generalizations and should be regarded as such. The rigging plan of your ship should always be your primary guide. In case of any doubt, refer to Steele's book or the *Young Sea Officer's Sheet Anchor*.

Chapter 12

Finishing Touches

The rigging of the ship is the last major operation in the building of a ship model. You could now put your model in a case and display it with justifiable pride.

With a little more effort, though, you can bring you model to life by adding small details. They take little time, and each individually probably adds almost nothing, but in the aggregate they bring life to the decks and a sense of perspective, telling a story of seafaring in the 19th Century.

DAVITS

Boats were discussed in Chapter 9 and instructions were provided for those boats lashed atop the core cabin. *Davits* are required to suspend boats capable of being hoisted outboard, and some ships carry empty davits to act as cranes or hoists for boats normally carried on skids amidships.

On older ships, the davits are usually nothing more than straight stout timbers fixed to the bulwarks so they angle up and outboard. If a boat is to hang in the davits, place them so that the ends are directly over the boat's ends.

On warships and large merchantmen with this type of davits amidships, you will often find a pair of davits piercing the transom. They anchor in the quarterdeck for the purpose of carrying the captain's gig, a small launch, outboard of the transom. Usually they have sheaves similar to those in the

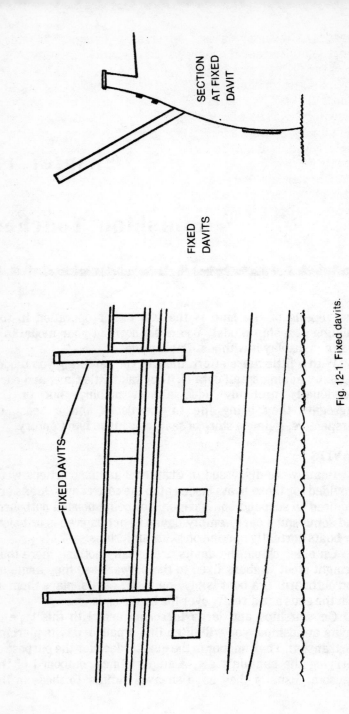

FIXED DAVITS

SECTION
AT FIXED
DAVIT

Fig. 12-1. Fixed davits.

catheads. Although almost universally equipped in this manner, warships seem to have seldom actually carried a boat here. See Figs. 12-1 and 12-2.

Whaling vessels also have fixed timbers as davits, but in this case the davits rise up straight and then curve outboard. Sheaves are used to accommodate the falls (tackles to hoist the boats). Because whaling boats are of thin wood and quite flexible, movable rests are fastened to the bulwarks to support the boats while hoisted in.

Newer vessels have socket-mounted metal davits. These davits rotate, so that by turning them, a boat may be either rested on deck or swung outboard for hoisting out. Sheaves are replaced by an eye to which a block is seized or shackled. The socket either rests on a flat surface, such as a deck or the gunwale, or else bolts to the side of the ship.

Setting up a boat in davits is a simple operation. Install an eyebolt at each end of the boat and attach to it a single becket block. Reeve the fall through the davit sheave or a double block on the davit eye. Bring it back down through the becket block, through the other sheave of the davit, and belay it to a cleat on the davit. Rig the falls, so that the boat hangs level just below the davit blocks. If these are socket davits, turn them to bend toward each other, leaving some extra in the falls as shown in Fig. 12-3.

Rig falls on socket davits even if they are empty. Set an eyebolt with a single becket block in the deck adjacent to the socket and rig the fall just as it is done on a boat. This adds a realistic aspect to an otherwise neglected-looking fitting. Don't bother, though, on fixed davits.

If the boat hangs inboard, fashion a pair of boat rests from scrap, and glue them between the garboards and the deck to give the appearance that the boat is sitting on them. On fixed davits, (except whaling ships, whose rests have already been mentioned and shown in Fig. 9-32) lash a spar to the inboard sides of the davits, which is the usual method of storing the boats mast. Lash the boat to the spar, so it won't swing.

HUMAN FIGURES

Human figures make a tremendous contribution to any model by adding not only the perspective of relative size, but a point of reference with which the viewer can personally identify.

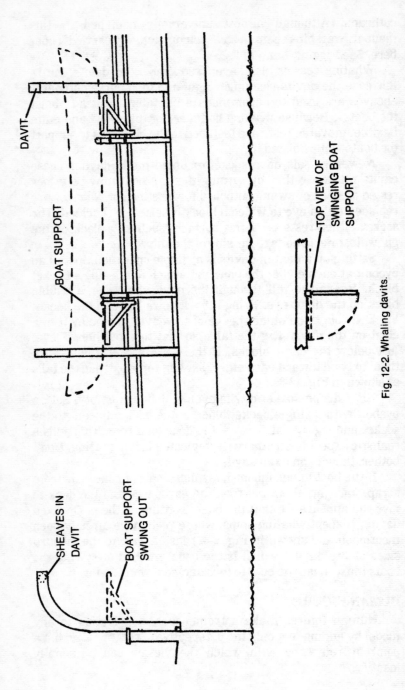

DAVIT

BOAT SUPPORT

TOP VIEW OF
SWINGING BOAT
SUPPORT

SHEAVES IN
DAVIT

BOAT SUPPORT
SWUNG OUT

Fig. 12-2. Whaling davits.

Figures are easy to come by. The partsmakers usually carry them in several scales and periods of attire. You can also use model railroad figures, which are generally better detailed and scaled than the white metal fittings. For 1/8" scale, use HO gauge; for 3/16", S gauge (harder to find, though); and for 1/4", O gauge.

Use care, though, in selecting model railroad figures. A man in a business suit or a woman in a short dress obviously doesn't belong on an 1815 warship. On the other hand, a conductor makes a very fine officer for your clipper's quarterdeck, and a laboring man with a shovel in hand can easily go to sea to swab a deck; just glue a little ballooner or a mop of threads to his shovel blade.

Even one figure will do nicely, but several are better. Avoid a bunch of lookalikes, though. Get people in various poses and positions and scatter them around the ship doing real jobs or walking purposefully from one place to another.

Get at least one man into the top hamper, even if he's just standing at the fore crosstrees or on a top. If you can find a climbing figure, glue him on the shrouds.

Some railroad figures come with a piece of ground as a base. Cut it off and trim the feet to proportion before you glue the man to the deck. Also, you may find it necessary or desirable to repaint clothing. Seamen in the last century usually wore odds and ends of clothing, even on naval vessels. The trousers should be blue, but the shirt can be any color. A straw hat was often worn but bare heads are okay, and so are billed baseball caps late in the century.

The impression of activity is important. Few people stand around with their arms at their sides on a ship. Put your people to work painting, hauling lines, repairing something, pumping the bilge. Be as realistic as you can. No one need man the helm if the sails are furled, but you better have a hand at the wheel if you're under sail, and an officer on deck too.

OTHER SIGNS OF LIFE

Signs of life can be given in other ways besides simply with people. A little realistic clutter really livens the old place up. Set up a temporary carpenter shop, for example, with a pair of sawhorses and a partially made part, and glue a bunch of small shavings from your scrap pile to the deck. Leave a few hanks of rope around the fife rails, especially where a man is

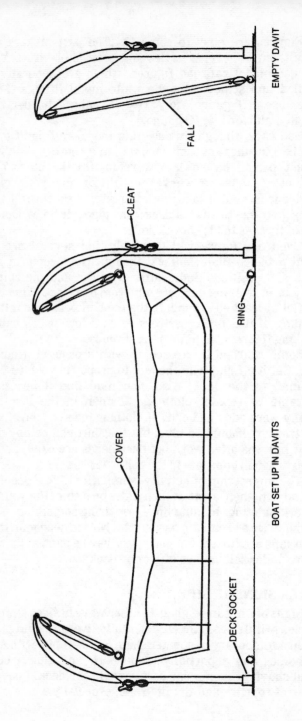

FALL

CLEAT

RING

COVER

DECK SOCKET

EMPTY DAVIT

BOAT SET UP IN DAVITS

Fig. 12-3. Socket davits.

348

at work. If someone is painting, make sure he has a bucket at his side and that you can see the old and new paint jobs.

Small touches like these can add not only realism from an activity viewpoint, but also tell something about what life was like under sail and the kinds of jobs that were commonplace.

A sailmaker, for instance, would tell an interesting story. Get a seated figure, put him on a hatch coaming, and heap a bunch of balloner on the deck at his feet and draped over his knees. A cooper is also appropriate. Show him assembling a cask with several completed barrels standing around and some staves stacked up in bunches. On a warship or armed merchantman, you can have people preparing to fire or moving a gun on deck with hauling lines.

It's possible to carry this idea to a fascinating extreme. Take a whaler, for example. You could have several men involved in a flensing operation, stripping blubber off a carcass and cutting it into chunks on deck, with all the attendant gore of the job. Have another man tending the try works. Such a touch would be quite a job, of course. I'm not saying it is necessary to take it this far, but it certainly would be rewarding.

Another realistic touch is the inclusion of farm animals. During the early part of a long voyage, sailing vessels usually carried a live steer or two, a couple of hogs, and a bunch of chickens. Pens were erected on deck, often atop the cargo hatches. Seamen who had run afoul of shipboard discipline shoveled the manure overboard, changed the straw, and tended the creatures' food and water.

Use your imagination to create scenarios of life on deck. Do some research to learn more about your ship, with an eye to recreating it in miniature.

EVERYDAY OBJECTS

Everyday objects found on the deck of a sailing vessel deserve mention here. Every ship has a scuttlebutt, a large tub found amidships and used as a drinking fountain. Somewhere around the forward deckhouse on a merchantman you will also find water casks. In clippers and other later vessels these are rectangular tanks. See Fig. 12-4.

All ships have many buckets. Several are found in racks at the deck breaks, in which case the buckets are of the usual shape. Freestanding buckets and sponge tubs are also

DECK BUCKET

SPONGE TUB

BELFRY

BUCKET RACK

WATER CASK

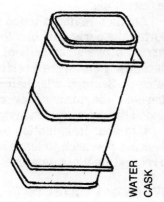

CASK

Fig. 12-4. Everyday objects found on ships.

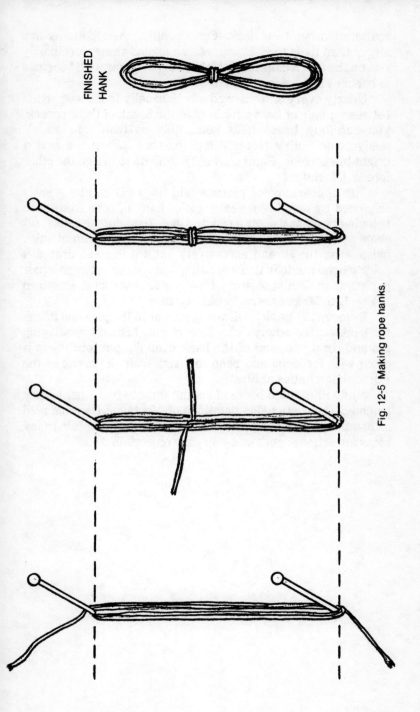

FINISHED HANK

Fig. 12-5 Making rope hanks.

scattered around on deck. For stability, their bottoms are larger than their tops. Shot racks on armed vessels ordinarily rest on the hatch coamings. Make them by gluing ball bearings or beebees into holes drilled in wooden strips.

Nearly every ship carried a bell, usually found suspended between a pair of heavy timbers at the break of the foredeck. You can buy brass bells separately or built into an already-made belfry from fittings makers. Leave the bell a bright brass color. Paint the belfry timbers to match the other foredeck furniture.

The appearance of pinrails and fife rails can be greatly enhanced by hanging a neatly coiled hank of rope from each belaying pin that ties off a running line. To make the hanks, set some sewing pins in two rows 1/4" apart in a scrap of thick balsa. Wax the thread excessively, until it is so saturated it holds a bend made in it. Take half a dozen turns between a pair of pins, then tie a knot around the center of the hank as shown in Fig. 12-5. Make several hanks at a time.

Remove the hank by drawing out one of the pins and lifting the hank off the other. Put a drop of glue behind the belaying pin and drop one loop of the hank over the pin top. Press it down with foreceps and bend the hank over the break of the rail so that it hangs naturally.

Study illustrated books of sailing ships to find other homey touches. The meticulous paintings of Montague Dawson, sold as prints in hobby magazines and catalogs, also contain many ideas for action scenes and everyday objects on deck.

Chapter 13

Care and Feeding

So now you've built a sailing ship model from scratch, a genuine work of art. It's something in which you can take pride for the rest of your life, a momument to yourself that will be looked upon with reverence by your descendants—*if you take proper care of it*.

THE TEN COMMANDMENTS

A sailing ship model is made for one purpose only; to be looked at through glass. Never, ever, under any circumstances, should it be left in the open, touched, or tinkered with by any save experienced and knowledgeable hands, nor should it be moved without the greatest care and planning.

As a guide to the care and feeding of a ship model, I offer the following Ten Commandments:

1. Thou shalt not suffer the sun to shine directly upon it.
2. Thou shalt permit no dust to settle upon it.
3. Thou shalt subject it to no extremes of temperature or humidity.
4. Thou shalt permit no dust to settle upon it.
5. Thou shalt never apply wax, nor any other chemical to its delicate skin or any part thereof.
6. Thou shalt permit no dust to settle upon it.

7. Thou shalt not move it overmuch, not lift it by any part save the base board, nor let it get out of a horizontal position.
8. Thou shalt permit no dust to settle upon it.
9. Thou shalt permit no oaf to lay upon it his cotton-pickin' hands.
10. Thou shalt permit no dust to settle upon it.

The great enemy, as you may have guessed, is dust. Dust on a model spells disaster. Dust on household surfaces looks bad; on a ship model it not only looks bad, but it brings deterioration.

Dust is awful stuff. It's oily and scummy and dirty and gritty. Dust will discolor paints and eat into surfaces. The oil will seep into porous wood and swell it, causing the finish to crack and the parts of the ship to warp. It will attack the cement bonds and make things fall apart. In the end, a model left unprotected in the open will literally fall to pieces, all from the silent enemy—dust.

A CASE

A case for your ship is an absolute necessity to protect it from dust. With a case you can also satisfy most of the other ten commandments as well.

A case kit from one of the partsmakers will set you back anywhere from $25 to over $100, depending on the size and exclusiveness of the glass. The money is well worth it. Weigh that against the hours you have invested in the model.

You can, however, avoid most of that cost if you are willing to sacrifice the aesthetics of mahogany moldings. With five sheets of glass cut by your hardware dealer, and a tube of silicone aquarium sealer, it is possible to build a perfectly suitable case for about one tenth the cost of a kit, and in considerably less time.

Measure the overall dimensions of your model, including the base board. Make the sides of the case two inches longer than the model, the ends two inches wider, and the height of all sides at least an inch greater. The top will be the length of the case by its width, plus one inch in both directions to create an overhang.

It's heavy stuff, so buy single-strength glass from your glazier so that you'll be able to lift the case. Be sure he finishes the edges so that there are no rough edges and irregularities.

Assemble the case on a large level surface. The only tools you need are masking tape and a piece of cardboard such as the backing from a tablet, cut so that it forms perfect right angles. Form the corners of the case by bonding the sides to the edges of the ends. (See Fig. 13-1.) For this step you need the silicone aquarium sealer. Run a bead along the edge of the glass, avoiding large accumulations, then bring the edge directly and firmly against the other piece to form a joint. Be as exact as you can, and try to avoid smearing the silicone. Around the outside of the top of the corner apply a piece of masking tape to hold the joint. Check that each corner is square by using the cardboard. Assemble the four sides and let

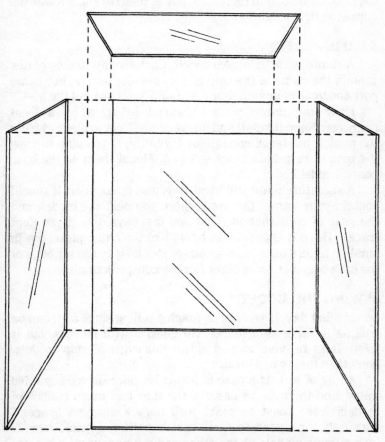

Fig. 13-1. A ship case made from five glass sheets.

the silicone cure for about an hour. Then, run a bead of silicone all around the top edges and set the top of the case in place with a uniform overhang on all sides.

The case will be firmly cemented in twenty-four hours. Remove the masking tape and turn the case over so it rests on the top. Use a razor blade to trim away and scrape off any excess silicone (take care not to cut into the joint!). Use window cleaner to remove the fingerprints inside and outside the case.

To protect the surface the case will rest on, cut very narrow strips of flocked adhesive paper and apply them to the bottom edges of the case.

This type of case is independent of the model. To encase the ship, first set it in its resting place, then *carefully* lower the case over it.

A NAME PLATE

A name plate is a nice touch. Customarily names plates contain the name of the ship and, in smaller letters, her home port and year of launch. For a warship, you can omit the port.

Have the name plate engraved in brass by a local engraver. Keep it small and discreet, so as not to distract from the model, but large enough for legibility. If you plan to view the model from both sides, get two. Mount them on the base board amidships.

A signature plate will identify you as the builder. It should contain your name, the town where you built the model, and the year of construction (first and last days, too, if you kept track). Have it engraved in brass like the name plate, but in smaller letters on a smaller plate. Fasten it to the aft edge of the base board or some other fairly inconspicuous place.

MOVING THE MODEL

Moving day, if you are as much a rolling stone as I, can be traumatic for a ship model. No quarrel with movers, but if they claim to have moved entire museums of ship models, don't take their word for it.

A tale of woe as a case in point: We once moved some 700 miles, and the movers assured me they had taken zillions of models from coast to coast with nary a snagged brace. I trustingly consigned to their vast expertise a brand new 37 inch clipper model. At the other end it came out of a carton.

And came out. And came out. They had simply rammed wadded packing paper around it indiscriminately, so shattering the rigging and the deck detail that it was utterly beyond redemption. I gave the pitiful remains to my young nephew to play with.

Move the model yourself. That way *you* control what happens to it, and if it does break you have only yourself to blame.

The best way to move a model is to put it on a board. Cut a piece of shelving stock ten or twelve inches wide to a length a little greater than the distance from spanker boom to jibboom. Tape the model to it using a very long piece of masking tape. Lay the tape across the gunwales amidships, stretched taut, and bring it around to the underside of the board on both sides, also stretched taut. If you can find another place fore or aft to guy it with a second piece of tape, so much the better.

Ideally, you should make a separate run carrying only the model and other delicate items to your new abode, and put the ship on an upper closet shelf until the commotion is over. If distance prohibits, build a plywood box of the case dimensions and strap it to a car top carrier with the model fastened securely inside. Wrap the box in a tarp for protection from the rain. Considering your time investment and the value of the model, the precautions are worthwhile.

After all, you have created a great work of art. That's exactly what it is. And to survive, like all works of art, it must be carefully protected from the ravages of time, environment, and clumsy man.

AND THEN...

If you're like the rest of us, you'll spend a lot of time admiring what you have done. But more and more you will notice not the tremendous accomplishments, but rather the annoying little mistakes. Others won't, but you'll know they're there, and sooner or later you will find yourself thinking, "It's okay, I guess, but I can do better." And you'll set out to prove it. When this happens, you're hooked.

I hope it does happen, for building model sailing ships from scratch is supreme among hobbies and one of the high forms of human creativity. If you get hooked, this book will have accomplished its objective and the lives of us all will be the better for it.

Glossary

Glossary of
Nautical Terms

abaft—to the aft of, stern.

amidships—to the center of the ship, especially with respect to the length.

athwart—running from side to side, perpendicular to the length of the vessel. When an object such as a beam is so positioned, it is said to rest **athwartships**

bark—a type of vessel rig in which all masts except the one closest to the stern are square-rigged.

barkentine—similar to a bark, except that only the foremast is square-rigged, and all the others are fore-and-aft rigged.

beakhead—the portion of the stem that thrusts farthest forward. The figurehead is often attached to the beakhead.

bee seat—a pair of timbers placed on either side of the bowsprit at its forward end. The bees are used to hold sheaves for the head tackle and as a place to secure standing lines.

bilge—the portion of the hull as viewed in cross section, where the downward curve turns in toward the keel.

billboard—a heavy timber or metal plate abaft the catheads, placed so that it protects the hull from the points, or bills, of the anchor as it is swung up on deck.

binnacle—a stand placed before or near the helm for holding the ship's compass.

bobstay—a chain or heavy rope running from the stem near the waterline to the underside of the bowsprit outboard end. This is a standing line which prevents the bowsprit from jumping or being pulled upward by the strain of the headsails.

boom—any spar that holds down the bottom edge of a sail, or is carried in a horizontal position, with one end secured and the other swinging.

boomkin—(also spelled bumpkin or bumkin) a small stout timber extending outboard from the hull and used as a point for securing rigging.

bowsprit—the spar anchored in the bow of the vessel and extending forward over the water, to which is anchored the jibboom.

breeching—a very heavy rope that passes around the cascabel, or breech, of a naval gun and fastens on either side of the gunport to heavy rings in the bulwarks. Its purpose is to arrest the recoil of the gun.

brig—a two-masted rig, in which both masts are square-rigged, and the mainmast (after-most) also carries a large fore-and-aft sail.

brigantine—a rig similar to a brig, except the mainmast carries no square sails. Also called a hermaphrodite brig.

bulwark—the side of the vessel, especially the part extending above the uppermost deck.

buttock—in seamen's terms, the rounding of the vessel's body around the stern. For naval architects, a buttock is a line on a ship's draft representing the vessel's shape if cut by an imaginary saw held vertically and slicing parallel to the centerline.

cap—a stout block of wood bound by a metal strap and used to secure two spars together at the outboard or upper end of a doubling.

carrack—a type of three-masted vessel popular from the Fourteenth to the early Seventeenth Centuries. The *Mayflower* is a late carrack.

cathead—a heavy timber angling outboard and forward near the bow. The cathead is used as a crane for lifting and handling the anchor.

chamfer—to cut the sharp edge off, or bevel the edge or end of a timber.

clews—the two lower corners of a square sail. The clewlines, often called simply the clews, haul the clews of a sail to the yard above when the sail is to be furled.

clipper—an extremely fast, slender, and graceful vessel that had a brief popularity in the 1850s. Most clippers were square-riggers, but a few were barks.

coaming—a raised sill in a hatchway or surrounding the hatch opening in a deck, to prevent water taken on deck from entering the vessel's interior.

crosstrees—timbers attached to a mast and running athwartships at the lower end of a doubling.

cutwater—the portion of the stem at the waterline.

deadrise—viewed in cross section, the rise of the ship's bottom from the keel to the bilges.

doubling—the point at which the upper end of a lower mast, and the lower end of a higher mast run parallel. The doubling is secured at each end to give the upper mast a rigid foundation.

down easter—a large and swift freighting ship that evolved from the clipper. Many naval historians regard the down easter as the pinnacle of sailing ship development, but they failed to gain widespread popularity due to competition with steam. Down easters were the last square-riggers produced as a class.

downhaul—a line used to assist gravity in hauling down a sail.

draught (or draft)—the drawing of a vessel, especially of her lines.

fiddlehead—a decorative carving sometimes used in lieu of a figurehead.

fife rail—the railing found at the foot of a mast, to which running lines are belayed.

fore-and-aft—the manner in which a sail is usually carried, in which its forward edge is secured to the mast, and it may be swung from side to side. A fore-and-aft rigged vessel has all her sails this way, e.g. a schooner or a modern sloop-rigged yacht.

forefoot—the most forward part of the keel, to which the stem attaches.

frigate—a three-masted square-rigged ship of war that carries guns on her spar deck and on a gun deck. Frigates were the most versatile warships under sail. Two early American frigates, the *Constitution* and the *Constellation*, both dating from 1797, still survive.

futtock—(also spelled futhook) in the hull frames, futtocks are the pieces of timber of which the frames are made by bolting them together. In the top hamper, futtocks are short shrouds, spreading from just below the hounds to the outer edges of the top.

gaff—a boom that angles upward for the purpose of securing and holding aloft the top edge of a fore-and-aft sail.

galleon—a type of ship that evolved from the carrack in the 1500's. The galleon carried three masts and high castles fore-and-aft, with a sleek bottom that gave her speed.

gammoning—a winding of heavy rope around the inboard end of the bowsprit and through a slot in the stem to secure the sprit. In later vessels, the gammoning became a heavy steel band.

garboard strake—the hull plank, or strake, that adjoins the keel on either side.

gudgeon strop—the straps fixed to the sternpost and the hull and forming loops into which the pintles, or rudder hinges, are inserted.

gun deck—the first deck below, on which the heavy guns of a frigate are carried. The gun deck may be entirely covered or open in the waist.

gunwale—(pronounced "gunnel")—the upper edge of a vessel's sides or bulwarks.

halliard—a rope or tackle belonging to the running rigging, and used to haul yards or fore-and-aft sails up the mast to drawing position.

hawse holes—the openings in the bow of the vessel through which the anchor cables pass.

hawser—a very heavy hemp rope used primarily as the anchor cable.

headrails—the decorative basket of railings carried on large vessels under the bowsprit. The headrails also held the "seats of ease" used by sailors, hence the naval term "head" as used to describe a bathroom.

hog—a condition found on most wooden vessels, and some modern ships, in which the keel droops at the ends. This is caused by the uneven strain along the keel, since the ends of the vessel have less buoyancy than the midships portion, and thus force the keel down at the bow and stern, while forcing it upward amidships.

hounds—heavy flat timbers bolted to the masthead to act as shoulders for the trestle trees, and thus support the top.

jackstay—a long strip of wood or iron bolted to the top of a yard or the underside of a gaff, to which the sail is bent (laced).

jibboom—the long spar projecting forward from the bowsprit.

kedge—a small anchor, usually of the iron stock type, used as an auxiliary anchor. To "kedge the ship," meant to winch her through shallows when the wind was calm. This was done by carrying the kedge well ahead of the vessel by longboat, then winching in the cable with the windlass, thus drawing the ship forward.

knighthead—a stout timber always appearing in a pair and usually projecting above the foredeck. Below, the knightheads support the bowsprit; above, they often serve as a tying-off point for running or standing lines.

knuckle—a point on a hull where the upward curvature takes a sudden change of direction.

martingale—a short spar hanging from the bowsprit cap to spread the headstays. Also sometimes called the dolphin striker.

packet ship—any vessel that operates according to a schedule. In the 1830s, a vessel type called the packet was developed, having a full hull but uncommonly sharp bows. It was from this type that the clipper seems to have evolved.

parral—a rope or iron collar that holds a yard to the mast, but allows it to move vertically and to swivel.

pintle—an assembly of a metal strap bolted around the fore edge of the rudder and a stout pin held to the leading edge. The pin points down and enters the loop formed by the gudgeon strops, thus completing a sort of hinge for the rudder to turn on.

rake—the angle at which a mast leans astern.

ratlines—light cord tied to the shrouds 14″ apart and parallel to the sheer of the ship to act as rungs of a rope ladder leading aloft.

run—the long finlike portion of a ship's underside, from amidships to the sternpost.

schooner—a rig in which the main drawing sails are rigged fore-and-aft, but some square sails may also be carried. Schooners were extremely successful as a type, and many operated into the 1950s as working ships.

scupper—a small drain hole in the deck near the waterways, used to carry water overboard from the deck.

sheave—a grooved wheel for carrying a line around a corner, as in a block or built into a cathead or bulwark.

sheer—the upward curve of a ship's deck, both directions from amidships.

sheet—a rope or tackle used to pull a sail's clews (lower corners) snug to the yard below and hold it so that it draws in the wind. On the spanker and other boom sails, the sheet controls the movement of the boom from side to side.

shrouds—heavy ropes or, occasionally, cables passing around the masthead and spreading to points of attachment below, for supporting the masts from the sides. The lower shrouds are fixed to the ship's sides, the upper, to the rim of the top or the crosstrees.

snow—a ship's rig very similar to a brig, the difference being that a brig carries her fore-and-aft mainsail directly on the mast, while a snow has a small spar fixed to the mainmast and parallel to it for carrying the mainsail. On fully-rigged ships of three masts, a similar mast for carrying the spanker on the mizzen is sometimes called the snow mast.

spanker—the large fore-and-aft sail carried over the stern of a vessel of three or more masts.

spar—any rounded timber used as a mast, yard, boom, or gaff.

spar deck—the uppermost deck of an armed vessel carrying guns on one or more gun decks below. The spar deck evolved from the joining of the foredeck and quarterdeck by gangways, which were gradually widened to make a single deck.

square rigger—a ship carrying square sails on three or more masts, so long as all masts carry square sails. A square rigger is also called a fully rigged ship.

stays—the standing lines that support a mast fore-and-aft.

steeve—the angle at which the bowsprit rises relative to the keel.

sternpost—the after extreme of the ship's frame, the sternpost is a heavy timber fixed to the keel and extending to the deck, on which the rudder is hung.

strake—a plank bolted to the frames of the ship from bow to stern and forming a part of the vessel's skin.

stunsails—(derived from "studding sails")—light auxiliary sails which are set outside the square sails in fair weather to increase the speed of the vessel.

taffrail—the railing that runs around the stern of the ship.

timberhead—an extension of a frame projecting above the deck line, to which the bulwark strakes are bolted.

top hamper—collectively, the entire rigging, spars, and sails of the ship.

transom—the upper part of the stern of a square-stern vessel, set above the counter.

tumblehome—the narrowing of a vessel above the waterline. Tumblehome increases stability, and also protects the chain plates and other intricate parts of the ship from damage by pilings, while at moorings.

waist—the portion of the vessel amidships.

wale—a strake, thicker than the others, and set at various intervals in the ship's sides for decorative or protective purposes.

waterline—a horizontal line corresponding to the surface of the water, with the ship afloat and under normal load. In drafts, several waterlines parallel to the load waterline are represented as points of reference.

waterways—timbers set above deck level along the joint with the bulwarks.

woolding—a rope winding about a spar, with loops seized in to act as a point of attachment for a line or block. In the early 1800s, wooldings were replaced by metal mast bands.

yard—a horizontal spar attached at its center to the mast and carried athwartships to spread a square sail.

yardarm—the outboard end of a yard.

Index

Index